Penguin Books
The Marsh Arabs

Wilfred Thesiger was born in Addis Ababa in 1910 and educated at Eton and Oxford where he got his blue for boxing. In 1935 he joined the Sudan Political Service and, at the outbreak of war, was seconded to the Sudan Defence Force. He later served in Abyssinia, Syria, and with the S.A.S. in the Western Desert, and was awarded the D.S.O. Since the war he has travelled in Southern Arabia, Kurdistan, the Marshes of Iraq, the Hindu Kush, the Karakorams, Morocco, Abyssinia, Kenya, and Tanganyika, always on foot or with animal transport. For his journeys he has received the Founder's Gold Medal from the Royal Geographical Society, the Lawrence of Arabia Medal from the Royal Central Asian Society, the Livingstone Gold Medal from the Royal Scottish Geographical Society and the Burton Memorial Medal from the Royal Asiatic Society. He is a fellow of the Royal Society of Literature and was awarded the C.B.E. in 1968, and the Third Class Star of Ethiopia.

His first book, *Arabian Sands*, was published in 1959 and is also published in Penguins.

Wilfred Thesiger

The Marsh Arabs

With 110 plates

Penguin Books

Penguin Books Ltd, Harmondsworth,
Middlesex, England
Penguin Books, 625 Madison Avenue,
New York, New York 10022, U.S.A.
Penguin Books Australia Ltd, Ringwood,
Victoria, Australia
Penguin Books Canada Ltd, 2801 John Street,
Markham, Ontario, Canada L3R 1B4
Penguin Books (N.Z.) Ltd
182–190 Wairau Road, Auckland 10, New Zealand

First published by Longmans, Green 1964
Published in Penguin Books 1967
Reprinted 1976, 1978

Made and printed in Great Britain by
Richard Clay (The Chaucer Press) Ltd,
Bungay, Suffolk
Set in Times Roman

For my Mother
To whose encouragement and understanding
I owe so much

Contents

	Chief Characters	11
	Introduction	13
1	A glimpse of the Marshes	19
2	Back on the edge of the Marshes	24
3	Hunting wild boar	34
4	Arrival at Qabab	44
5	First impressions of the Madan	52
6	In Sadam's guest house	58
7	Bu Mughaifat: a Marsh village	67
8	Crossing the Central Marshes	78
9	In the heart of the Marshes	88
10	The historical background	94
11	Winning acceptance	102
12	Among the Fartus	111
13	Feuds in the Marshes	117
14	Return to Qabab	123
15	Falih Bin Majid	132
16	Falih's death	141
17	The mourning ceremony	149
18	The Eastern Marshes	155
19	Among the Sudan and the Suaid	164
20	Amara's family	172
21	1954: the Flood	182
22	1955: the Drought	193
23	Berbera and Mudhifs	200
24	Amara's blood feud	209
25	My last year in the Marshes	215
	Glossary	221
	Index	225

List of Maps

Iraq   16–17
Southern Iraq   31
The Marshes   62–63

Chief Characters

Majid al Khalifa	Sheikh of the Al bu Muhammad on the Majar river
Falih bin Majid	Majid's son. Lived on the Wadiya
Abd al Wahid	Falih's son
Khalaf	Falih's brother
Muhammad al Khalifa	Majid's brother. Lived at Majar
Abbas	Muhammad's son
Hamud al Khalifa	Majid's brother. Lived at Majar
Hatab	Hamud's son. Lived on the Wadiya
Dair	Falih's retainer and canoeman
Abd ar Ridha	Falih's coffee-maker
Sadam bin Talal	Majid's representative at Qabab
Sahain	A Feraigat *qalit*, or headman. Lived at Bu Mughaifat
Jasim al Faris	Sheikh of the Fartus at Awaidiya
Falih	Jasim's son
Daud	Jasim's nephew
Hashim	Daud's father. Served ten years in Amara prison for murder
Maziad	Sheikh of the Al Essa
Abdullah	Maziad's uncle. His representative at Saigal
Tahir	Abdullah's son
Amara	One of my canoeboys. Lived at Rufaiya
Sabaiti	One of my canoeboys. Lived at Rufaiya
Yasin	One of my canoeboys. Lived at Bu Mughaifat
Hasan	One of my canoeboys. Lived at Bu Mughaifat
Thuqub	Amara's father
Naqa	Amara's mother
Reshiq	Amara's brother. Cultivated rice
Chilaib	Amara's brother. Looked after the buffaloes
Hasan	Amara's brother. Went to school
Radhi	Amara's brother. A small child
Matara	Amara's sister
Lazim	Sabaiti's father
Badai	Amara's cousin. A nomad Feraigat
Radhawi	A nomad Feraigat. On bad terms with Badai
Hasan	Radhawi's son. On bad terms with Badai
Khalaf	Radhawi's son. Killed by Badai

Introduction

I lived in the Marshes of Southern Iraq from the end of 1951 until June 1958, sometimes for as long as seven months on end. 1957 was the only year when I did not go there. Although I was almost continuously on the move this is not properly a travel book, for the area over which I travelled was restricted. Nor does it pretend to be a detailed study of the Marshmen among whom I lived, for I am not an anthropologist nor indeed a specialist of any kind. I spent these years in the Marshes because I enjoyed being there. During this time I lived among the Marshmen as one of themselves, and inevitably over the years I became to some extent familiar with their ways. From my recollections, helped by my diaries, I have tried to give a picture of the Marshes and of the people who live there. Recent political upheavals in Iraq have closed this area to visitors. Soon the Marshes will probably be drained; when this happens, a way of life that has lasted for thousands of years will disappear.

The Marshes cover some six thousand square miles of the country round Qurna, where the Tigris and Euphrates join above Basra to form the Shatt al Arab. They consist of permanent marsh where *qasab* (*Phragmites communis*) is the predominant vegetation; seasonal marsh, most of which is covered with bulrushes (*Typha augustata*) and dries up in the autumn and winter; and temporary marsh, which is only inundated during the floods and is later overgrown with a sedge (*Scirpus brachyceras*). This area can be conveniently divided into the Eastern Marshes, east of the Tigris; the Central Marshes, west of the Tigris and north of the Euphrates; and the Southern Marshes, south of the Euphrates and west of the Shatt al Arab. There is also some permanent marsh below Shatra on the Shatt al Gharraf, a river that leaves the Tigris at Kut and flows south-west in the direction of Nasiriya;

some seasonal marsh on the plains to the north-east of Amara, where the floods from the Tib and Duarij flow down from the Persian foothills and disperse; and a little seasonal marsh in the Al bu Daraj country, fifteen miles north of Amara to the west of the Tigris. At the height of the floods great tracts of desert adjoining the Marshes are covered by sheets of open water that vary each year in size but can extend for a distance of more than two hundred miles from the outskirts of Basra almost to Kut. As the floods recede most of this inundated land reverts to desert.

In spring the melting snow on the high mountains of Persia and Turkey causes the Tigris and Euphrates to flood, and the Marshes are the centuries-old result of the overflowing and dispersion of these two rivers. The Eastern and Central Marshes draw their water from the Tigris, and eighty per cent of the discharge at Baghdad disperses into them. The Euphrates itself disperses below Nasiriya through numerous canals, its scattered waters gradually draining into the Haur as Sanaf, and thence into the Shatt al Arab down the channel of Qarmat Ali, a few miles above Basra. The old channel between Suq ash Shuyukh and Qurna is still known as the Euphrates, but in fact the water in it has escaped from the right bank of the Tigris. Until recently it was believed that the Tigris and Euphrates used to flow separately into the Persian Gulf and that the build-up of their silt had gradually pushed the coast-line farther and farther south. The present theory, first advanced by Dr G. M. Lees and N. L. Falcon in 1952, is that the weight of accumulated silt causes a corresponding subsidence of the earth's surface and that the coast-line has therefore remained largely unchanged since Biblical times. On the Tigris the annual flood reaches its height in May, on the Euphrates a month later. From June on, both rivers begin to fall, and they reach their lowest level in September and October. In November there is usually a slight rise, increasing throughout the winter, and sudden short floods may occur during the winter and spring.

The Central Marshes, perhaps because I started there, is the area I came to know best. Indeed, I thought of it as home. In the course of years I must have visited nearly every settlement, however small, and most of them I visited again and again. When I acquired a canoe, my canoeboys came from there. Accepted by them, I was accepted by their fellow tribesmen. They remained with me throughout, and their villages were the bases to which I returned after expeditions. I travelled almost as extensively in the Eastern Marshes but never knew the people there so well. I remained a stranger, although welcome for the medical help I could give them. Of the Southern Marshes I saw but little.

I owe a great debt of gratitude to John Verney for all the help and advice he gave me with this book during the months I was with him in Florence. He read through successive drafts with infinite patience and made many improvements. I also wish to thank Val ffrench Blake and George Webb for many valuable suggestions and for their kindness in reading and correcting the proofs. Graham Watson drove me to write the book, and he too gave me much encouragement and advice. My thanks are also due to K. C. Jordan who drew the maps, to the firm of James Sinclair of Whitehall who have always given much care to the developing and printing of my photographs and who produced the prints for this book, to the staff of the Natural History Museum and many others who have helped me with information.

W. T.

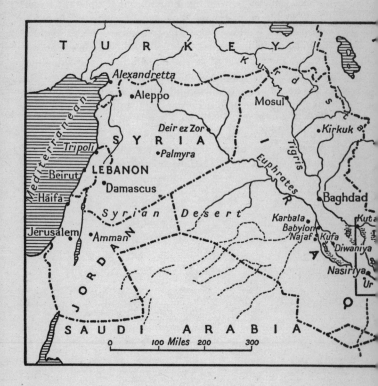

1. A Glimpse of the Marshes

All day we had ridden across a flat plain, and the dust rose from under the horses' hooves and choked us. The rains had failed, as they so often did, and the plants that had come up lay crumbling on the gaping soil. There was not a bush, nor even a rock, to serve as a landmark to measure our slow progress towards the horizon. Our saddles, of the usual Arab design, were hard as boards. The stirrups, being hung far back, forced us to sit forward on our forks and pressed us into the pommel which stuck up like those on cowboy saddles. Indeed, it struck me that the American saddle had probably derived from such as these, the Arabs introducing the design into Spain and the Spaniards taking it with them to the New World.

We kept our horses at a walk for my companion had not ridden before. He was Dugald Stewart, British Vice-Consul at Amara. Though only twenty-nine and obviously very gifted, he maintained that he had no ambition except to end his career as Consul at Split, where he could get all the wild-fowling he wanted. We exchanged memories of Eton, as Old Etonians will. He had been a scholar and in spite of a game leg, made worse by two operations, had won many school colours, whereas I, with two sound legs, had never managed to get any.

We camped that night among the Bazun, sleeping on the ground in the sheikh's guest tent after an enormous meal of rice and mutton. Except that it was supported on eleven poles and was far larger, the tent did not differ from the other black goat-hair booths pitched all around us. Open along one side, all faced the same way and most had a shackled horse or two picketed in front. A solid mass of sheep and goats pressed around, and often partly inside, each tent. I had watched them being driven in at sunset by the shepherd lads, each flock moving in a golden aura of dust. Throughout the night their bleating made a background noise against which the barking of dogs rose and fell.

I was on my way south from Iraqi Kurdistan, where I had gone to try to recapture the peace of mind I had known in the deserts of Southern Arabia. There I had lived with the Bedu for five years, and with them had travelled ten thousand miles across country where no car had ever been – until seismic parties, the vanguard of modern progress, began to arrive in search of oil.

In Iraqi Kurdistan, which I had always wanted to visit, I had ridden from one end of the country to the other, accompanied only by a young Kurdish servant. The scenery was wild and beautiful, and the Kurds who lived there still wore the finery of tribal dress – tasselled turbans and baggy trousers, short jackets and cummerbunds, of every colour and pattern – hung with daggers and revolvers and crossed with decorated bandoliers, heavy with cartridges. I had slept in terraced villages that hugged the mountainsides where the flat-roofed houses rose from the roofs below, and in the black tents of the nomads on bare mountaintops where gentians grew among the grass, and snowdrifts lay throughout the summer. I had followed tumbling rivers through oak forests where bears grubbed in the thickets, and I had looked down on a herd of ibex, threading its way along a three-thousand-foot wall of rock, while huge griffon vultures swung past, the wind whistling in their pinions. I had seen the glory of the Kurdish spring, valley-sides covered with anemones, and mountains crimson with tulips. I had gorged on grapes, freshly picked and warmed by the sun or cooled in a nearby stream.

But having seen Iraqi Kurdistan I had no desire to go back. Travel was too restricted, rather like stalking in a Highland deer forest. Across this stream was Turkey, beyond that watershed lay Persia, where uniformed police waited at the passes demanding visas I did not possess. I was fifty years too late. Half a century earlier I could have gone up through Rowunduz to Urmia, and on to Van, and the only effective hindrance would have been brigands and warring tribes. Admittedly the Marshes, for which I was now bound, covered a smaller area than Iraqi Kurdistan, but they were a world complete in itself, not a fragment of a larger world to the rest of which I was denied access. Besides, being fond of Arabs, it was probable that I could never really like Kurds. Although the landscape appealed to me the people did not. Admittedly I was hampered by not speaking their language, but even had I done so I felt that I should still not have liked them. As people are more important to me than places I decided to return to the Arabs.

Next day we rode on again, southward this time towards the Marshes across the unchanging plain, stopping at midday at some tents to feed ourselves and change horses. Dugald was re-mounted on a magnificent but restive grey stallion. When I protested that it would be too much for him, the sheikh clearly thought I wanted to ride it myself, and said he had brought it for 'the Consul'. A little later Dugald inadvertently jabbed the stallion with his heel and it bolted. To save himself he dropped the reins and grabbed the pommel with both hands. Our companions started to gallop in pursuit, but, realizing that they would only excite it further, I shouted to them to stop. Dugald had already lost both stirrups. It seemed only a matter of time till he came off. The ground was hard and I pictured a ghastly accident, but two miles farther the horse stopped exhausted, with Dugald still clinging to the saddle. When we caught up with him he had dismounted and was looking at his hands. The palms had been scraped raw by the decorative nails in the pommel. 'Now I am bloody well going to walk,' he announced, and no assurances that our horses were quiet would induce him to change his mind and ride one of them.

The sun was still high. Past floods had covered the ground, which was fissured with deep cracks. While the sheikh kept up a flow of remonstrances, Dugald lurched and limped along: 'Oh for God's sake get him to shut up,' he implored me. The sun set and there was still no sign of the Marshes nor of the village for which we were bound. It was dark when we saw lights moving in the distance. The Bazun had warned Maziad bin Hamdan, sheikh of the Al Essa, to expect us, and he had sent out a search party at dusk. They led us to his encampment on the edge of the Marshes. Beyond the tents we could sense rather than see water.

Maziad himself came out to welcome us (Plate 4). A small man, stockily built but standing very upright, he conveyed at once an impression of dignity and authority. The guest tent was lit by a hurricane lamp and filled with men, most of them armed with rifles. They rose as we came in. Maziad showed us to a place opposite the hearth. While we were served with coffee and tea, Maziad asked the conventional questions about our health and journey. Everyone sat very still and upright and no one else spoke. We were in the presence of desert Arabs, who are always formal in public and conscious of their dignity. We fed at last, it seemed hours later, from an enormous platter heaped high with the usual rice and mutton. It was not a delicate meal, but Arabs appreciate quantity rather than quality. We ate first with some old men, and as soon as we had all finished Maziad summoned others by name to take our places. As host, he himself stood until all had finished. They fed in relays and when the last was done he called in children from the dark outside the tent. The smallest, quite naked, cannot have been more than three. They stuffed themselves with the rice that was left and gnawed at bones that had already been picked clean. Then they cleared the dishes, scooping what was left into bowls they had brought with them. The bones were thrown to the dogs. Towards the end, the coffee-man saved a small helping and set it aside on a plate. Maziad now drew a little apart and took his frugal meal, while we were once more served coffee and tea. As host it would not have been seemly for him to eat until the last of his guests had done so, and next day at meal time I watched him standing before his tent to ensure that no one passed by without coming in. Twice daily he killed a sheep for his guests, who might number a hundred. These shepherd tribes still held to the customs, and judged others by the standards, that they had brought with them from the deserts of Arabia.

In the following years I came back many times to Maziad's guest tent, and visited many other encampments of his tribe. During the worst of the summer months, I would escape from the Marshes, borrow horses and move about among the shepherd tribes. I got to know most of them – the Bani Lam, the Bazun, the Al Essa, the Al bu Salih and others. Some would cross the frontier in the spring and move up into the Persian foothills, where the new green grass was bright with anemones; others moved down into Saudi Arabia and to the outskirts of Kuwait for the winter, the men and boys herding the sheep and goats, while the black-robed women drove donkeys loaded with tents and poles, carpets, bedding, small wooden chests, cauldrons, dishes and kettles. Often I saw them moving through the mirage across a plain that was as empty as the sea.

After the meal, Maziad showed us to a nearby cabin, neatly built of reeds and matting, where mattresses and colour quilts were spread for us to sleep – an unexpected privacy for which Dugald and I were both grateful. All night the wind, cold off dark water, blew through the lattice, and half asleep I heard waves slapping on a shore.

As I came out into the dawn, I saw, far away across a great sheet of water, the silhouette of a distant land, black against the sunrise. For a moment I had a vision of Hufaidh, the legendary island, which no man may look on and keep his senses; then I realized that I was looking at great reedbeds. A slim, black, high-prowed craft lay beached at my feet – the sheikh's war canoe, waiting to take me into the Marshes. Before the first palaces were built at Ur, men had stepped out into the dawn from such a house, launched a canoe like this, and gone hunting here. Woolley had unearthed their dwellings and models of their boats buried deep under the relics of Sumeria, deeper even than evidence of the Flood. Five thousand years of history were here and the pattern was still unchanged.

Memories of that first visit to the Marshes have never left me: firelight on a half-turned face, the crying of geese, duck flighting in to feed, a boy's voice singing somewhere in the dark, canoes moving in procession down a waterway, the setting sun seen crimson through the smoke of burning reedbeds, narrow waterways that wound still deeper into the Marshes. A naked man in a canoe with a trident in his hand, reed houses built upon water, black, dripping buffaloes that looked as if they had calved from the swamp with the first dry land. Stars reflected in dark water, the croaking of frogs, canoes coming home at evening, peace and continuity, the stillness of a world that never knew an engine. Once again I experienced the longing to share this life, and to be more than a mere spectator.

2. Back on the Edge of the Marshes

Six months later I was travelling down a branch of the Tigris towards the Marshes in a leaky bitumen-coated canoe paddled by two Arabs. One of them was a gaunt old man, dressed in a patched shirt of indeterminate colour, that reached half-way to his calves. The other, a stocky boy of fifteen with a squint, wore the remains of a European jacket over a new white shirt hitched up through his belt to prevent it trailing on the ground. Both wore headcloths of the kind generally used by the Shia tribesmen of Southern Iraq, a three-foot square with a black net pattern on a once-white base. Not having head-ropes, they had twisted the cloths, folded into a triangle, round their heads. The old man sat on the raised stern. I sat on the bottom of the canoe at his feet, cross-legged on a piece of matting with my luggage in front of me. It consisted of two black tin boxes, one filled with medicine, the other with books, films, cartridges and odds and ends. On top of the boxes a Kurdish saddle-bag, woven in rich colours, was stuffed with blankets and spare clothes. Propped against it were my shotgun and a ·275 Rigby rifle in a canvas cover.

The river was thirty yards wide, fast-flowing and obviously deep. The tips of my fingers were in the water as I grasped the sides. A stiff breeze blew upstream, raising small waves that splashed on to me and my luggage. I sat very still, convinced that the smallest move on my part would capsize us. The two Arabs, however, shifted about with complete unconcern, never disturbing the balance of the canoe.

The boy stopped paddling, turned and crouched down to shelter while he lit a cigarette. The old man stood up, looking for a friend working in the fields. From the bottom of the canoe I could see nothing but the steep-sided banks three or four feet high. They were intersected at intervals by irrigation channels of various sizes draining out of the main stream, and were crowned with thorn scrub, two or three feet tall and a dusty bluish-green. Terrapins slithered back off shelves on the banks and flopped into the opaque brownish water. Some of them were flat in shape, with soft shells as much as two feet across which undulated at the edges as they moved; others, smaller, resembled more conventional tortoises. Pied kingfishers darted past or hung in the air with rapidly beating wings before diving, kites circled above us, and the occasional flock of rooks rose noisily from the cultivation behind the banks. A dusty haze toned down the sky and everything was a drab earth colour.

We passed a small settlement of reed huts, grey like weathered ricks, where dark-clothed women washed dishes at the water's edge among a fleet of black canoes drawn up on a mud bank. A man came out of a hut and the elder of my Arabs called out a greeting, 'Salam alaikum' (Peace be on you). The man replied, 'Alaikum as salam' (On you be peace), and added, 'Filhu' (Stop and feed). We answered, 'Kafu, Allah yahafadhak' (We have fed, God protect you). Half a dozen dogs raced along the bank beside us, barking and snarling hysterically until stopped by a ditch too wide for them to jump.

I had left Amara that morning, in the first week of February 1951, and had hired the canoe at Majar al Kabir to take me five miles downstream to Falih bin Majid's house on the edge of the Marshes. His father, Majid al Khalifa, was one of the two paramount sheikhs of the great Al bu Muhammad tribe, that numbers 25,000 fighting men. I was hoping to spend some months in the Marshes, and Dugald Stewart had told me that Falih would be the best person to help me.

Squatting uncomfortably in the bottom of the canoe, I looked hopefully ahead as we rounded each bend to see if the Marshes were yet in sight, but the brown river flowed on through an interminable flatness.

Yet another bend and the river divided. A row of large well-constructed reed dwellings fronted the main stream. On the open ground behind stood a single-storied brick house, flat-topped like a fort. But what struck me most was a barrel-vaulted building, roofed with honey-coloured matting. At either end four tapered pillars broke the roof line. The building was sited on the promontory between the two streams. 'Sheikh Falih's *mudhif* (guest house),' said the old man. A lad in the doorway stepped inside and a moment later several men came out and waited for me to land. 'Sheikh Falih,' said the old man, indicating a thick-set figure who wore a finely woven brown cloak over a surcoat of heavy dark cloth.

The boy jumped skilfully ashore as the nose of the canoe touched the bank, and held the canoe until it had swung along-side. The elder man then stepped out, went up to Falih and kissed his hand, saying, 'An Englishman from Amara, *Ya Muha-fadh* (O Protector).' Falih looked down at me and said, 'Wel-come.' He had a powerful, virile face, clean-shaven except for a close-clipped moustache, with dark bushy eyebrows which nearly met over a prominent fleshy nose. His face was framed in the folds of a conventional black and white headcloth, kept in place by a heavy black head-rope. As I stood up, the canoe wobbled and water poured over the gunwale. Falih said, 'Wait a second,' and to the canoemen, 'Go on, hurry. Help him.' He held out a strong hand to pull me up the bank, repeating 'Welcome.' Turn-ing to a man beside him, he ordered, 'See that they bring the Englishman's things into the *mudhif*.' Then he led me towards the doorway. 'Be pleased to enter. Make yourself at home.' Kicking off my shoes, I passed between the pillars. Eight feet in girth, each pillar was formed by a bundle of giant reeds, the peeled stems bound so tightly together that the surface was smooth and polished.

The great hall smelt acrid with smoke and the light was dim, after the bright sun outside. Shadowy figures stood along the walls. I called out, '*Salam alaikum*' and they answered together, '*Alaikum as salam*.' We seated ourselves on some gaudy rugs spread on the matting and the others settled themselves along the walls. Those that had rifles placed them in front of them. I no-ticed two lovely old rugs of blue and gold farther down the room, relegated there from the place of honour, in favour of the modern ones on which we sat. Against the wall at the far end was a wooden chest and near the entrance a large pitcher of porous clay filled with water and supported in a wooden frame. There was no other furniture. The hearth was a third of the way into the room and in the centre. Here beside a small fire a dozen coffee-pots were ranged, the largest about two feet high. Into this in accordance with Arab practice the grounds of previous brews were emptied, the discoloured liquid being used to fill the other pots. Fresh coffee, brewed in the smallest pot, was always prepared on the arrival of any guest of importance. An old man in a white shirt, the only person besides myself not wearing a cloak, busied himself making it in conformity with a time-honoured ritual. As soon as the beans were roasted he ground them in a small brass mortar, beating out a rhythm as he did so. This pleasant sound was an intimation that coffee was being served in the sheikh's guest house, and an invitation to any man within hearing to partake. Then holding the pot in his left hand, and in his right two small china bowls, little bigger than egg cups, he poured a few drops into the top cup and offered it to Falih, who told him to serve me first. I in turn refused. When Falih insisted, however, I drank while the old man poured a second cup for him. The coffee tasted strong and bitter. Knowing Arab custom, I accepted three cups before shaking the cup slightly to show I had had enough. The coffee-man moved slowly round the room serving the others in the order of their importance. Falih and I and the two canoemen who had brought me were also given tea, black and sweet, in small narrow-waisted glasses with a gold rim. Falih's eldest son, a sixteen-year-old boy, came in. He had his father's heavy nose but a narrower, weaker face. Falih introduced him to me as 'Your servant'. Falih told him to see about lunch, saying to me, 'I am ashamed not to give you a proper meal, but you came without warning. Forgive me, but I expect you would rather eat what is ready, than wait while we slaughter a sheep, for you must be hungry after your long journey.'

Among Arabs long periods of silence are never embarrassing between host and guest. Falih asked me two or three times, 'How are you?' and I gave the prescribed answer, 'The praise be to God.' He also asked me more than once, 'Your journey, was it good?' and I answered, 'It was good, the praise be to God.' Otherwise no one in the room spoke. After a while he occupied himself once more with the morning's business, for these *mudhifs* were more than guest houses; they were the audience chambers where the sheikhs sat morning and evening, running their estates and settling disputes between their tribesmen.

A few sheikhs, such as Majid al Khalifa, Falih's father, owned vast properties that brought them in hundreds of thousands of pounds each year. Once the land had belonged to the tribes, and a sheikh ruled only as long as his tribe would follow him, but in recent years the sheikhs had virtually acquired possession. Now, among the settled tribes, they had become landlords, while their tribesmen were reduced to labourers farming the fields in return for a share of the crop and without any security of tenure. In theory all land in Amara Province belonged to the State, which leased it to the sheikhs. These, however, paid their taxes and regarded it as their own, and as long as they were powerful no one questioned their title.

Although the sheikhs were no longer supposed to have judicial powers, few cases between tribesmen (except murder, and not always that) found their way into the Government courts. The tribesmen preferred the arbitration of sheikhs whom they knew to the jurisdiction of officials with whom they had nothing in common, and on the whole the Government was content to leave well alone.

Falih dealt with various cases. He gave orders for a bank to be strengthened before the river rose, discussed an allocation of land for the coming rice harvest, and warned a man to pay the share of his crop that was still outstanding. However, finding the dialect difficult to follow, I studied the faces opposite, struck by the difference between their broad rather heavy features and those of the fine-drawn Bedu of Arabia – the difference between a cart-horse and a thoroughbred. But it was hard to form an opinion of them under such conditions. Each man sat quietly wrapped in his cloak, his headcloth crowned by the thick black head-rope that was fashionable in these parts. They struck me as a good-tempered and humorous people, ready to accept discipline, but I suspected that they could be both stubborn and quick to anger when roused.

The *mudhif*, which I later measured, was sixty feet long, twenty feet wide and eighteen high, but gave the impression of far greater size, especially when I first entered it. Eleven great horse-shoe arches supported the roof. Like the entrance pillars, these were made of the stems of giant reeds, bound closely together, and were nine feet in circumference where they emerged from the ground, and two and a half feet at the top. These reeds, I dis-covered, could grow to twenty-five feet in height. To complete the framework, further reed bundles, married so as to resemble two-inch cables, were lashed, one above the other, along the entire length of the building on the outside of the arches. The contrast between this horizontal ribbing and the shape of the vertical arches made a striking pattern seen from within. The roof itself was covered with overlapping reed mats, similar to those on the floor and sewn on to the ribs in such a way as to ensure a fourfold thickness. The sides of the room were the colour of pale gold but the ceiling was darkened by smoke to a deep chestnut and gave the effect of being varnished.

Supervised by Falih's son, several servants appeared and laid in front of us a circular mat, some five feet across, woven of soft rushes. On this they arranged a round tray heaped with rice, dishes of vegetable stew, three roast chickens, a grilled fish and dates, as well as plates of custard, bowls of buttermilk and jugs of sherbet. Most of the people had already left the *mudhif*. I had expected them to stay because tribal Arabs generally congregate when a meal is being served, but I learnt later that in these parts only the sheikhs of nomad tribes kept open house in their guest tents. The others, except on special occasions, expected their retainers to feed themselves and only entertained travellers from afar. Now, only three old men remained as guests, besides my-self and my canoemen.

Falih and his son ate with us. A servant brought round a basin and ewer and in turn we washed our hands. Falih then said, 'Come on, make yourself at home,' and leaning forward poured a dish of stew over the rice. He broke up a chicken with his hands, placing a large piece on a plate that had been specially laid for me together with a spoon and fork. Since the others ate from the dishes with their right hands, I did the same. Falih said at once, 'Use the fork and the spoon, it will be easier for you.' But I told him that I had fed with my hands for years and was well accus-tomed to Arab ways, to which he answered, 'Then you are one of us.' When we had finished we washed again and were served with coffee and tea.

Noticing that Falih was eyeing my rifle I passed it to him and asked what he thought of it, as all tribesmen are interested in guns. He felt its balance, aimed with it, exclaimed, 'This is a good rifle' – which indeed it was – and showed the usual Arab curiosity about its price. At last, as I had hoped, he raised the question of my plans and I told him that I wanted to go into the Marshes to see the Madan.

'That is easy, I will send you to Qabab. It is a large village in the heart of the Marshes where the reeds for this *mudhif* came from. Sheikh Majid, my father, has a representative there and if you want to spend the night he has a proper house. At Qabab you will see how the Madan live; nothing but buffaloes, reeds and water. You can only go about in a canoe. There is no dry ground anywhere. There will still be duck if you like shooting.'

I thanked him but explained that I hoped to spend several months with the Madan. 'Qabab is all right; Sadam has a *mudhif*, but the Madan live like their buffaloes,' he continued. 'Their houses are half under water, filled with mosquitoes and fleas. If you try to sleep in one of them you will probably get your face trodden on by buffaloes during the night. The Madan are poor people; they have no proper food; rice and milk are all they eat. Much better stay here where you can visit the Marshes whenever you feel inclined. I can make you comfortable; this place is yours for as long as you wish. I have boats and men to take you wherever you want to go. Spend the nights here and the days in the Marshes. That is the sensible thing to do.'

I told him that I had already spent a few days in the Marshes with the Consul from Amara the previous year. I had come back now because I was interested in the Madan and wanted to know them better, which I could only do by living among them. 'I have been travelling all my life in wild places and am used to discomfort. I spent the last five years in the Empty Quarter. That was hard enough, always hungry and thirsty. Here at any rate I shall have all the water I want. '

Falih laughed. 'Yes by God, you won't be short of water; you will sleep in it. You English are a strange people! One night in the Marshes is enough for me when I have to go there on the Sheikh's business. I don't sleep there for pleasure. Anyway, stay with me tomorrow and I will arrange a pig hunt. I will send you to Qabab the day after and tell Sadam to look after you. This evening you might like to walk round the cultivations with me

Southern Iraq

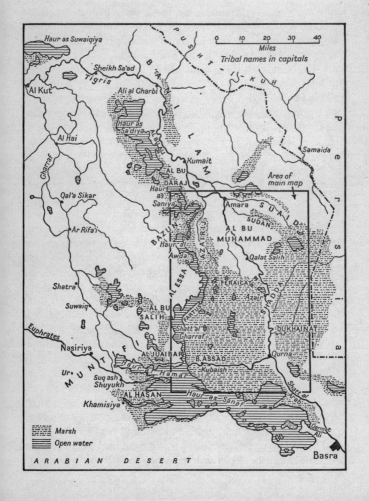

and see if we can shoot some partridge. I will leave you now to rest.'

'Have you ever shot pig?' asked Falih. 'Watch out, they are dangerous. Only last week one attacked and killed a man near here while he was looking at his crops. I doubt if we shall see any today, though we should find some partridge.'

We were walking in single file along the top of a dyke that bordered a wide irrigation channel, and led towards a grove of palms dark against the sky. This man-made dyke raised us above the interminable flatness of the alluvial plain that is Southern Iraq. To the east, the plain stretched for 100 miles to the Persian foothills, south for 150 to the sea; north for 200 to Baghdad; and west beyond the Euphrates to merge into the Arabian desert. Every now and again we had to jump across a gap where water was fed to the fields below us. For a while we plunged about under the palms through a wilderness of matted thorn bushes, three or four feet high, then moved to more open country beyond. Here the ground was slippery and white with salt, and was generally covered with a species of salt bush. We flushed a few black partridge but they were wild and gave us no chance of a shot. On the way back to the village three duck flew over us, coming in very high from the Marshes. Falih fired and got one. I congratulated him, and wondered whether this was a fluke, but discovered later that he was a fine shot.

We got back to the village at dusk. A lamp was burning in the *mudhif*, hanging from the ceiling by a cord. There were half a dozen lads sitting about inside. Falih said his sunset prayer facing the entrance, for the *mudhif*, as always, was orientated on Mecca. Moslems are supposed to pray at dawn, at midday, in the afternoon, at sunset and again two hours later. Few people in these parts bothered to pray at all, and those that did were mostly old men. Having finished his prayers Falih sent for dinner. This was similar to the earlier meal, except that there was roast mutton instead of chicken and some meat in the stew. Soon afterwards the servants who had cleared away the dishes came back carrying armfuls of mattresses, bolsters and heavy quilts, lined with green, red or yellow silk. Two of the old men were still there spending the night. Falih ordered a boy to fetch his rifle and to remain on guard until dawn, wished me good night and crossed to the brick building where he and his family lived.

The boy put out the lamp, drank what was left of the coffee and sat poking at the fire. He had a heavy, rather Mongolian face that was disturbingly beautiful. When one of the old men began to snore, he called to him insistently to shut up. At last the old man turned over with a grunt, but a few minutes later he was snoring again. The boy grinned at me and said, 'Old men always snore.'

3. Hunting Wild Boar

Abd ar Ridha, the coffee-maker, appeared in the grey dawn and lit the fire, which soon filled the room with smoke. The boy had gone. The two old men got up hawking and spitting. After performing their ritual ablutions, they said their prayers and then crouched over the fire. It seemed cold, so I stayed where I was until two servants came to remove the bedding, when I joined the others and was handed a cup of coffee. A servant brought breakfast – thin pancakes of rice flour on a grass platter and hot sweetened milk in a kettle. He laid our portions on the carpet in front of us as the sun rose gilding the entrance pillars.

An hour or two later, Falih, accompanied by a throng of armed retainers, came in to fetch me for the promised pig shoot. After they had all drunk coffee, I got into the same canoe as Falih and his son.

She was a beautiful craft that could carry as many as twelve people. Thirty-six feet long but only three and a half feet at her widest beam, she was carvel-built, flat-bottomed and covered outside with a smooth coating of bitumen over the wooden planks. The front swept forwards and upwards in a perfect curve to form a long, thin, tapering stem; the stern too rose in a graceful sweep. Two feet of the stern and of the bows were decked; there was a thwart a third of the way forward, and a strengthening beam across the boat two thirds of the way forward. Movable boards covered the floor. The top part of the ribs was planked along the inside and studded with five rows of flat, round nail-heads two inches across. These decorative nails were the distinguishing mark of a *tarada* (Plate 9) which only a sheikh may own. Years later, in Oslo, I saw the Viking ships preserved there and was at once reminded of the *taradas* in the Marshes. Both types of craft have the same beautiful simplicity of line.

Four men punted the canoe, two in the stern and two in the bows, moving rhythmically in time as they drove their poles into the water on the same side and changing over as one man when necessary. They had laid their rifles in the canoe beside them and had taken off their cloaks. Each wore a bandolier filled with cartridges and a curved, narrow-bladed dagger in the front of his belt.

The Marshes lay three miles below Falih's *mudhif*, and as we approached them we passed a large village that extended for some 200 yards along the left bank of the stream. Built of mats fastened over arches of reeds, the houses were ranged parallel with the bank and often very close together. In front of them, a few buffalo calves were tethered and some cows wandered about. I noticed two or three horses, each with its body enveloped in a rug and its front feet shackled with an iron bar. Falih's own horses had been shackled in the same way and when I asked him the reason, he explained, 'It stops people from stealing them. If you fasten a horse with a rope, the thief can cut the rope, jump on its back and then both disappear. Our horses are thoroughbreds; they are valuable and we take care of them.'

'Why are they wrapped up like that? It isn't cold.'

'To stop the flies biting them.'

Dogs raced along the bank above and stopped every ten or fifteen yards to bark at us in a sort of gibbering frenzy, their lips drawn back over their teeth. Each group of dogs handed us over at its boundary to a fresh lot. Children watched silently and women, none of them veiled, looked out from the houses. There seemed to be few men about. We drew into the bank under a large house and one of Falih's retainers shouted: 'Zair Mahaisin!' An elderly man came out fastening his headcloth. 'Welcome! Welcome *Ya Muhafadh*! Come in! Come in!' Falih refused, although the man pressed us to drink coffee. Falih asked: 'Have you sent the men down to the marsh in their canoes?'

'Yes, *Muhafadh*, they are all there and waiting for you at the mouth of the stream.'

'Are there any pigs in the reeds?'

'Yes, but very scattered. The water is too low for them to have collected on the reed islands.'

'Come on, in you get,' and Zair Mahaisin climbed neatly into the canoe and sat on the floorboards.

Passengers always sit in the bottom of a canoe, the place of honour being that nearest to the stern against the rear-thwart. When the crew paddle, two sit in the stern on the raised deck one in front of the other, the third on the forward-thwart, an uncomfortable narrow beam, while the fourth kneels in the bows. I asked Falih: 'Are these people Madan?' He exchanged a smile with Zair Mahaisin and said: 'No, they are *fallah* (cultivators). The Madan live in the Marshes. You will meet them later when you get to Qabab.'

We had left the fields of wheat and barley behind us before we came to the village. The channel which we were following had little water in it and the canoemen kept the *tarada* moving with difficulty. The earth banks were lower and by sitting up straight I could see over them. On either side a couple of hundred yards of weed-carpeted mud glistened in the sun, and past them lay the reedbeds. A small flock of cattle-egrets showed up snow-white against this background; two buff-backed herons sat, humped and brooding, on the edge of a small ditch, and some pied crows quarrelled noisily round a piece of garbage. Falih remarked: 'This is where they plant their rice; they will start clearing the fields soon.'

Ahead of us I could see a large number of men and canoes. When we were near them we climbed out and stood precariously on the last crumbling vestiges of the dyke. A few old men, better dressed than the others, waded through the mud and water, to greet Falih and to kiss his hand. The rest, many of them boys, sat or stood in their canoes a short way off in the deeper water. Some had coarse black or brown cloaks wrapped round their waists but were otherwise naked; the rest wore the long Arab shirt, tucked high up round their thighs; two, who were pulling a canoe through shallow water, lifted their shirts up under their armpits, exposing their nakedness with complete unconcern. Most had some sort of rag round their heads and many wore daggers. Several boys were also armed with clubs, weighted with lumps of bitumen. Seeing me look at his, one of the boys passed it to me with an engaging smile. In general these people were powerfully built and of moderate height, with light skins darkened by the weather, frank, open faces, wide-set eyes and rather broad noses.

Their bitumen-covered canoes were mostly small (Plate 12). The generic terms for all canoes was *mashuf*, though each type and size had a special name. A few, low in the water and called *mataur*, would carry only one man and were used for wild-fowling. Others, slightly larger, would seat two, while some were the same size as the canoe in which I had travelled from Majar al Kabir. Many of the men punted their canoes with fish-spears, the butt end in the water. These spears were formidable-looking weapons with bamboo shafts as long as twelve feet, and five-pronged heads like giant toasting forks, but with each prong barbed.

Falih had suggested that I should arm myself with my shotgun, as it would be dangerous to use a rifle with so many people about. Now I was glad to see that only his four canoemen carried rifles, though in fact the villagers possessed plenty of firearms. During the First World War the local tribesmen had acquired a large number of British and Turkish rifles picked up on the battlefields, and afterwards had never been disarmed. Ammunition for the Lee-Enfield rifles was still procurable because the Iraqi army and police were equipped with them. Ammunition for the Turkish rifles was practically exhausted. In some villages there were craftsmen who could reload an empty cartridge case using locally manufactured powder and bullets, but with the Turkish ammunition the cases themselves were becoming dangerously thin.

In the Second World War there had been very little fighting in Iraq and consequently small chance of loot for the tribes. In Persia, however, the army and police force had largely disintegrated before the British advance and each man had taken his rifle home with him. The tribes, too, had looted the armouries of the various garrisons. Later, remembering Riza Shah's methods and fearful that they would be ruthlessly punished if found with weapons, they had smuggled many of them into Iraq. They could then be bought in Iraq for as little as five dinars, the equivalent of £5; now, I was told, one would fetch a hundred dinars. Of Czechoslovakian make, they were known as Burno from the mark Brno on the barrel. I noticed that the rifles which Falih's canoemen carried were of this type.

Falih had been listening to an involved complaint about the distribution of some rice-land and said: 'That is enough. Come tomorrow to my *mudhif*, early, two hours after sunrise, and tell Hasan to come too.'

Then he asked: 'Is Adhaim here? Call him.' A short man with a slight limp climbed out of one of the farthest canoes and splashed towards us. He tried rather obsequiously to kiss Falih's hand. 'Have you given the ten dinars to Jasim which I told you to pay him?'

'I was going to do so tomorrow, *Ya Muhafadh*.'

'I told you to do so ten days ago.'

'I have been ill; for two days I have been . . .'

'Yesterday I heard you were at Majar.'

'I went there to see the doctor and buy medicine.'

'You never went near the doctor, you spent the day at Nisaif's wedding.'

'I swear by Abbas I went to the doctor. I will . . .'

'Dog, son of a dog, I told you that if you did not refund this money to Jasim at once I would punish you; you are a cheat and a liar. Yasin, take him to Khazal and tell him to keep him till I come. Tell him to tie him up. Take him! Go! You black dog, I will teach you to obey my orders.'

When someone else came forward with another complaint, Falih said: 'Enough. Come show us the pig. I wish to see how the Englishman shoots.' To me he said: 'You go in that *mashuf*. Be careful how you move about in it. This man will paddle you.'

I climbed into a small canoe which had been drawn up at my feet. Falih and his son each got into another, and we started towards the reedbeds, followed by the rest. When the water deepened, each man laid down the pole or fishing spear with which he had been punting, settled himself in the canoe and started to paddle with short quick strokes. When more than one person was in a boat, they dipped in time together on the same side.

The haze of the previous day had disappeared and the sky was a pale luminous blue, touched here and there with semi-transparent wisps of cirrus cloud. The paddles dug a succession of tiny whirlpools and the sparkling drops fell back into the clear water, which looked very cold. We had left the muddy flow from the stream's mouth behind us, among the beds of grey, battered bulrushes that grew in the shallows. Now we were among the *qasab* (*Phragmites communis*) which covered most of the permanent marsh. This giant grass, which looked like a bamboo, grew in the dense reedbeds to a height of more than twenty-five feet. The stems, each terminating in a tasselled head of palest buff, were so thick that the marshmen used them as punt-poles. At this season the reedbeds bordering the narrow waterways were light and airy. Relics of the past year, they were pale gold and silvery grey, except at their base where the new growth, as yet only a few feet high, was very green. Small parties of coot scuttered along the water ahead of us to the shelter of the reedbeds; pigmy cormorants and darters, sitting with their dark wings spread out to dry on reed stumps, white with droppings, took fright and dived into the water or flew off low above it; herons rose with a noisy disturbance of dry reeds to flap away with their long legs trailing behind.

The canoes, of which there must have been at least forty, jostled and bumped as they crowded down the narrow lanes, or spread out on the more open stretches, the crews racing each other with shouts and laughter.

Soon I could not tell whether we were travelling deeper into the Marshes or parallel with the shore, for the reedbeds closed in on us and the waterways became narrower and more tortuous. Suddenly we were out of the reeds and on to a small sheltered lagoon. Mallard rose quacking and flew back high over our heads. Many small islands, some only a few yards across, others covering an acre or more, enclosed the far end of the lagoon. The Marshmen called such islands *tuhul*. Some were anchored, others were loose and drifted about. All were smothered under a mass of *qasab*, here only eight to ten feet high, tall clumps of sedge, the leaves sharp-cutting as razors, brambles, a few small willow bushes, and several different kinds of creeper. Underneath all this was a carpet of mint, sow thistle, willow herb, pondweed and other plants.

The ground looked solid but felt very soggy. Actually it consisted of a layer of roots and decomposed vegetation floating on the surface. Some years later I shot a large boar feeding on a similar island that had been burnt not long before. He stood there as if on firm ground, but when we passed the place an hour later the corpse was gone. 'I can't have killed him. He must have recovered and gone off.'

'No, no,' my companion answered. 'He was dead enough. He has sunk.'

At one of these islands Falih's canoe drew alongside mine. 'This is the place,' he said and shouted to the others: 'Come on, get into it and see if there is anything there.' Several men stepped ashore holding their spears in front of them. They drew blank, so they tried another island and then a third. I was watching two warblers, hopping about among the reeds, when I was startled by several loud crashes, followed by shouts. 'There he is! Quick! Look out! By God! Four of them.' Then a splash and silence.

'Where have they gone?' asked another voice.

'They have taken to the water. One got up right under my feet, by God! As big as a donkey, by Abbas!'

Someone else cried: 'I threw my spear and just missed; a sow with three young.'

More shouts, 'They have gone in here. Get round quick and cut them off.'

We were wedged in a narrow passage between two islands, but my canoeman backed out hurriedly into the open water where several more canoes joined us. The hunt had moved on to another island and, as we hastened towards it, there was more excitement. Then a piercing squeal cut off short, a laugh and a man shouting: 'I've got it; one of the small ones; I have speared it. It was in the water; I am drowning it.'

Falih's canoe went past. He had taken off his cloak and was himself paddling. 'Where has the big one gone, Manati?' he asked a vigorous old man who had led the hunt so far.

'Into the large island over there I think, *Ya Muhafadh*. . . . Yes, here are its tracks. Come on. Let's get it out!'

Manati plunged out of sight into the jungle of reeds followed by two others. I could hear them moving about. One of them called, 'It has not gone this way,' and a little later Manati shouted, 'Here are its tracks.'

Nothing happened, however, and I thought they must have lost it when a series of splintering crashes came from the far side and a voice screamed, 'It is killing me! It is killing me!'

Someone shouted, 'It has got Manati. Come on lads. Quick! Where are the warriors?'

Many people answered his call, splashing through the reeds.

Falih, I and some others paddled frantically to the far side of the island where we found Manati being helped into one of the larger canoes. His shirt, covered with blood, was torn half off and he lay with his eyes closed. There was a hole in his right buttock I could have put my fist in. Falih leant over him and asked anxiously, 'How are you, Manati?' The old man opened his eyes and whispered, 'I am all right, *Ya Muhafadh*.' Falih gave orders to go back at once to the mouth of the Khirr, which luckily was not far.

As we paddled back, a boy said, 'It was a sow that bit him. A boar would have slashed him with its tushes and killed him.'

Someone else said, 'It was a good thing he managed to fall on his stomach. I saw a man two years ago in the Al bu Bakhit country after he had been killed by a sow. She had dragged out half his guts.'

Another said, 'The boar that killed the young *Sayid* last year in the wheat cultivation cut him to pieces. He was alone and un-armed and must have trodden on it. The crops were high, just before we harvested them. He crawled back towards the village but died before he got out of the field.'

A boy asked, 'Do you remember when Hashim rode the pig?'

'Yes, by God,' answered my canoeman, 'he and his brother were inspecting their barley when they saw a boar, an old one, grey coloured. Hashim's brother wanted to shoot it. He had just bought a rifle from the Feraigat. Hashim tried to stop him but he fired and wounded it in the stomach.'

'Yes,' interrupted another man, 'he is a very bad shot.'

My canoeman continued, 'The pig charged and knocked him down; it slashed his arm badly. Hashim got behind it and stabbed it in the shoulder with his dagger. When it turned on him, he dropped the dagger and jumped on its back. The pig made off with him riding it. He held on to its ears. It took him all the way to Sayid Ali's garden and collapsed trying to cross the big ditch. Hashim said he never wanted to ride a pig again!' and the audi-ence laughed.

'Pigs, they are the foe,' said an older man. 'They eat our crops

and kill our men. God destroy them! Look at Manati; he will
never be any use again. That sow has finished him.'

We arrived at the stream's mouth. Falih's *tarada* with a small
crowd was waiting for us where the embankment was high and
fairly wide. We landed and drew up the canoe with Manati in it.
He was lying on his side, a man supporting his head and shoulders. He seemed to have bled very little for the water in the bottom of the boat was only tinged with pink, but the wound was a
ghastly looking mess, the torn ends of muscles sticking out from
the oozing flesh. Manati moved slightly to look at his injury but
said nothing.

In my boxes at Falih's village was a large supply of drugs. I was
not qualified as a doctor, but after twenty years in wild places,
where everyone assumed, as a matter of course, that I would treat
their sick and injured, I had acquired some experience of medicine. Furthermore, I had always taken every opportunity to go
round wards of hospitals and to watch operations and in that
way had picked up quite a bit of surgical knowledge. I was to
acquire a great deal more during the years I spent in the Marshes.

Now I said to Falih: 'We had better get him back as quickly
as we can to your *mudhif*, where I can give him morphia and try
to patch him up, not that there is much I can do for him. We
must send him to hospital in Amara.'

'Don't send me to hospital,' Manati pleaded, 'not hospital. Let
me stay in my village. Ask the Englishman to doctor me.'

I said, 'Let's get him back anyway to your village,' but Falih
insisted that the meal was ready, 'Let us first eat and then go.'

I was getting angry when Manati smiled at me and said, 'Eat,
Sahib, eat; I am all right,' and added, 'Anyway I am hungry. I
want some food myself before I go any farther.'

I gave in and walked over to where the food was spread out on
a reed mat. There was a great dish of rice and joints of mutton, as
well as roast chickens and dishes of stew. I found it impossible to
eat and rose quickly, hoping that now we could be off, but the
others sat down in turn until everyone had fed; after that there
was coffee and tea. Unable any longer to conceal my irritation
and impatience, I walked over to Manati. He was holding a
mutton bone. I wondered whether he had really eaten anything.
He looked ghastly.

Back at Falih's village Manati begged again not to be sent to hospital, but Falih eventually persuaded him to go. The pig appeared to have bitten a great lump out of his buttock. I gave him an injection of morphia, washed his wound and sprinkled it thickly with sulphonamide powder. Then we made him as comfortable as we could in a canoe and sent him off to Majar al Kabir on his way to Amara.

I met him again a year later when I lunched in his village and was horrified to find him permanently crippled, unable to move unless he supported himself on a pole. I asked how long he had been in hospital and he answered, 'When I got there they wouldn't let me in, so I came back. Thanks be to God, your medicine cured me. It was all I had.'

I suspected, however, that he had never been near the hospital but had returned to his village from Falih's *mudhif*.

4. Arrival at Qabab

Falih sent me to Qabab the following morning in a canoe paddled by three men. 'They will take you to Sadam. Come back whenever you are tired of living among the Madan. Remember this house is yours. Go in peace.'

We started off down the main river and passed another large *mudhif*, which my canoeman told me belonged to Sayid Sarwat. I was soon to discover that he was the most revered of the local *Sayids*, that his reputation extended throughout Southern Iraq, and that in consequence his *mudhif* possessed the sanctity of a mosque. Today any townsman in Iraq with pretensions to learning calls himself *Sayid*, as in Turkish times he would have called himself *Effendi*. In this sense *Sayid* simply meant Mr and had no religious significance. To the tribesmen, however, *Sayid* was still a venerated title, meaning a descendant of the Prophet.

Below Sayid Sarwat's *mudhif*, a small village straggled along the river bank, a drift of grey smoke showing above the line of houses. Buffaloes, black, sullen-looking brutes, heavy-bodied and shaggy-coated, stood beside the river or rested in the water with only their noses, the tops of their heads and their thick, curved horns showing. Canoes of various sizes were moored along the bank, and drawn up on dry land were the rotten remains of others, the planks fallen from their ribs. The usual collection of pi-dogs chased us, barking from the water's edge. A man watched silently from the entrance of a house. 'Go on, Sahib, greet him,' said one of the canoemen.

I called out, '*Salam alaikum*,' and he answered, '*Alaikum as salam*,' and added, 'Stop and eat.'

I replied, 'We have fed, God protect you.'

'Good,' said the man behind me, 'you must learn our ways. You see it is the custom for the man in the boat to greet the man on the shore, and for the boat going downstream to greet the boat coming up.'

Below the village, willow trees, bare as yet, except for a touch of green bursting from their buds, lined the bank on either side; their lower branches trailed in the muddy water, dipping to the current. Behind them were jungles of untended palms and in one place reed houses in a clearing. Here the river forked once more and we took the smaller right-hand branch. Fields of wheat and barley, another village, mud flats and then the Marshes' edge and beds of bulrushes, the same scene as the previous day.

We followed a narrow twisting channel through the reeds, and for the first mile passed many canoes returning, so deeply loaded with soaking piles of *qasab* shoots that little was visible of the canoes themselves. They were paddled by half-naked men and boys, sometimes two in a canoe but more often one. '*Hashish* (fodder) for their buffaloes,' said the man who had appointed himself as my instructor. He was called Jahaish (little donkey). This was not a nickname but his proper name. Many of these tribesmen had wildly improbable names; Jahaish was one of the least odd. I was to meet at various times men or boys called Chilaib (little dog), Bakur (sow) and Khanzir (pig), startling among Moslems, who regarded both dogs and pigs as unclean. Others had such strange names as Jaraizi (little rat), Wawai (jackal), Dhauba (hyena), Kausaj (shark), Afrit (Jinn) and even Barur (dung). In order to avert the evil eye unattractive names like these were often given to boys whose brothers had died in infancy.

We passed a place where they were gathering *hashish*, the Arabic word for grass applied here to young reeds used for fodder. A naked boy stood in the bows of a canoe cutting the green shoots with a saw-edged sickle, and piling them, dripping wet, into the canoe behind him. Every now and again he drew his canoe forward a yard or two by pulling on the bigger stems. Beyond the curtain of the reeds I could hear voices and laughter. A boy's voice, very clear and true, sang a lilting song; my canoe-men stopped to listen. 'That is Hasan,' one of them said appreciatively. The song ended and someone called out, 'Give us another.'

It was a scene which was to become familiar during the next

seven years. Sometimes the setting was winter, the water icy cold with a chill wind sweeping across the Marshes from the Kurdish snows. Sometimes it was summer, the air saturated with moisture; then it was unbearably hot in the tunnels at the bottom of the dark, towering reeds, and mosquitoes danced in hovering clouds. It seldom seemed to be spring or autumn, for those are brief periods in this part of the world. But whether it was winter or summer, I associate the sounds of laughter and song with the reedbeds, where the Marshmen toiled gathering fodder for their insatiable buffaloes.

'That boy has a lovely voice,' Jahaish said, as they picked up their paddles.

'Yes, one of the best, better than Chilaib at Qabab.'

'Yes, indeed, a better voice, but he cannot dance. Did you see that *dhakar binta* at Abd al Nabi's wedding? By God, it was a treat to watch him dance.'

I asked what a *dhakar binta* was; the words appeared to mean a male girl. Jahaish explained that a *dhakar binta* was a professional dancing boy who was also a male prostitute and there were two or three at Majar al Kabir who were hired to dance at weddings and other festivities. When I asked if they lived among the tribes, he said 'No, no never. Of course, plenty of our boys dance, but they aren't *dhakar binta*.'

One of his companions added, 'Well, there is *one* at Saigal. What is more, his son Mazan is also going to be a wonderful dancer. He is still a child but, by God, he is better even now than his father ever was.'

We passed no more canoes and moved slowly, almost drifting, down the still lanes between the golden reeds. Except when one of us spoke, there was hardly a sound other than the subdued splash of the paddles and the whisper of water under the prow. Gradually the lane broadened and we found ourselves at the edge of a small lake, three-quarters of a mile wide. The water was a vivid blue in the sunlight. Jahaish said, 'We will go straight across; there is no wind.' A large band of coots rested on the lake and beyond them a lot of duck, too far off to identify. I picked up my gun but the duck rose as we emerged from the shelter of the reeds.

'They are very wild now,' Jahaish said. 'You should come here in the autumn when they have just arrived; then you could shoot as many as you wish. Falih got a lot this winter.'

The reeds across the lake looked like low sandstone cliffs along a much indented coast, while those in the distance behind reminded me of fields of ripe corn. On the far side we plunged again into the reedbeds and met two large boats. They were stacked with dry reeds and left us only just space to pass. Both were very roomy, with high sides, about thirty feet long, and with a decoratively carved stern and prow (Plate 31). Each carried a crew of three who propelled the boat slowly forward by setting their poles in the water and then moving step by step along the gunwale, from bow to stern. Having reached the stern they walked back and started again.

'Is Sadam at Qabab?' shouted Jahaish.

'Yes, he got back the day before yesterday from Khalaf's.' Khalaf was Falih's younger brother. 'Where are you going?'

'To Sadam; we are taking the Englishman there from Falih's.'

'Where is Falih?'

'At home.'

'And Majid?'

'Still in Baghdad.'

'We call these boats *balam*,' Jahaish told me. 'They come from Qabab with reeds for Majid's new *mudhif*.'

Soon afterwards we overtook canoes loaded with *hashish*, on their way back to Qabab. The channel was evidently shallower, for bulrushes grew among the *qasab*. It broadened out; we rounded a promontory of rushes and there, on a shining expanse just rippled by the breeze, was the village; the houses were reflected in the water. A haze of white smoke merged into the pale-blue sky above them and a wall of yellow rushes lay beyond. There were sixty-seven houses scattered about the lagoon, sometimes only a few yards apart. From a distance they appeared to be actually in the water, but in fact each was constructed on a soggy pile of rushes, resembling a giant swan's nest, just large enough for the building and a space in front (Plates 14 and 15). Two buffaloes stood before the nearest, water dripping from their black coats; others lay more or less submerged near by. Like those on the mainland, the houses were all made of mats, fastened over an arched framework of *qasab*. They were open at one end and we could look into them as we paddled past. Some were of a fair size; others were mere shelters hardly to be classed as houses at all (Plate 17). The newer ones were the colour of fresh straw but most were dirty grey.

Everywhere people climbed in and out of canoes, to get from one small artificial island to another. Men and boys were carrying armfuls of *hashish* ashore, to pile it in front of their houses. We called a greeting to them and they answered: 'Welcome; welcome; stop and eat.' I watched a boy of four or five step into a canoe, pick up a pole, push off and punt towards a reedbed. A young woman with a child in her arms called to him as he passed. She had a lovely face, tapering to a delicate chin, and wore a black dress, with a coarse black cloak thrown over her head. In front of another house two girls in long gowns of patterned cloth, one red, the other green, pounded grain in a wooden mortar with long heavy pestles. They struck in turn, bending their bodies forward from the hips, and grunted rhythmically with each blow.

Sadam's *mudhif* was at the far end of the village on the edge of the reedbeds and a little apart from the other houses. The largest building in Qabab, it was the only one on dry ground, for it occupied a small sheer-sided island of black earth that rose five or six feet above the surrounding water. This island was evidently an ancient site, for brickwork showed near the water-level. There was sufficient room for another smaller house in which Sadam and his family lived. As we approached, he came out, shouting over his shoulder to a boy to hurry up and bring carpets. 'Welcome, welcome,' he called, and helped me ashore. He was a tall, lean man, his face lightly marked with smallpox, and clean-shaven except for a thin moustache. He was dressed in a white shirt under a brown cloak and he wore a headcloth and head-rope. With him was his son Auda, a self-possessed child of ten.

I kicked off my shoes at the entrance and went in. The *mudhif*, the only one in Qabab, was roughly built, had seven arches and was open at the southern end. From its raised position, it commanded a view of the entire village. Some rather tattered reed mats covered the floor, and a hurricane lamp with a blackened glass hung on a reed stuck into the wall.

'Where is that boy? God curse him,' Sadam exclaimed impatiently. A stupid-looking youth appeared with two large carpets and some cushions. 'Come on, boy, hurry up; can't you see that we have guests? Give those to me and go and get the other carpet, the good one.' The boy came back with a small prayer-rug of fine quality. Sadam spread this against the far wall, put a cushion, shaped like a bolster and covered with red silk, beside it, and asked me to be seated. I heard him whisper to the servant. 'Tell them to prepare lunch, and then go to the merchant and see if he has any fish. Mind you get a good one, and bring back six packets of cigarettes, and more sugar and tea. Take the small canoe.'

A large, heavily built man came in. He had a curiously indeterminate face, which had probably been handsome when he was a a boy but was now effeminate and flabby. Accompanied by his son of about fifteen, he greeted us and sat down. 'Come on, Ajram, lend a hand,' Sadam said to the boy, a cheerful-looking lad. 'Boil water for coffee. There it is in the big pot. Get a fire going; the *qasab* is over there in the corner. Here are some matches.'

When his servant came back, Sadam tossed a packet of cigarettes in front of me, and one in front of each of my companions. He opened the other packets and threw a cigarette to each of the people in the room.

Several men had come in while he was giving us coffee, and more arrived now, until there were twenty or thirty, similar in type to the villagers who had gone pig-hunting with me and Falih. What struck me most was the breadth of their faces; several, and one tall youth in particular, were almost Mongolian in appearance. All the grown men had moustaches and a few of the old ones little grey beards. Their hair was cropped. They were dressed in the usual headcloth and shirt and most of them wore a coarse cloak.

Sadam went out and returned, followed by Auda, Ajram and his servant, carrying two bowls of soup, two boiled chickens and a large round tray heaped with glutinous rice. He placed the dishes on a round mat in front of me. Ajram and the servant reappeared with a grilled fish, two feet long, and half a dozen thick discs of unleavened brown bread, burnt in places and smeared with ashes. As was customary, Jahaish invited Sadam to join us but he refused saying, 'Eat, eat.' He poured the soup over the rice and broke up the chickens, piling the meat in front of us. Bedu always roll rice into a solid ball in the palm of the hand before popping it into their mouths, but here they used only the tips of the fingers. I noticed they ate rice with the chicken, and bread with the fish. At the end, each person rose independently, washed his hands and rinsed out his mouth.

After we had finished, Sadam invited the others to feed, but one after the other they pretended to refuse, saying, 'Thank you; we have already fed.'

'Nonsense; come on, feed,' Sadam urged them.

'No. Never. No, no,' they answered with apparent indignation.

Finally Sadam took a man by the arm, as if to drag him forcibly, whereupon he rose and went over to the food. After more protests, some of the others joined him, but a few said, 'No, really Sadam, I promise you I have fed. By your mother's milk I have fed' – a curious oath that seemed peculiar to the Al bu Muhammad tribe. Of those who eventually ate, hardly one had not first declared that he never would. I also noticed that they immediately chased a dog out of the room, but allowed a cat to sit beside them and even gave it scraps.

After more tea and coffee, my three canoemen stood up and Jahaish said, 'Remain in the safe keeping of God, Sadam.'

'What? You are going? Nonsense; spend the night,' Sadam exclaimed.

'No, we have work to do; we must get back.'

'I beg you to stay.'

'No, really,' and they repeated, 'Remain in the safe keeping of God.'

Sadam said, 'All right, go in peace,' and I added, 'Salute me to Falih.'

'God give you peace,' they answered, picked up their paddles and poles which they had stacked in a corner of the room, went out and boarded their canoe.

As the rest left, an old man came up and said to Sadam, 'Bring the Englishman to my house to drink tea this afternoon.' I noticed that, in accepting the invitation, Sadam addressed him as *Zair*, a religious title used by the Shias.

In Islam the split between Sunni and Shia is as fundamental as that between Catholic and Protestant in Christendom. Today, Northern Iraq is Sunni, Southern Iraq Shia, a division of considerable political importance. In Arabic the word Shia originally meant a party, but came to be used exclusively to denote the Party of Ali, the Prophet's cousin and son-in-law, whom the Shias regard as his first legitimate successor, whereas the Sunnis affirm that the Prophet was succeeded by Abu Bakr, the first Caliph.

5. First Impressions of the Madan

Muhammad united the warring tribes of Arabia for the first time in their history. Within ten years of his death in A.D. 632, the same poverty-stricken and intensely individualistic tribesmen erupted from the desert, destroyed the disciplined armies that opposed them, and wrested Syria and Egypt from Byzantium, Iraq from Persia. In less than a hundred years their empire stretched from the Pyrenees to the borders of China, and covered a greater area than was ever ruled by Rome. Their achievement was the more remarkable since the state which they set up was torn by rivalries and feuds from its earliest years.

Trouble started when Omar – who succeeded Abu Bakr, the first Caliph – was murdered in 644. Othman, the next Caliph, a man of feeble character but the representative of powerful families in Mecca, was murdered in 656. Ali succeeded him, but was widely suspected of being implicated. Civil war broke out and Muaiya, who was Othman's nephew and governor of Syria, joined the rebels. Intermittent fighting and inconclusive negotiations followed one another until, in 661, Ali himself was murdered in his new capital of Kufa, in Southern Iraq. His body was buried in the desert.

Hasan, Ali's eldest son, was weak and self-indulgent and needed little persuasion to renounce his claims. Muaiya, the powerful governor of Syria, became Caliph and founded the famous Omaiyad Caliphate of Damascus. The new régime was soon unpopular in Iraq where most of the population, although converts to Islam, were not Arabs and resented the arrogance and oppression of their Arab rulers. When Muaiya died, the people of Kufa planned revolt. They sent messengers to Husain, Ali's second son, imploring him to come to Iraq and head the rebellion, and promised him universal support. Husain agreed and set out across the desert from Mecca with a small party, including women and children. On the way he learnt that the plot had been betrayed and that the ten ringleaders had been arrested and executed. Undeterred, he marched on and arrived at Karbala on the Euphrates. He was faced by four thousand men, lined up along the river, whom the new Caliph, Yezid, had sent to intercept him. Certainly Yezid had not ordered his death nor did he desire it. Husain could safely have withdrawn or he could have surrendered. Instead he chose to fight and by so doing altered the history of Islam.

Not one of those on whose support he had counted moved to his assistance. Only a lone Frank, tradition says, joined the little band, impressed by their bravery. On the tenth day of the Arabic month of Muharram, A.D. 680, Husain and his party advanced against their enemies. 'It did not take long,' an eyewitness told Yezid. 'Just time enough to slaughter a camel and have a short nap.' Husain's severed head was carried to Kufa and shown to Yezid's governor, who slashed it across the mouth with his cane. In the appalled silence that followed, an old man raised his voice. 'Alas that I should have lived to see this day – I who saw those lips kissed by the Prophet of God.'

Shiism had started as a political movement among Arabs to advance the claims of Ali and his descendants to the Caliphate. But after the martyrdom of Husain, it established itself as a new religious movement and soon became especially powerful in Iraq and Persia, embodying the social discontent of the indigenous population with the Arab aristocracy. In time, Shiism split Islam as decisively as the Reformation divided the Catholic Church. Whereas the orthodox Sunnis recognize Ali as the fourth of the Caliphs, or successors to Muhammad, the Shias regard the first three Caliphs as usurpers. They believe in an apostolic succession of Imams who followed the Prophet. Most of them believe in twelve of these, of whom Ali, Hasan and Husain were the first three, the others being Husain's descendants. According to the Shias, the last Imam was Muhammad al Mahdi who mysteriously disappeared at Samarra and whose return they await in the fullness of time as the Mahdi or Expected One.

The Holy City of Najaf grew up in the desert, round Ali's tomb, over which the Faithful built a great mosque with golden

domes, that even today no infidel may enter. From as far away
as India, men still bring their dead to rest in this hallowed earth;
for to many, Ali the Saint is a semi-divine figure, greater even
than the Prophet himself. To the original Moslem declaration of
faith, 'I affirm that there is no God but God, and that Muhammad is the Prophet of God,' the Shias add, 'and that Ali is the
Vice-Regent of God.' Husain's body was buried at Karbala
where he fell. Soon afterwards men began to visit this place to
pray, a town arose, and then a splendid mosque housing the remains of the greatest Shia martyr. Both Karbala and Najaf became the goal of pilgrims from across the world.

The Marshmen, when I first visited them, were extremely suspicious of the outside world. From Qabab they would go to the
market in Majar, but few had been to Amara, twenty miles beyond, and only one or two had seen Basra or Baghdad. All,
however, hoped to visit Karbala and Najaf, and every man would
have wished his body to be taken to Najaf and buried there.

On our way to the *Zair*, Sadam suggested that we should visit
the merchant. We got into Sadam's canoe and, paddled by Ajram,
went towards the nearest group of houses. Two of them were
built on a single 'island', and a piece of white cloth, like a small
flag, was fastened to a reed stuck in the roof of the larger one. 'A
shop is always marked like that, then a stranger can see where it
is,' said Sadam. Two small brown cows and three rather be-
draggled sheep chewed at a heap of green reeds. The merchant
himself came to the edge of the island to greet us and hold the
canoe; the cut rushes on which he stood sank several inches under
his feet into water which was dirty with floating pieces of dung
and other oddments. Near by a lavatory was built out over the
water, a precarious reed platform inadequately sheltered from
sight by a strip of torn matting. This was a refinement of civilization. Ordinary Marshmen paddled to the nearest reedbed and
squatted over the side of the canoe, a knack not easily acquired.

As we stepped ashore, the merchant's son cowed a dog into
silence by waving a paddle over its head, and two chickens flew
up on to the roof. The shop door was made from packing-cases:
a padlock hung on a chain. Inside, the merchant dragged forward
an empty tea chest for me to sit on and told his son to prepare tea.

There was not much to buy. Two sacks, one marked Sugar and the other sprinkled with flour, a large package of dates, a chest of cheap Indian tea, a tin of kerosene, packets of Iraqi cigarettes and matches, some bars of soap and a dusty head-rope. I remembered having seen the merchant in Sadam's *mudhif*; one of his eyes was inflamed and now he kept dabbing at it with a corner of his headcloth.

Through the doorway I noticed, with misgiving, a girl filling a kettle with water from beside our canoe, having scooped some solid pieces of muck aside. But the tea tasted like any other. While we waited for it I asked Sadam what qualifications a man required to call himself *Zair*, and he explained that a pilgrim must have visited the shrine of Ali ar Ridha, the eighth Imam, at Meshed er Ridha in Khurasan, in North-eastern Persia. It so happened that I had been in Meshed the previous winter and had been lucky enough to see the mosque and do the circuit of the shrine. This was the building which Robert Byron thought one of the most beautiful in Persia when he entered it in disguise in 1933. Even in 1950 it was very difficult for a non-Moslem to get in. In the same mosque is the tomb of the famous Caliph, Harun ar Rashid who is execrated by the Shias for having caused the death of the Imam Ali ar Ridha. In Southern Iraq generally, far more pilgrims had been to Meshed than to Mecca, although the distance is much the same. During my years in the Marshes I met many *Zairs* but I only remember three *Hajis*.

Although Shias count Karbala and Najaf more holy than Meshed, in Southern Iraq a pilgrimage to them conferred no title. Some years later, when I was in Central Afghanistan among the Hazaras, who are also Shias, I found that any man who had been to Karbala was called *Karbalawi* whereas a pilgrimage to nearby Meshed brought no titular distinction. It appears to be a question of distance.

The *Zair*'s house was one of several, separated by ditches of dirty water a few feet wide. Before the open end of each, a soggy farmyard covered a larger area than the house itself. Its floor, a mixture of decayed vegetation and manure, rose a few inches above water-level and was contained by a reed fence less than a foot high. On the outside walls of the house, rows of dung cakes dried in the sun. An old woman in black and two small girls in coloured dresses sat in the sunlight at the entrance. We landed, stepping over the fence and entered the house, pushing past buffaloes that swung their heads away but otherwise paid no attention. One of their calves stood inside and a brood of chicks scuttled under our feet. Another woman, dressed in black like all the older women in the village, said 'Welcome Sadam,' and lifted a small, naked child to make room for us to pass.

The interior was about six yards long, two yards wide and eight feet high, with seven arches. I learnt later that all houses and *mudhifs* are traditionally made with an odd number of arches. The room was divided in two by a low bed-like structure of *qasab* stems, built against the left-hand wall, on which were piled goat-hair sacks containing grain, and an assortment of quilts, odds and ends of clothing and other rags. Some canoe poles rested on top. The near half of the house belonged to the women and there they did the cooking. We picked our way past a wooden mortar, a butter churn made out of a skin bag suspended from a wooden tripod and a circular grindstone with a wooden handle. A lot of dishes, trays and pots were scattered beside a small fire. At the far end, the *Zair* was saying his afternoon prayers, his cloak spread before him as a prayer-rug. This was the men's half where guests were entertained. Two frayed, dirty rugs were laid on the reed mats, also several woollen cushions, bright with coloured geometrical designs, but stuffed overfull for comfort. Sadam, acting as host, said, 'Sit down; make yourself at home.' At length the *Zair* finished his prostrations, sat back, muttered a final prayer, stroked his beard, looked over his right and left shoulder, stood up, picked up his cloak and said, 'Welcome.'

He was a distinguished old man, tall but stooped, and with a lined ascetic face, beaked nose and white beard. He wore nothing except a headcloth and a long white shirt so thin as to be transparent. Picking up another cushion, he put it on top of the one beside me and said, 'Now lean on that, you will be more comfortable.' He lit a fire in a gap in the matting on the floor of trampled rushes and, when it was going, added dried cakes of buffalo dung, propping them one against the other like a card house. A pungent, whitish smoke filled the room, making my eyes water. Sadam said, 'That bit is still wet,' and took it off, but the fire smoked just the same.

The *Zair* fetched the tea things and sat beside the fire, washing the glasses, saucers and spoons in an enamelled bowl. The tea was in a screw of paper and the sugar in a small tin. While the *Zair* and Sadam discussed the levy of reeds which Falih had demanded for his father's new *mudhif*, the *Zair*'s son arrived back. He unloaded the *hashish*, feeding some of it to the buffaloes and piling the rest just inside the house. He looked about twenty, was bare-headed, his short hair cut in a pudding-bowl style, and was naked except for a cloak wrapped round his waist. Leaning his fishing spear in a corner, he put on a shirt before joining us.

'I will go to Bu Mughaifat and see Sahain tomorrow,' Sadam said. 'He must produce two more boatloads of reeds from his village.'

'Yes, by God, Sadam, so far *we* have produced it all,' the *Zair* exclaimed.

'Sahain's people always get out of everything,' his son added. 'It is the same with all the Feraigat. All they can do is to make trouble.'

That evening, back at Sadam's *mudhif*, I stood watching the sun go down behind reedbeds that stretched to the world's end. High overhead, banks of cirrus cloud, blown to tattered streams, ranged from ebony to flaming gold and the colour of old ivory, against a background of vermilion and orange, violet, mauve and palest green. From all around, as if the Marshes breathed, came the massed voices of frogs, an all-pervading pulse of sound, so sustained that the mind ceased to take note of it. More than any other, even than the crying of geese in winter, this was the sound of the Marshes. A dog barked; a buffalo grunted with a noise surprisingly like a camel's; a man called out a long, and to me, unintelligible message; a pause, and someone answered. More buffaloes swam across the open water towards the village, only their heads showing and each leaving a wake. Among the houses columns of dense smoke spread upwards from small fires, lit to keep the mosquitoes away from the herds. A boy, late back from the reedbeds, paddled down a waterway, a path of shining gold leading from the setting sun. He sang softly as he came towards me, the notes lingering in the air.

Sadam called and I went inside.

6. In Sadam's Guest House

During the last year I had read what I could about the Madan. It was little enough. The only book seemed to be *Haji Rikkan: Marsh Arab* by Fulanain (S. E. Hedgecock), a sympathetic description of a Marshman's life at the end of the First World War. Otherwise I found nothing but occasional references to them, all unflattering, in various accounts of the Mesopotamian campaign. Certainly the Madan had a bad name with Arabs and Englishmen alike. In Arabic the word meant a dweller in the *Adan* or Plain, and the nomads of the desert used it contemptuously to signify any of the Iraqi river tribes, while the cultivators along the rivers used it disparagingly of the Marshmen. All Arabs are snobs. The greater the pretensions of any tribe to pure Arab descent, the more its members despised the Marshmen for their dubious lineage, and the readier they were to impute to them every form of treachery and evil. Townsmen, too, travelling up and down the Tigris and Euphrates, feared them, shunned them, and believed all they heard against them. Even among the British in Iraq their reputation was bad – a legacy, I suspected, from the First World War, when, from the shelter of their Marshes, they had murdered and looted both sides indiscriminately.

During the few years that the British administered Iraq, the political officers had been too busy with more urgent matters to concern themselves much with the Madan. Several of them had travelled widely in the Marshes, but their visits seldom lasted more than a few days. In recent years a number of Europeans from Basra and Baghdad had come for the duck shooting, but they stayed with the richer sheikhs on the edge of the Marshes. As for Iraqi officials, I felt certain that none of them had been farther into the Marshes than was absolutely necessary. I was probably the first outsider with both the inclination and opportunity to live among the Madan, as one of them.

Like many Englishmen of my generation and upbringing I had an instinctive sympathy with the traditional life of others. My childhood was spent in Abyssinia, which at that time was without cars or roads, and then, after leaving Oxford, I lived for the next eighteen years in remote parts of Africa and the Middle East. All this made it easy for me to consort with tribal people, to adapt myself to their ways and to find an interest in their lives, but difficult for me to feel at home with those who had discarded their own customs and were trying to adapt themselves to Western civilization. In Iraq, as elsewhere, this change was inevitable and I knew that others, broader-minded than myself, found the process interesting and believed in the value of its results. All the same, I preferred to see as little of the products as possible. For example, I generally felt bored and frustrated when I had to spend a night with Iraqi officials – for which I blamed myself, since my hosts were friendly and extremely hospitable. But their preoccupation was with Iraqi politics about which I knew little and cared less, while my interest in the tribes appeared to them incomprehensible or even sinister. We would talk for hours about the United Nations, the attractions of a holiday in Paris, different makes of motor-car or the development of their country, and for the sake of good manners I would be forced to utter insincerities. Their houses, comfortable compared with many places I had slept in, were too often jerry-built bungalows in execrable taste. Their education had taught them to judge civilization entirely by material progress and they were, in consequence, ashamed of their background and anxious to forget it. A suburbia covering the length and breadth of Iraq was the Utopia of which they dreamed.

My own tastes went, perhaps, too far to the other extreme. I loathed cars, aeroplanes, wireless and television, in fact most of our civilization's manifestations in the past fifty years, and was always happy, in Iraq or elsewhere, to share a smoke-filled hovel with a shepherd, his family and beasts. In such a household, everything was strange and different, their self-reliance put me at ease, and I was fascinated by the feeling of continuity with the past. I envied them a contentment rare in the world today and a mastery of skills, however simple, that I myself could never hope to attain.

I had spent many years in exploration, but now there were no untouched places left to explore, at least in the countries that attracted me. I therefore felt inclined to settle down among a people of my choosing. In Arabia I had been very close to my companions, but constant journeying had prevented me from getting to know any particular community as well as I could have wished. What little I had seen so far of the Marshmen appealed to me. They were cheerful and friendly and I liked the look of them. Their way of life, as yet little affected by the outside world, was unique and the Marshes themselves were beautiful. Here, thank God, was no sign of that drab modernity which, in its uniform of second-hand European clothes, was spreading like a blight across the rest of Iraq.

Sadam was alone in the room, brewing coffee. As I sat down he handed me a cup and pushed the flaming end of a long bundle of reeds farther under the pot.

'What are your plans, Sahib?' In Arabic *Sahib* simply means a friend. 'Falih sent me a message that you wish to see the Marshes. Do you work for the Government?'

'No. I travel because I enjoy seeing different places and different kinds of people.'

'Who pays for your journeys? What salary do you get?'

'I have no salary, and I pay for my own journeys.'

'How strange,' and Sadam said nothing more for a minute or two.

I could tell that he did not believe me so I added, 'I have travelled in many countries, in the land of the Habash, in the Sudan and in Arabia. I have just come here from Kurdistan. I seek knowledge.'

I hope it sounded impressive. He certainly would not believe me if I said I travelled for fun.

'Do you seek knowledge among the Madan?' he asked, looking sceptical.

'Knowledge is to be found in all places,' I replied sententiously.

After another pause he said, 'Do you know Grimley? He was Consul in Amara.'

'Yes, we were together in the war.'

'He is my friend. He enjoys a party. Where is he now?'

'I don't know.'

'Do you know Ditchburn in Baghdad?'

'I met him once in Syria.'

'Do you know Edmonds?'

'Yes, in England.'

'Edmonds is a good man. He is our friend; he is very wise. Is he well?'

'Yes, praise be to God he is well. He sends his salutations.'

In Iraq, at that time, the British still had a considerable legacy of good will, the result of our close association with the country between the two world wars when Englishmen worked there as administrative officers and advisers. Many of the older inhabitants continued to feel respect and affection for individuals. Tribesmen were, on the whole, too courteous to embarrass a guest, but I was sometimes bitterly attacked by townsmen or Government officials over British policy – Palestine or Suez, for example. On such occasions, the mention of an Englishman they had known could turn bitterness to friendly reminiscence.

'What have you got in those boxes?' Sadam continued.

'Medicine.'

'You are a doctor?'

'I know about medicine.'

'Have you a medicine for my head? It hurts.'

I opened the box and gave him two aspirins.

'More, Sahib, this is very little.'

I allowed him six more, but warned him only to take two at a time.

'And for my stomach? I have a pain here too.'

I gave him some soda-mint tablets.

'What is this?' and he pointed to a bottle.

'That is iodine.'

'And this?'

'That is gentian violet, for burns,' and I firmly shut the box.

Another pause, while he handed me more coffee, and then he asked, 'Where do you wish to go?'

'I would like to cross the Marshes to the Euphrates and return

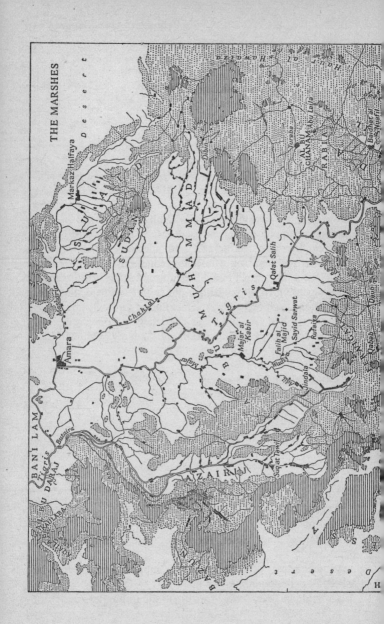

THE MARSHES

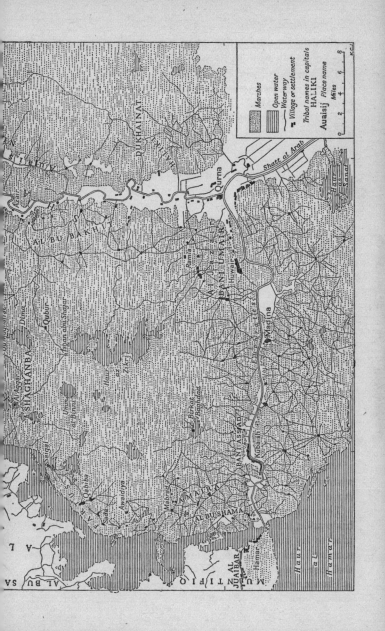

through the Fartus country, where I travelled last year with the Consul.'

'Did you meet Jasim al Faris?'

'No, he was away when we visited his village. His young son Falih entertained us.'

'I do not know him. Stay here; it is much better. We will go shooting together, duck, pig, whatever you wish.'

'Thank you, Sadam. I will certainly come back, but first I want to see the Marshes.'

'The Marshes are big, Sahib, beyond the Tigris they stretch far into Persia. You would not see them in a year.'

'All the same I hope to see what I can now.'

'Very well. Tomorrow we will go to Bu Mughaifat. I have work to do there. We will lunch with Sahain. The next day I will take you to the Euphrates by way of Zikri. It is a big lake, a bad place when the wind blows. Many Madan have been drowned there.'

At dinner, which we ate alone, Sadam offered me a bowl of buffalo's milk. I had not tried it before and found I preferred it to cow's milk. Afterwards the room filled up and I sat back against the wall, listening to the talk. Most of it was beyond me, as yet, for they discussed the cultivation of rice, using terms I did not know.

I asked, 'Do you grow rice in Qabab?'

'We did in the past, but the floods no longer carry down silt. Qabab is finished for rice growing. You can't grow it except on fresh silt. This year we shall ask Majid to give us land to cultivate near the river's mouth.'

'Do you mean you will leave here?'

'Of course not. This is our home. We are Madan. Those who wish will grow rice on the edge of the Marshes but they will all come back here.'

Two men started an angry argument about the payment of a bride price, still outstanding. Everyone joined in. Ajram's father tried to lay down the law. Sadam turned on him. 'Husain, to-morrow I and the Englishman are coming to lunch with you. We shall expect a good lunch.' There was a silence. Everyone looked at Husain, who fidgeted, said 'Welcome' in an unconvincing tone and then hurried on, 'By your mother's milk, Sadam, tomorrow

I have to go to Majar.' Several people smiled and I sensed that
Husain was being baited. I learnt later that he was notoriously
mean.

'Go to Majar the following day. Tomorrow the Englishman
honours your house.'

'I am honoured,' Husain replied unhappily.

Sadam said, 'At midday then. Meat and milk and rice.'

Husain appealed to the others. 'You all know that I have to
go to Majar tomorrow. I have an appointment with my wife's
cousin.'

'The one that died last year?' Sadam asked.

'No, really, Sadam. I swear on your life. By Abbas,
Sadam.'

'By God, Husain, the day you entertain a guest will be a day to
remember. You are a disgrace.'

I felt sorry for Ajram.

When at last the guests left, Sadam detailed Ajram and another boy to spend the night in the *mudhif*.

'Put the Englishman's luggage between you, and the lamp on
top of it. One of you stay awake, and I'll kill you if anything is
stolen. His guns I will take to my house for safe keeping.' To me
he said, 'You will be all right here, but the Madan are thieves.
Last week some of them stole my canoe, God burn them! I still
haven't got it back. Then a month ago they broke into the merchant's shop at night and cleared it out. When you are in the
Marshes sleep on your guns, otherwise they will be stolen; not
by the people of the house; by others, probably from another
village. A few years ago the Regent himself came to Majar. All
the sheikhs were there with their men, an enormous crowd. One
of Majid's men had a new Burno, for which Majid had paid more
than a hundred dinars. The man was very proud of it and showed
it to everyone. A Madan asked to look at it. He handed it to him,
and the Madan just dived into the crowd. He was never seen
again, nor the rifle. Majid was furious.'

Sadam's servant brought a mattress and a quilt. 'Put it there,'
Sadam told him. 'No, there, you fool, and get the cushion.'

I said I had blankets.

'You will not need them here. This is your house.' He arranged
the cushion, bade me good night and warned Ajram, 'If you sleep

I will flay you'; a threat he seemed quite capable of putting into effect.

I too went outside before lying down. There was no moon and the night was very dark. Ajram called, 'Look out for the dog.' The stars glittered, diamond bright, and were reflected in the water at my feet. The air was sharp with a lingering touch of winter, and in a few houses the light of fires still flickered through the doorways. Duck landed with a splash near by and I was conscious once more of the rhythmic croaking of the frogs.

7. Bu Mughaifat: A Marsh Village

The sun was not up when I woke. Ajram had relit the fire with buffalo dung and the pungent smoke eddied about the room.

'Good morning, Sahib. You slept well?'

'Good morning, Ajram. Yes, very well indeed; and you?'

'I did not sleep; I guarded your things.'

He folded the bedding, took a kettle and, in a corner of the room, poured lukewarm water into my cupped hands, so that I could wash my face and rinse out my mouth. Sadam called to him to come and milk the buffaloes and I went out to watch. The smoke of many fires hung in a haze over the village. The lagoon was glassy, the colouring everywhere subdued, the air chilly and rather damp. The milk pail, cut from a block of wood, tapered at the base to a point so that it could not be stood upright. Sadam's servant handed it to Ajram who squatted against the buffalo's flank, holding the pail between his knees. There were four buffaloes and a calf. I wondered why Sadam had called Ajram instead of detailing his servant. I had not realized that only some boys knew how to milk, a curious shortcoming in a people whose life centred round their buffaloes. Some families in Qabab owned as many as fifteen, but the usual number seemed to be between six and eight, and there was at least one in front of every house.

It did not surprise me that women were not allowed to milk buffaloes, for among the Bedu of Southern Arabia they were never allowed to milk camels. On the other hand, among the shepherd tribes outside the Marshes, and also among the Kurds, men would not milk sheep or goats; they merely held them for the women. No Marshman would ever pound or grind grain, nor would he make dung cakes for fuel; and he would only cook or fetch water if there was no woman there to do it for him. Such prohibitions are common among all primitive peoples. A Catholic Mission in the Shilluk country of the Southern Sudan once lost all its adherents when the priests disregarded the boys' protests that only women plastered the inside of a house with mud.

When Ajram had finished, we breakfasted off flaps of rice bread, and the buffalo's milk, heated and sweetened with sugar. Sadam then sent him to fetch a canoe with three men to take us to Bu Mughaifat. Here in Qabab, Sadam possessed almost despotic power, fining or flogging the villagers at will and levying tolls on merchandise passing through. He was Majid's representative, and in the Marshes the Government was content to leave authority in the hands of the sheikhs.

Majid was one of the two paramount sheikhs of the Al bu Muhammad, a settled tribe numbering a hundred and twenty thousand that lived along the main stream of the Tigris and the many branches that flowed into the Marshes, from Amara as far south as Azair. The other sheikh was Muhammad al Araibi, a very old man whose domain was on the east side of the Tigris. In Turkish times the tribe had relied on the rice crops, sown on land inundated by the spring floods. More recently, with the introduction of mechanical pumps, many of them grew winter crops of wheat and barley. Although nearly every family kept some buffaloes, the tribe, except for a few sections that lived inside the Marshes, were reckoned to be Fallah and not Madan. Only two or three families of Al bu Muhammad lived at Qabab itself. The village's other inhabitants belonged to the Feraigat, Shaghanba or Fartus. These three tribes and such Al bu Muhammad as lived elsewhere in the Marshes, were reckoned Madan, despite the fact that many of them cultivated rice.

In Amara Province, sheikhs whose lands bordered the Marshes had acquired a right over the villages inside, even when these were inhabited by other tribes. The sheikhs took a share of the rice crop, when there was one, allowed no one to trade who did not pay for the right, and insisted that the villagers sold fish only to men they had authorized to buy it. They requisitioned dry reeds for the building of their houses and *mudhifs* and, in some cases, levied a tax on the buffaloes. Their representatives, of course, levied further tolls to benefit themselves. The villagers grumbled at this system but accepted it.

In return the sheikhs and their representatives kept the peace and gave the tribes the justice they understood. The tribesmen dreaded being involved in a court case where they would have to pay heavy lawyers' fees and bribes and would be kept from home as long as it lasted. If convicted, they might be jailed in a town far removed from their kinsmen, a terrifying prospect, since few of them had ever been more than a dozen miles outside the shelter of the Marshes. The sheikh might fine them, have them flogged or even imprison them for a while in his village, but he would deal with them in his *mudhif*, in surroundings with which they were familiar and in the presence of their fellows. Few people were convicted who did not, in fact, deserve it.

Sadam was Majid's cousin. Generally a sheikh gave such a post to one of his trusted slaves. In Iraq all slaves were legally free, but the tribesmen still reckoned a man a slave whose ancestors had been so. This did not mean that he was ill-treated or even despised. Many slaves were enrolled among the sheikh's retainers, a few had great power and prestige and I often heard them spoken of with envy. Some were foster-brothers to the sheikh or his sons. Many, having much Arab blood, were almost indistinguishable from the local tribesmen in colour and appearance. But although it was common for Arabs to take a slave girl, it was death for a slave to touch a freeborn woman. To avenge the insult, her relations would hunt him down and kill him, even if he had married her.

As I soon realized, Sadam was extremely unpopular. He was overbearing and tyrannical, and his temper when roused was ungovernable. The villagers complained that he made full use of his position to enrich himself, but any of them would have done the same. They admitted his generosity, admired his strength of character and were also amused by his sense of humour, which could be outrageous. On one occasion he scandalized the neighbourhood by making his canoemen sing a catchy couplet, as they passed a village where the brother of a man he disliked had just died, and where the mourning was in full progress – 'May God burn your brother, who died yesterday, you son of a dog.'

In the end he overreached himself. A sailing boat loaded with packages of dates went through Qabab on its way from Qurna to Amara. Sadam came out of his house and peremptorily ordered the owner to stop and hand over three packages, before the boat continued. The man answered that he would have been delighted to give Sadam some dates as a present, but he was damned if he would hand them over now. Sadam rushed indoors, fetched a rifle and fired just over his head. The man complained to Majid, who removed Sadam in disgrace the next day. I met him a number of times after that. He was in poverty but still as hospitable and welcoming as when he ruled in Qabab.

Bu Mughaifat was a couple of miles from Qabab. We set off there from Sadam's *mudhif* along a lane of water that ran like a highway between the two villages. I asked Sadam if these passages through the reedbeds were natural or man-made. He explained that when the water was low the Madan drove buffaloes through the reeds to make a track, which later was kept open by the coming and going of canoes. We came on a dozen buffaloes, submerged in the middle of the waterway, and the man in the bows jabbed at their heads with his pole to try and move them, but they paid little attention, even when the canoe scraped over their backs.

'Can the buffaloes touch bottom everywhere here?' I asked.

'Not everywhere, but they have to be able to stand in the water to feed. Besides, they like being in the water, like those we have just passed. Sometimes, when the floods are very high, they have to stay on the platform in front of the house, but then the flies worry them and they lose condition. Also, unless they can graze, it is difficult for their owners to get them enough food. As it is the Madan spend all day cutting and fetching fodder for the buffaloes at night. That is the life of the Madan, cutting reeds for the buffaloes to eat.'

I learnt that, when they were grazing, they fed on *qat* (*Polygonum senegalense*), *kauban* (*Jussiaea diffusa*) and *lisan al thaur* (*Potamogeton lucens*), as well as *sijal*, a kind of sedge (*Cyperus rotundus*) and a variety of grasses that grew in the shallows along the edge of the watercourses.

There were eighteen houses in Bu Mughaifat, clustered together, with the reedbeds pressing in upon them. We landed at one of the largest, scrambled up a slippery black bank, and squeezed through a narrow slit into the house. Several people were inside, all getting in each other's way as they laid down rugs and scattered cushions about. 'Welcome. Welcome, Sadam. Welcome, Sahib,' said Sahain, our host (Plate 25), whose name meant 'little dish'. All crowded forward to shake hands. Like all Madan, their shirts were either white or dark. Only the children wore gay colours. The interior resembled that which I had been in the day before, with one important difference, the significance of which Sadam explained to me. An entrance was in the north wall, which showed that the house was a *raba*, a combination under one roof of private dwelling and guest house. Among the Madan, as among the other tribes, a stranger could stop anywhere for a free meal or for a night's lodging and would never be turned away. When, however, there was a *mudhif*, he was expected to go there, unless he had friends in the village. In a village without a *mudhif*, he was expected to go to a *raba*. Anyone could turn his house into a *raba*, or indeed build a *mudhif*, but to do so required a certain status in the village. Later they told me of a young man who having made money in Basra returned to his village on the mainland and built himself a *mudhif*. This was considered presumptuous and when his son and then his wife died within the year the villagers were not surprised. 'His father never had a *mudhif*, no not even a *raba*,' they said. 'If he had to build one he should have got a *Sayid* to bless the enterprise. To do so otherwise was bound to be unlucky.'

I commented on Arab hospitality. Sahain told us that a few years before, three Madan from Qubur, a nearby village, visited Basra. They were young men and none of them had been out of the Marshes before. They walked down the main street in the town, feeling bewildered and rather frightened; they knew no one in Basra. They were hungry and looking for a *mudhif*. Suddenly a jovial man, with a great fat stomach, stepped out of a house into the road, and said, 'Welcome! A thousand welcomes! Come this way.' He led them into a large room, where many people, on chairs, were eating at small tables. 'Make yourself at home. What can I get you? Soup, vegetables, fish, meat, sweet? Will you drink sherbet? Just say and I will bring you whatever you order. Welcome; welcome.' The three lads thought this was a strange way to behave. Who had heard of a host asking his guests what they would have? However, he was very friendly and this was obviously how civilized people acted.

'We will have it all,' they said.

'Good, good. Soup, fish, vegetables, chicken, will that do? And of course a sweet, and sherbet to drink. Just a moment if you please.'

One of the Madan turned to the other. 'By God, these townspeople are good. Where would you find such hospitality in the Marshes? What did our parents mean when they warned us that the townspeople were bad?'

Their host came back carrying many bowls of food, which covered the table, and brought them water to wash, but they refused to allow him to pour it over their hands himself. Then, 'Go on, eat, make yourself at home,' he said. Never had they tasted such a meal. They ate and ate.

'Let me get you a little more soup. Let me get you another chicken.'

'Thank you. Thank you.'

'What a man,' they exclaimed, as he fetched more food. Finally, they assured him they were satisfied. They washed and then he brought them coffee and tea. Then they rose to go, saying—'God reward you.'

'Hi stop! Wait a minute. God reward you indeed! Where is my money? Two dinars, that is what you owe me.'

'What do you mean? Owe you money? This is your *mudhif*. We were walking past and you pressed us to come in.'

'Dogs! Give me my money. Madan, dogs, thieves! You wait till I get the police.'

In the end they were forced to pay a dinar and a half. They had no money left for the bus and had to walk back to Qurna.

'We are Madan,' one of Sahain's listeners said. 'What would we know of the town?'

Sahain said, 'I have been in Basra. People everywhere, and cars, thousands of them, each up the arse of the next.'

'Is it true there are no *mudhifs*? How does a stranger live?'

'You pay for everything, as you do in the coffee shops in Majar.'

Tea was handed round. Several more villagers had come in, crowding our end of the room. At the other end, the women were cooking lunch. Sadam told Sahain that Bu Mughaifait must contribute two boatloads of *qasab* towards Majid's new *mudhif*.

At once there were protests and arguments as to who should produce them. They were a wild unkempt crowd and the boys were as vociferous as their elders. Sadam, who was playing with a small amber rosary, intervened blandly, 'And I want it by the day after tomorrow.' This provoked a fresh outburst, which was interrupted by the arrival of lunch, two dishes of soggy rice and two chickens.

Bu Mughaifat was a Feraigat village and Sahain was *qalit*, or head man, of the section that lived here, an important and hereditary position. About forty years old, and distinguished by an air of quiet authority, he was smaller than most of the others but sturdily built, and during the argument before lunch was the only person not to get excited. He wore a small clipped beard on the point of his chin and the usual short moustache. His brother, Hafadh, who was about eighteen, brought in the food with two other boys.

The year before, while guarding his rice crop at night, Hafadh had heard what he thought was a pig. He fired and going to look found the body of a woman shot through the head. She too was a Feraigat from a nearby village. Her family eventually agreed to accept blood money, which, I now learnt, was reckoned in women. Among the Feraigat the price was six, of whom the first, known as the *fijiria*, needed to be a virgin of marriageable age, that is between fourteen and sixteen; the other five were known as the *talawi*. The *fijiria* has to come from the family of the killer, or, if he had no suitable daughter or sister, from his nearest relative. She was always married to the victim's brother or cousin. The bereaved family could choose how many *talawi* they would demand, or whether they would accept money instead. This was assessed at fifty dinars each for the first two and twenty dinars for the other three. The women or money were found by the section of the tribe to which the killer belonged. When I remarked that six women seemed a disproportionate price for one life, Sadam said, 'Compensation among the Al bu Muhammad for one of the sheikh's family is fifty women and seven years' banishment.'

The Arabic word for blood money is *fasl*, but compensation is a better translation. The degree of guilt did not affect the amount of *fasl*. I heard of a case where it was demanded, and paid, for a death which followed twenty years after an accidental injury. In the event of murder, the dead man's relations would almost certainly refuse to accept it and would seek blood for blood. *Fasl* was assessed on a varying scale for any injury; an eye at the equivalent of half a life; a tooth at one woman; and so on. It was paid for all fingers, except, for some reason, the middle one. It would be paid for a face slapped in public. Sadam even told me that if someone killed another's dog on purpose, he would be involved in a blood feud which could only be settled by three women.

I was curious about the origins of the Al bu Muhammad. Sadam described how, fourteen generations ago, one of the Zubaid Aza tribe, called Muhammad, had killed his cousin and, accompanied by his daughter Basha, sought refuge with the Feraigat. He lived with them for fifteen years and fell in love with Mahaniya, the beautiful daughter of the Feraigat sheikh. Eventually the sheikh agreed to give him his daughter in marriage, provided that Muhammad let him marry Basha. Muhammad agreed, but on the day of the marriage the sheikh substituted his uncouth daughter, Kausha, for the beautiful Mahaniya. The marriage party, singing and dancing as was the custom, brought her to Muhammad's house and there handed her over. On unveiling her, he discovered the deception, but instead of repudiating her, he took her as his wife, exclaiming, 'The praise be to God. This is the one that has fallen to me.' Kausha gave him two sons, Saad and Abud, from whom are descended the two branches of the great Al bu Muhammad tribe, the Amla and the Al bu Abud. Sadam added, 'We, the Al bu Muhammad, have as our battle cry, "I am the brother of the Basha."' This, like many other of their customs, obviously originated with the Bedu in Arabia where a man takes as his battle cry either his sister's name or his favourite camel's.

Before we left, a *Sayid* came in. A middle-aged man with stubble on his chin, he had been cutting fodder and was dressed in an old torn shirt. Everyone rose and Sadam's canoeman went across and kissed his hand. There are innumerable *Sayids* in Southern Iraq, as in most parts of the Arab world. In the Marshes there were few villages that did not boast at least one family descended from the Prophet. Certain small villages consisted entirely of *Sayids*; and I was to meet whole sections of Madan nomads who claimed such descent. There seemed little need to produce evidence to support the claim. Later, among the Fartus, I stayed with a family of so-called *Sàyids*. Several people in the village told me, 'They are not *Sayids* at all; we all know where they come from. It was only the other day the old man dyed his headcloth green.' In spite of this, they already called him *Maulana*, the form used to address a *Sayid*. Probably, in a few years, no one would question the family's pretensions.

Sahain's house was built on an island which I assumed to be either natural or the site of some ancient village, but I noticed, as we left, that it consisted of alternate layers of earth and decomposed reeds. It was in fact an elaboration of the same kind of rush platform that formed the foundation of the *Zair*'s house in Qabab. The method of construction was first to enclose an area of water large enough for the house and yard with a fence of reeds, perhaps twenty feet high; next to pack reeds and rushes within this fence; and when the stack rose above water, to fracture the reeds of the containing fence and lay them across it. The Madan then piled more rushes on top and trampled them down as tightly as possible. When satisfied with this foundation, they built the house, driving the reeds to form the arches individually into the ground, before tying them together in a bundle. If the floor flooded, because it had sunk or because the water-level had risen, the owner had only to lay down several armfuls of newly cut reeds. Such a site was called a *kibasha* (Plate 87).

For a more permanent site, the Madan covered the foundations with mud scooped up from under the water. They did this when the water was at its lowest, in the autumn, and then only where it was not too deep. They covered the mud with further layers of rushes. The *kibasha* had now become a *dibin*. If the family that built a *dibin* left it unoccupied for more than a year, they forfeited possession and anyone could use it. Over the years the alternate layers of mud and reeds formed an island like that on which Sahain's house stood.

On our way back to Qabab, some mallard rose out of the reeds close to us. Unfortunately I had not been expecting a shot and my gun was unloaded. Sadam was obviously disappointed and when we got back that evening, I offered to look for some. 'Good,

I will send Ajram with you. He knows where to go. . . . See that the Englishman does not upset the small canoe!' he called as we paddled away. 'He is not used to them' – an unnecessary comment, since my lack of skill must have been already obvious to Ajram.

We met occasional canoes returning to the village loaded with *hashish*.

'Where are you going, Ajram?'

'We're after duck.'

'Try the edge of the lagoon, there are many there.'

After a while Ajram said, 'Is your gun ready? This is the place.'

And indeed there were plenty of duck in sheltered inlets, but extremely wild. Hugging the edge of the reeds and moving very slowly, we succeeded at last in stalking a small bunch of mallard. I got two on the water with the first shot, but missed with the other barrel. Ajram paddled over and we picked them up.

'Look out, there are more coming,' he said.

Disturbed by the shots, many duck were circling and I fired at one which fell some distance inside the reedbed. Ajram pulled off his shirt, jumped into the water and crashed about among the reeds. I was not surprised when he came back empty-handed. He waded, chest deep, to the canoe and scrambled in. Had I tried this, I should certainly have turned the canoe over, but he hardly rocked it. He did not bother to put on his shirt, picked up the paddle and headed down another waterway. His skin, where it had not been darkened by the sun, was nearly as white as mine.

We got two more mallard before returning to Qabab, where a small party of men and women were waiting outside the *mudhif*. A girl in black held a baby in her arms, covering it with her shawl.

Sadam explained, 'This poor little thing is badly burnt. They want medicine. Can you help?'

The woman uncovered the baby and held it towards me – a boy about a year old. His chest, stomach and left leg and arm were coated with wet buffalo dung.

'When did this happen?'

'Now, a few minutes ago,' the girl said. 'I was cooking rice for the evening meal. The water was on the fire. I turned for a moment and he pulled the pot over. Sahib, he is our only child. God preserve you, Sahib. Save him, Sahib, save him. God protect you.'

They had been married two years, Sadam told me.

As I could see better outside, I fetched the box of medicine from the *mudhif*. I told the mother to sit on the ground and hold the child, who was whimpering softly. Then, as carefully as I could, I wiped off the wet manure. The child started kicking and screaming and the young father squatted beside me and gripped his feet. The burns were very extensive. In places the skin had come away and lay like crumpled tissue-paper on the exposed flesh; in others there were great blisters. I spread gentian violet paste smoothly on the whole surface.

'Don't put any cloth on that now. When it is quite dry cover it lightly with this,' and I handed her a large piece of gauze, also an aspirin which I told them to dissolve in water and give to the child to drink. They climbed into their canoe and went back to their house. Several others then asked for medicine. One had a septic cut on his foot, two complained of headaches, another of piles. The merchant we had visited wanted medicine for his sore eyes. It was nearly dark when the last of them had gone.

The ducks which we ate for dinner were excellent. Afterwards, we divided into two sides of five and played *mahaibis*, or hunt-the-ring. The side that had the ring sat in a row with their hands under a cloak. One of their opponents faced them and tried to guess who held the ring and in which hand. While eliminating them in turn, he kept up a flow of patter in a loud high-pitched voice, 'I see it in the hand of so-and-so, I see it in the hand of so-and-so.' Understanding very little of this patter, I found the game infinitely boring, but the others enjoyed it immensely. I had to play hunt-the-ring on many occasions and in many different villages and almost invariably it ended, as now, in accusations of cheating and a general loss of temper.

Finally Sadam turned them out saying – with some truth – that the Englishman was tired and wished to sleep.

8. Crossing the Central Marshes

Next morning, as promised, Sadam started with me across the Marshes to the Euphrates. It was still early; the sun had not been up much over an hour. A stream of canoes was leaving the village to fetch *hashish*, each with a fishing spear laid prongs-forward in the bows. He and I travelled in one canoe, Sahain in another, each paddled by three men. They all had rifles. In the Marshes, men did not willingly go unarmed when passing through another tribe's territory.

When the others left me at the Euphrates, I would be quite alone with no one to look after my things and no one to introduce me when I arrived in each new village. I had tried to persuade Ajram to come as my companion, promising we would return to Qabab in about six weeks, but he refused. 'He was afraid,' Sadam explained to me. 'No one will go with you. The Madan are ignorant. They live here in the Marshes like their buffaloes and are scared of the Government. I have met the English and know them to be good people, but the Madan are suspicious of all strangers. Ajram thought you would take him away and conscript him into the Army.' Not having expected any difficulty in finding a companion, I now felt rather daunted.

A fifteen-year-old boy, paddling his canoe beside us, said, 'Take me with you, Sahib; give me money and take me with you. Then I need no longer weary myself cutting *hashish* all day in cold water.'

'No, don't take him; he is no good; he is lazy; take me,' another boy called out.

'Rubbish, they are both no good. Take me, I can sing and I can dance. I will keep you amused,' exclaimed a smaller boy who looked about thirteen, and paddled on the other side of us. He had a snub nose, a big mouth, laughing eyes and was very skinny.

'They are only joking,' Sadam said to me, and then to the small boy, 'Go on, Helu, sing.'

'I don't know how to, Sadam.'

'Go on, sing, Helu. Keep us entertained until you get to the reedbeds.'

Sahain also called out from his canoe, 'Sing, Helu.'

Sadam told me he had a sweet voice, using for *sweet* the same word as the boy's name. The child gave us an impudent grin and then began in a clear treble, 'The Arabs told me of you, a tyrant from your earliest days.' The song had a fascinating tune, lilting and rather mournful. Sadam explained, rather hurriedly I thought, that it had been composed about a sheikh beyond the Tigris by a wife whom he had ill-treated and divorced. Perhaps he was afraid I might suppose the song was directed at him – as it may well have been.

In the Marshes a song was in vogue for six months or a year. Then people got tired of it and another took its place. Usually there were half a dozen current at the same time. This was an easy favourite. During the next two years I heard it everywhere, at wedding celebrations, in the evenings at impromptu dances, and, as now, on the way to the reedbeds.

'Go on, Helu, another; give us another'; and Helu sang again. Several canoes waited for us to catch up with them. There must have been twelve or fifteen bumping into each other as they paddled beside us down the waterway. Two boys were paddling stern first. Later I noticed Madan often did this when alone in a canoe (Plate 33). Each time Helu stopped, his audience shouted, 'Come on, Helu; another.' A beautiful girl of fourteen sat by herself in one of the canoes, her black cloak draped over her head and shoulders. When a boy pushed the nose of her canoe aside with his hand, sending it into the reeds, she turned on him angrily. I could not hear what she said, but the others laughed and encouraged her not to stand any nonsense. In another canoe, a smaller girl was paddling with her brother, sitting behind him as women always must. I asked if women helped with the *hashish* and Sadam said, 'Yes, but only if a family is short-handed.' At length the canoes turned off into the reeds one after the other. Helu called out jokingly as he left us, 'Don't you want me with you, Sahib?'

Ahead stretched an expanse of water about two miles across. The surface, stirred by a rising breeze, was a dark, sparkling blue. Sadam told me it was known as Dima. The local Madan had an individual name for every piece of open water, even if it was no bigger than a pond, and for almost every waterway and reed-bed, but their knowledge was generally confined to the neighbour-hood of their homes.

'Round or across?' Sadam asked and Sahain, after studying the lake and the sky for a few seconds, said, 'Across; we shall be going into the wind; we shall be all right.'

Above us three eagles soared against a cloudless sky. I watched a mass of duck flying about at the far end of the lake. Some were circling high up, and those that came near I identified as mallard and shoveller. Others, either teal or garganey, dipped and rose in compact formation above the reedtops, the undersides of their wings flickering white as they turned together in a single move-ment. I wondered what had disturbed them, until I noticed two canoes a long way off near the reeds. I asked if they were shooting but Sahain, after a glance in their direction, answered, 'No, they are poisoning fish. They are from Qubur, the village where we are going to lunch. Paddle hard, we want to cross before the wind gets any stronger.' We were half-way when he called out, 'Get your gun ready, Sahib,' and pointed to our left, where several hundred coots were packed closely together. As we watched, an eagle flew low above them and stooped, but the coots drove him off by beating the water with their wings, so that it rose like spray from a breaking wave.

The wind was growing stronger and as we turned towards the coots, the water began to splash over the sides of the canoes. The eagle stooped two or three more times before we were in range of the coots, which paid no attention even when we were only forty yards away. I fired both barrels into them. They scattered and rose into the wind, leaving a trail of dark, floating bodies. While we picked up the dead, the others hunted down the cripples, which dived whenever the canoe neared them. Sahain, standing in the bows, collected them one by one with his fishing spear, as they surfaced, jabbing at those within reach, and throwing the spear at those farther away. As each bird was picked up, one of the men cut its throat, facing towards Mecca and muttering, 'In

the name of God; God is most great' – an invocation that made
the birds lawful food for Moslems; otherwise even Madan would
have regarded them as carrion and thrown them away. Lawfully,
all the birds should still have been alive in order to bleed when
their throats were cut, but these men were not over-particular.

'Is this one dead?' one of them asked, fishing out a bird whose
head had been under the water for ten minutes.

'No, of course it is not. Go on, hurry up and cut its throat.'

Carrion, pork and blood are forbidden to all Moslems. Also,
there are many prohibitions which vary from place to place
and from tribe to tribe. For instance, some Moslems will not eat
birds with webbed feet, and in Iraq the Shias would not eat hares,
whereas the Sunnis would. The Madan ate cormorants and
darters but not pelicans; ibis, herons and cranes but not storks;
dabchicks but not the other grebes; and they would not eat
catfish.

When we had collected all the dead coots, Sadam told our
crew to hurry, for our canoe, with two passengers and my boxes,
was shipping a lot of water. I was thankful when we reached the
shelter of the reedbeds. There Sahain's canoe joined us and we
counted our bag. Between us we had picked up eighteen. 'That
will give us plenty for lunch,' said Sadam with evident satisfaction.

By the time we reached Qubur, a grey haze had spread across
the sky, the wind whistled through the reedtops and the weather
had turned unpleasantly cold. The village resembled Qabab and
was about the same size. We went to one of the larger houses.
The narrow entrance was at the top of a greasy black slope five
feet above. Inside, two boys warmed themselves at a small fire.

'Is your father at home?' Sadam asked.

The older one answered, 'Yes, but he has just gone over to the
merchant's'; and to his brother he said, 'Go quickly and tell
Alwan we have guests.'

In spite of my coat, shirt, sweater and grey flannel trousers, I
was bitterly cold and glad to sit beside the fire. Alwan's son, a
tall, slim boy of sixteen, was dressed only in a flimsy cotton shirt.
He went to the other end of the house and brought back some
rugs and cushions which a girl handed to him.

'Let me bring in your luggage,' he said to Sadam.

'No, we are going on to Abu Shajar after we have fed.'

'You cannot do that. Stop here tonight. It is bad weather for travelling and anyway it is a long time since you have honoured us.'

Sadam sent one of his men to fetch twelve of the coots which he gave to the boy.

Alwan himself, middle-aged and friendly, arrived a few minutes later. He too urged us to fetch in our things and to stop the night, but Sadam insisted that we must go on.

'Are the Madan still at Abu Shajar?' he asked.

'Yes,' Alwan answered. 'The floods are late this year and they haven't yet moved.'

He brought the tea-things, remarking, 'You shot a lot of coots.'

When Sahain told him about the eagle, he said, 'One nested in the reeds this year and attacked anyone who used the waterway. The boys always went there to gather *hashish*, so they set fire to the reeds and burnt the nest.'

While he talked he fingered a long chain of ninety-nine small black beads. This was a religious rosary, whereas the thirty-three amber-coloured beads, which Sadam fingered, were merely for fiddling with. Most people carried such beads in their pocket and played interminably with them when they had nothing else to do. Sadam threw his across to me and, when I tried later to give them back, said, 'No, keep them, they are yours. I have others at Qabab.' From then on, I too caught the habit.

We ate nine coot for lunch. I thought the meat delicious, tasting like duck, but that may have been because I was cold and hungry. Sadam and Sahain, in spite of my protests, kept giving me pieces off theirs. Afterwards we poured the gravy over the rice and when that was finished, soused what was left of the rice with buttermilk. I found it difficult to eat this mess with my fingers but the others ate just as untidily, and there was much scattered rice to be swept up when the dishes were finally removed. Alwan piled the remains of the rice and the broken carcasses on to one dish. One of his sons fetched more buttermilk, and then they sat down in their turn. After more tea, we got into our canoe and bade him farewell, but no one thanked him for the meal – it would have been unheard of to do so.

We travelled along barely discernible passages through wind-threshed reeds and above us the tasselled reedheads, pale against a paler sky, streamed like pennants in the gale. One of the canoe-men, encouraged by Sadam, sang ballads. He had a powerful, raucous voice and the cords of his throat stood out while his face became alarmingly congested. The ballads were interminable and without apparent rhythm. To appreciate them as the others appeared to do it was obviously necessary to understand the words, but these were beyond me.

After an hour and a half, we reached Abu Shaja, an island of dark, bare earth, three hundred yards across and perhaps ten feet high at its highest point. The shore was surrounded by reedbeds. Thirty or forty houses had been erected close together in a hap-hazard manner along the water's edge. Buffaloes stood wherever there was a space, a series of small pits round each house pre-venting them from actually rubbing against the walls. The people here were Shaghanba.

After a discussion as to which was the most prosperous-looking house, we beached our canoes in front of it. A man and a boy came out, welcomed us and helped to carry my things ashore. The others had brought nothing with them except their rifles. We also took the poles and paddles inside since, by accepted practice, any passer-by could help himself to them. The poles were only qasab stems, but suitable ones were not easily found and a man grew used to his own. The paddles, made from shovel-shaped pieces of board nailed to lengths of bamboo, could seldom be replaced locally.

As usual, the small house soon became crowded. Our host asked a few questions, but the others just sat, watching me im-passively with their dark eyes. I sensed their distrust; 'Who is he? Where does he come from? Why has Sadam brought him here?' When, in due course, Sadam and my host took me round the island, a babble of conversation broke out behind us.

The soil was impregnated with salt and nothing grew on it. There were no stones or pieces of rock, indeed I saw none any-where in the Marshes. Judging by bricks and bits of pottery that lay about on the ground, Abu Shajar appeared to be the site of some forgotten city. Sadam said, 'They say there is gold buried on this island; the Madan have hunted for it. Look, do you see where they have dug?' and he pointed to some shallow pits. He added, 'They have not found any.'

Our host interrupted, 'Last year a Shaghanba family were digging holes for their house on Al Aggar and found two jars filled with coins.'

I asked where Al Aggar was.

'Over there to the west. It is an island like this. Many Shaghanba live there.'

'What happened to the coins?'

'I don't know. I expect they hid them so that the sheikhs should not take them.'

Sadam said, 'A few years ago, when we were building my *mudhif* at Qabab, we found a stone idol – the figure of a woman, you could see her breasts. It was this long,' and he held his hands nine inches apart.

'Have you still got it?'

'No, Majid took it.'

While I was in the Marshes, I never tried to collect objects of archaeological interest. But once I was given a Hittite seal and another time a small piece of lead sheeting covered in scratches that proved to be Phoenician characters. The man who gave it to me said it had been part of a huge roll which they had melted down for bullets. On a third occasion I was taken with much secrecy into a house and shown the terracotta figurine of a dog. Underneath was printed, 'Made in Japan'.

The sun was low, the wind had fallen and the interminable reeds were a desolate scene in the grey light. In several places to the north and east, dense clouds of smoke showed where Madan had fired the reeds to provide a new growth of pasture for their buffaloes.

'Have you ever heard of Hufaidh?' our host asked me.

'Yes, but tell me more about it.'

He waved towards the south-west. 'Hufaidh is an island somewhere over there. On it are palaces, and palm trees and gardens of pomegranates, and the buffaloes are bigger than ours. But no one knows exactly where it is.'

'Has no one seen it?'

'They have, but anyone who sees Hufaidh is bewitched, and afterwards no one can understand his words. By Abbas, I swear it is true. One of the Fartus saw it, years ago, when I was a child. He was looking for buffalo and when he came back his speech was all muddled up, and we knew he had seen Hufaidh.'

Sadam said, 'Saihut, the great Al bu Muhummad sheikh, searched for Hufaidh with a fleet of canoes in the days of the Turks, but he found nothing. They say the Jinns can hide the island from anyone who comes near it.'

I made some sceptical comment, but Sadam said emphatically, 'No, Sahib, Hufaidh is there all right. Ask anyone, the sheikhs or the Government. Everyone knows about Hufaidh.'

We strolled back to the village, along the water's edge, on a brittle carpet of white, convoluted shells, half an inch to an inch in length. I found they were empty, but wondered if they had belonged to the freshwater snails that in summer carry the parasites that cause bilharzia. These minute flat worms live in the water during the warm weather. If they are given the chance, they penetrate the human skin and find their way into the bladder, where they multiply, causing loss of blood and often intense pain. Eventually the eggs pass out of the body in the urine, ready to start their life cycle once again. Bilharzia is the scourge of the Marshes and all the Madan suffer from it as an inevitable consequence of their way of life.

Several girls were fetching water, carrying the earthen jars on their heads. They only waded out a few feet before filling them. The foreshore was used as the public lavatory, and each jar must have contained an interesting sample of the local germs. Theoretically, everyone in the Marshes should have been infected with dysentery and a number of other endemic diseases, but, in fact, most of the Madan had acquired some immunity. In any case the strong sunlight probably killed off a number of germs. Personally I found it impractical to take precautions, except to avoid wading about near the villages in summer. I ate their food and drank the same water; often I used their bedding and at all times I was bitten by mosquitoes, sandflies and fleas. During all the years I was there, I once had sinus trouble and once a mild attack of dysentery which I cured after four days. Otherwise I suffered nothing worse than a headache.

It was useless to worry about the diseases I might catch, but sometimes it was more difficult not to feel squeamish about the food and water. Two occasions in particular upset me, both in the middle of summer when I was travelling on horseback among the cultivators north of the Marshes. On the first I had followed a shallow irrigation ditch for several miles towards the village that was my destination. The ditch contained a foot or two of water flowing sluggishly in the same direction. I passed a dead dog lying in it and farther on a dead buffalo calf; the skin had soaked off its ribs. Both smelt horribly. Near the village, the edge of the ditch was foul, since Arabs always try to defecate near water so as to be able to wash afterwards. The *mudhif* was on the edge of the ditch, and the water there was almost stagnant under a covering of green slime. Even they won't drink that, I thought.

I arrived in the middle of a grilling afternoon. They brought me a drink from the pitcher at the end of the room and it tasted cold and fresh. Hearing I was there, many people came to the *mudhif*, some just sociably inclined, others wanting treatment. After the usual courtesies, I moved outside into the shadow of the building, where I operated, injected and distributed medicines. There was a slight breeze but it was still unbearably hot, for in summer the temperature on these plains rises to over 120° in the shade. Needing more water, I gave a bowl to a boy to fetch some. Seeing him go to the ditch I called impatiently, 'No, not that filthy stuff, bring me some clean water from the *mudhif*,' which he did, after giving me a surprised look. Later, I watched the pitcher being filled again from the ditch and reflected unhappily that I had agreed to remain another day.

On the second occasion, I was staying with a sheikh who was a friend of mine. I had arrived at his village the evening before and the usual crowd of patients turned up early next morning. It was stiflingly hot and humid, with never a breath of air. Even sitting still, the sweat trickled down my face and body. The sheikh, a hospitable old man, killed a sheep to feed his guests who by now were a hundred or more. Four men, one of them a large black slave, staggered into the room, bent double with the weight of a copper dish, four feet across and heaped with rice, on top of which was a boiled sheep, with lolling tongue and soggy eyes. As they carried the dish in, the sweat was dripping off their noses and chins on to the rice, and I knew they must have carried it like that a distance of a hundred yards or more. Pouring a bowl of liquid butter over the rice, the sheikh turned to us. 'Welcome, welcome to my guests. Today is a blessed day.'

As I sat down to the dish he said, 'Now, Sahib, the more you like me, the more you will eat!'

9. In the Heart of the Marshes

The sun had just gone down when Sadam and I got back with our host to his house. Sahain was reciting the sunset prayer. Among the Madan some old men, mostly *Zairs*, prayed regularly. A few others, like Sahain, compromised by saying the dawn and sunset prayers. Most of them, however, did not pray at all. When they did pray, they first placed in front of them a small rectangular tablet of sacred earth from Karbala, which they touched with their foreheads as they prostrated themselves. The tablets were always kept in a little basket hanging on the wall.

Having finished his prayer, Sahain returned the sacred tablet to the basket, built up the fire with dung cakes and told me to come and get warm. A boy brought a lamp, a bottle half-filled with paraffin with a wick of shredded cloth held in its neck by a lump of squashed dates. Two men talked quietly together next door. I could hear every word they said. The walls of the two houses, each a single thickness of matting, were not more than two feet apart. I soon found that these people had no privacy in their lives and never expected any. They accepted the fact that whatever concerned one of them concerned them all. If a family had a row among themselves their neighbours at once turned up, offering advice and taking sides, and thereby adding more raised voices to the original din. The only way to have a private conversation was to go out in a canoe with someone. Even so, the subject of conversation would soon become generally known, for they were both extremely inquisitive and quite incapable of keeping a secret.

After dinner, the visitors started to arrive. When there seemed no room even for another child, two or three more would push in, step with difficulty between us and sink down into the crowd. The mat walls bulged outwards a little farther and they were accommodated. There was only a space left by the fire. While our canoeman sang, everyone else talked, raising their voices to make themselves heard. Our host handed round cigarettes, and even tiny children smoked if they could pick up a stub. More tea was brewed, more fuel was stacked on the glowing fire from which columns of blue smoke rose and drifted against the matting overhead. It was all very primitive and uncomfortable, but I felt content.

Wedged in a corner, I was half asleep when at last they scrambled to their feet and crowded out past a woman nursing a small child beside the dying embers of another fire. We rearranged the mats and the tattered pieces of carpet, and I pulled the blankets out of my saddle-bag. Our host fetched bedding from the other end and we lay down side by side to sleep, while he sat by the fire to watch over us. A hard lump of earth pressed into my side, mosquitoes tried persistently to settle on my face and many fleas moved about inside my shirt. A dog barked and buffaloes moved restlessly a few yards from my head. Then I was asleep and did not wake until my companions roused themselves at dawn.

The wind had died during the night, and outside it was a clear sunny morning. The buffaloes were already leaving unattended for the grazing grounds. Among the settled Madan, as opposed to the nomads, they were not herded but were left free to come and go at will. Inside the house Sahain and Sadam argued whether to cross Zikri or avoid it. I pressed them to go by Zikri, which I wished to see. Sadam said, 'You won't wish that if we are caught there by a wind. These big lakes are very dangerous. Last year a wedding party returning to Qubur was surprised by a storm on Dima; two canoes and eight people, all were drowned. You have seen Dima; it is small, not like Zikri.'

Sahain joined in. 'Yes, Sahib, they are dangerous. We live here and we know. Four years ago, at this time of year, two men were drowned, the third scrambled on to a small floating island of *qasab*. He was there five days before he was found. Twice he had seen canoes, but they did not hear his shouts. He was just about dead from hunger and cold.'

After we had breakfasted, our host and his son watched us carry my luggage down to the canoe, but made no move to help.

When I later commented unfavourably on this, Sadam explained that a host should always help guests to carry their things into the house, but not out, which would look as if he were in a hurry to get rid of them. He said, 'We shall cross Zikri since you wish to see it, and should spend the night with the Bani Umair at Ramla. But if the wind gets up, we shall take the longer route.'

We reached the lake after travelling for two hours along a series of small, inconspicuous waterways through the tall reeds. When I saw open water ahead of us, glittering in the sunlight, I was at first disappointed, for the lake appeared to be no larger than Dima, which we had crossed the day before. Beyond the open water was a wall of *qasab* and we were half-way there before I realized that it was growing on a multitude of small floating islands, many of them some distance apart. Beyond this fringe of islands lay Zikri itself. From the floorboards of a canoe I could not judge whether it was three miles across or six. The breeze was very slight, but the others stopped paddling and seemed uneasy. I was inclined to be impatient, not realizing how deceptive such a calm could be.

Four years later, at the height of the floods, I happened to be crossing a great sheet of flood water twelve miles wide and six feet deep, that covered the desert along the western edge of the Marshes. We started at dawn. The lake was dead calm and there was not a breath of wind. I had by then acquired my own *tarada*. Half-way across Amara, one of my four canoeboys, suddenly exclaimed in a scared voice, 'God! Do you hear that?' I listened and heard the wind coming at us out of the north across the still water. Ahead I could just discern a line of palms, perhaps six miles away, marking the village for which we were bound. Behind us, the reedbeds were no longer in sight. Then one of the boys called out excitedly: 'Look! There is a sailing boat. The praise be to God! Quick, Sahib, fire off your rifle and attract their attention.' Our canoe was already half-under when the boat reached us. The crew hoisted my boxes aboard and took the empty *tarada* in tow. By the time we reached the village large waves were breaking on the shore, and the palm trees were bending to the force of the gale (Plate 85).

Now, as I looked at the still waters of Zikri, I urged the others to cross it. Finally Sadam said, 'All right, but we will go round the edge. We can get into the reeds if it starts to blow. It is farther but safer.'

I had assumed that Zikri, like Dima, would have a well-defined border of stable reedbeds, but as we paddled from one group of floating islands to the next, I realized that what appeared to be the border was, in fact, another chain of islands that masked more open water and yet more islands. The water, eight or ten feet deep, was very clear. Below the surface dark tangles of rubbery weed, like seaweed, swung to the current's tow. This was holly-leaved naiad (*Najas marina*) which the Madan called *suwaika*. They said that such beds were favourite breeding-places for fish. A score of pelicans, very white and clean in the strong light, paddled purposefully away, turning their big yellow bills as they watched us. Sadam begged me to shoot one since the Madan used their pouches as skins for drums. But they looked so comically indignant that, to spare them, I said a shot would frighten the duck sitting in dark lines on the water beyond. A goliath heron rose noisily from some reeds out of range and flapped away with slow heavy wing-beats, his long legs trailing behind him. Someone said, 'If you had shot that, it would have fed us all. It has as much meat as a sheep, and strong-tasting meat, too.' Ahead, several eagles soared on motionless wings. In the Marshes there were nearly always eagles in the sky, as in Africa there are vultures.

At the far end of Zikri, in a small bay, we came on three canoes each paddled by a boy. Near them several apparently dead fish floated on the water. One of Sahain's men suggested picking them up, but Sahain replied impatiently, 'Don't be a fool. We don't know these people. We don't want to anger them. Let us ask them and they will be sure to give us some.' The boys told us they were from Ramla, close to the Euphrates, and gave us half a dozen fish, each about two pounds. These fish, called *binni*, were barbel. They were golden-coloured and, unlike others here, had no feelers. Madan poisoned fish in the winter, and in the spring before the water in the Marshes began to rise. They used datura which they bought from the local merchants and mixed into pellets with flour and chicken droppings or inserted into fresh-water shrimps. The datura stupefied the fish, which rose to the surface and were easily collected. These boys were using shrimps.

. When I asked Sadam if the Madan fished with nets, he said,
'No, never. Only the Berbera use nets. Tribesmen spear fish.'

'Who are the Berbera?'

'Oh, them, they are just Berbera, low-class people who fish
with nets. They live among the tribes. There are many among
the Al bu Muhammad.'

Sadam recited a couplet to the effect that the Berbera, like
weavers and pedlars, ironworkers, market gardeners and
Sabaeans, were beyond the pale, not fit to associate with tribesmen because they were engaged in trade. Among the Madan
themselves, as among all tribal Arabs, wealth as such was held in
little account and trade was fundamentally a despised activity. A
man's status depended wholly on his character, virtues and
lineage.

Leaving Zikri, we were back in thick reedbeds. Long before
Ramla, the water shallowed and the men kept the canoes moving
with difficulty. The *qasab* poles were fragile. When I tried punting with one later, I broke it with the first push, but these men
leant on them with all their weight as they forced the canoes
forward a foot at a time. The poles, the same giant twenty-five-
foot *qasab* that the sheikhs used for their *mudhifs*, were only found
in certain parts of the Marshes. The Madan always carried a few
spare poles, but a man would often keep the same one for months.
Stepping clumsily into the canoe that morning, I had broken
three.

When we reached Ramla at last, we were across the Marshes.
Although reeds and bulrushes grew close to the village and men
came and went in canoes, there were palms among the houses and
beyond the village an open plain. We stopped at a *mudhif*. Our
host took me for a stroll round the village, which was intersected
by deep ditches full of water and bridged with palm logs. We
passed the merchant's shop hidden behind piles of reed mats, and
a little farther stopped to watch a family making them. An old
man sat cross-legged on the ground beside a pile of dry *qasab*
canoes, each about eight feet long and as thick as my middle
finger. These he split in half with a curved knife before tossing
them over to a woman, who pounded them with a wooden
pestle to make them pliant, using the weighted end with its short
heavy cross-piece. She pounded about twenty at a time, laying

them side by side. A boy then wove them in a herring-bone pattern (Plate 30). The mats were roughly eight feet by four feet and my host told me that each took two hours to make and fetched fifty fils, or the equivalent of a shilling.

We walked out across the open plain. The fact that the ground was covered with fallen sedge, like straw from an abandoned harvest, showed that it had been flooded. Now it was iron hard, with hoofprints like plaster casts. Plovers rose crying into the wind, wheeled and settled again; herons and white cattle egrets took off as we approached and a pallid harrier drifted, banking and turning, a few feet above the ground. In the distance dark clumps of palms marked the villages along the Euphrates. My companion pointed to a far-off mound and said, 'The Turks had a cannon there when they fought us; they shelled our village and killed many people.' Probably this had happened during some punitive expedition that went up from Basra, for the Turks were always having trouble with these tribes.

We went back to the *mudhif* at sunset. The guests left early, saying we must be tired after our journey, and we settled down to sleep. Somewhere in the village a woman lamented for her dead child. Without a pause, hour after hour, she repeated the words 'Oh my son, my son,' an agony of grief that poured out into the night and found no comfort.

The next day the others would return and leave me on my own.

10. The Historical Background

It was on the edge of the Marshes that human history in Iraq began. Far back in the darkness of time a people, already socially and culturally advanced, moved down from the plateau of Iran and settled in the Euphrates delta, where, in the fifth millennium B.C., they built reed houses, made boats, and harpooned and netted fish. They lived there as men do today, in an environment that has changed but little. Some fifteen hundred years later they were absorbed or displaced by another race that moved into Iraq from Anatolia. The newcomers brought with them the domestic buffalo, a knowledge of metalwork, and the art of writing. Each race left in its distinctive pottery a record of its journeyings. Then, about 3000 B.C., the Flood covered the face of the land. But somehow man survived and the Sumerians founded their cities on the sites of ancient villages buried under feet of silt, and developed what was perhaps the world's first civilization.

The centuries passed; Babylon rose and Sumer fell. In 728 B.C. the terrible Assyrians, with horse-drawn chariots and weapons of iron, wiped out the Amorites and razed Babylon to the ground. They in turn, worn out by war and conquest, were overthrown by the Medes. In 606 B.C. the mighty Assyrian city of Nineveh was stormed and 'became a desolation and a place for beasts to lie down in'. Babylon, risen again under the Chaldeans, outlasted Nineveh by seventy years, until it was destroyed by Cyrus, who gave Nebuchadnezzar's Hanging Gardens to the flames. Other races too, had invaded Iraq during the same two thousand years; the wild lawless Gutti, who devastated Sumer; the Cassites; and the Hittites who once sacked Babylon; the Mittanians, bringing with them strange gods from India; and the people of Elam.

After Cyrus captured Babylon in 539 B.C., Iraq passed under foreign rule for more than a thousand years, sometimes as an important province of an empire, sometimes as a battleground of contending powers. Persians, Greeks, Seleucids, Parthians, Romans and then again the Persians, marched their armies across the land, seeking to hold it or to wrest it from others. When, at the beginning of the seventh century A.D., the Arabs surged out of the desert on a wave of conquest and overran Iraq, they added but another name to this list of alien conquerors.

Hope of plunder was the incentive, and membership of Islam, their new religion, the bond that held the nomad tribes together. Welcomed by the indigenous population, or received with indifference, the new government appropriated the state lands, but left anyone who acknowledged its rule in possession of his own. Far from being fanatics, determined to proselytize, the Arabs regarded Islam as the prerogative of their race, and at first allowed no one who was not an Arab to be converted, unless he became affiliated to an Arab tribe. Such pseudo-Arabs were known as Mawalis. Non-Moslems paid a special tax and mass conversions were not encouraged. For the next hundred and sixteen years, Iraq was a province of the Arab Empire, governed first from Al Madina in the Hejaz, and then from Damascus, except when Ali, the third Caliph, ruled briefly at Kufa. During these years the Arab inhabitants constituted a small warrior aristocracy based on the towns, most of them being employed as soldiers or government officials. Arrogant and often oppressive, they treated the local population with contempt. When Shiism was born, after Husain had been massacred at Karbala in A.D. 681, it appealed especially to the Mawalis of Iraq, since it expressed in religious terms their discontent with the established order. By the time that an Abbasid Caliph founded his dynasty in Iraq and built his new capital at Baghdad in A.D. 750, his empire, although Moslem, was no longer Arab in any true sense of the word. The magnificent court life that surrounded a Harun ar Rashid, the gorgeous robes, the elaborate etiquette, the ceremonial, the eunuchs and the court executioners, all were utterly unlike the stark simplicity in which the early Caliphs had lived in the Hejaz.

The Abbasid Caliphate lasted for five hundred years, sinking from the glories of its early reigns to the chaos of later times. The last of its Caliphs was executed after Hulagu captured Baghdad in 1258, his death adding but one more body to the 800,000 butchered by the Mongols when they sacked the city. In 1401 Baghdad was sacked again, this time by Timur-leng, the last of the great Mongol conquerors, and if the slaughter was less that was because there were fewer people in the city. After him came the Turkomans, first the White Sheep and then the Black, and after them in 1509 the Persians, to be followed in 1534 by the Turks, who held the country until they were driven out by the British in the First World War. But by then the fortunes of Iraq had sunk low indeed. From a few small towns, Turkish officials tried to assert some semblance of authority over unruly tribes in this destitute province of a tottering empire.

For thousands of years, since the time of the Sumerians, Iraq had been a settled land of towns and stable agriculture. Conquerors had sacked cities and massacred the inhabitants, but, until the Mongols came, they had always built anew, making their own contribution to the civilizations that had gone before; above all, they had cared for the canals in which the irrigation water flowed. But the shambling yellow horsemen, whom Janghiz Khan conjured up from the deserts of Outer Asia and loosed upon the world, took pleasure only in killing. Their monuments were pyramids of human skulls. When this whirlwind of destruction finally blew itself out over Iraq, the work of centuries had been destroyed and the irrigation system, on which the prosperity of the country depended, had been irreparably damaged. Much of this damage was deliberate, but even more was probably the cumulative effect of sheer neglect. Organization and endless labour had been required to dredge the canals, to strengthen and restore the banks and to build the barrages that regulated the floods. After the Mongol hordes had passed, the survivors were too few and too broken-spirited to repair the damage. The fields reverted to desert and the precious water dispersed in swamps. Men still cultivated along the river banks, but Iraq ceased to be an agricultural and became a pastoral country. Cities that had been among the greatest in the world degenerated into squalid villages.

Arab nomads, from the desert beyond the Euphrates, drifted into the country and grazed their herds on mounds which were once the palaces of kings. Whereas the original Arabs had settled

2

3

2. A shepherd encampment on the northern edge of the Marshes
3. The guest tent of the Al Essa sheikh
4. Maziad bin Hamdan, sheikh of the Al Essa
5. One of the Al Essa

6. In the Marshes
7. A boy from Qubur
8. Sunset on the edge of the Marshes
9. A *tarada*
10. Rufaiya, a village on the northern edge of the Marshes

11. One of the Fartus
12. Hunting pig in the Marshes

13. In the heart of the
Marshes, near Zikri
14. Qabab, a Madan village
in the Central Marshes

15. A Marshman's
house
16. A Feraigat family
at Bu Mughaifat
17. Madan dwellings
at Qubab
18. At Bu Mughaifat
19. Mats for export
among the Bani
Assad

20

21

22

3

20. A merchant's shop
in the delta of the
Chahla
21. A Feraigat boy
from Qabab
22. One of the Al bu
Daraj
23. Bringing home a
load of dry reeds
24. Feraigat girls

24

25. Sahain, the Feraigat *qalit* at Bu Mughaifat
26. Jasim al Faris of the Fartus
27. The daughter of an Al bu Muhammad sheikh
28. A Suaid village in the Eastern Marshes
29. Weaving mats

28

29

30. A reed mat woven from split *qasab* stalks
31. The prow of a *balam*
32. Returning in the evening with fodder for the buffaloes
33. Going out in the morning to gather fodder
34. A Madan family on their way to market

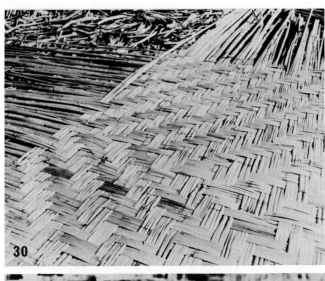

30

31

35

36

35. Madan going off to
spear fish
36. Al bu Muhammad boys
just after their circumcision
37. A loom in the Marshes
38. A young Sayid after his
circumcision

38

39

40

41

39. A war dance among the Fartus
40. The Al Essa celebrating the end of Ramadhan
41. Canoes at Al Aggar
42. A Fartus boy in the reed beds
43. Fartus fishing on Umm al Binni

44

45

44. Water-crowfoot in
the Eastern Marshes
45. A zaima
46 to 49. Among the
Suaid Madan. Rafts
made from bulrushes

50

51

52

50. A Sabaean boat-
builder
51. One of the Amaira
in the Central Marshes
52. Repairing boats
53. Amara bin Thuqub,
one of my canoeboys
54. A Feraigat boy
55. Yasin, another of
my canoeboys

56. A Suaid boy, a
skilled dancer
57. My *tarada* in rough water
58. My *tarada*
59. Spring in the Marshes

56

57

58

59

60. Winter in the Marshes
61. With the Sudan
62. With the Bani Lam
63. Hasan's mother, Afara,
of the Bait Makenzie
64. A *sitra* at Abu Laila:
dwelling house at the left end

63

4

65

66

67

65. At Qubur in a year of very low water
66. Buffaloes at Abu Laila
67. A herdsboy of the Rabia, the nomad Feraigat
68. The encampment of the Rabia at Abu Laila
69. Qabab, buffaloes resting at midday

70

71

70. A brick-kiln on the Tigris near Azair
71. At Huwair. Repairing a *balam*
72 Building a canoe at Huwair
73. The first stage

72

73

74. Haji Hamaid
75. Re-coating my *tarada* with bitumen
76. My *tarada* skirting a lagoon
77. Travelling in the Marshes in summer
78. A woman of the nomad Suaid
79. A boy of the nomad Suaid

80

81

82

80. In the Eastern Marshes
81. Marriage celebrations at Rufaiya
82. Al bu Muhammad dancing the *hausa*
83. Near Majar al Kabir
84. An Al bu Muhammad village on the Adil, a branch of the Majar

85

86

85. A gale near Hamar
86. The market at Fuhud on the Gharraf
87. Suaid nomads pulling down their house preparatory to moving

87

88. Suaid nomads setting up their village on dry ground
89. Azairij dismantling their house to go harvesting
90. Binding the arches

91

92

93

91. Building a *raba*, the first stage
92. Feraigat spearing fish
93. Berbera netting fish on Umm al Binni
94. A *mudhif* at Hamar during the height of the floods
95. A *mudhif* among the Al Hasan

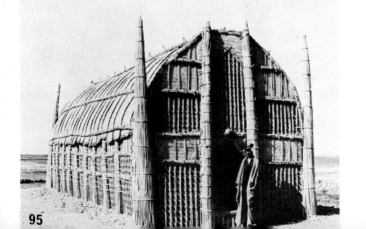

96

97

96. A *mudhif* among the Al Juaibar
97. Interior of a *mudhif* on the Euphrates
98. Interior of a *mudhif* on the Euphrates
99. A *mudhif* on the Euphrates during construction

100. The coffee hearth
101. Among the Muntifiq
102. The doorway of a *mudhif* on the Euphrates, from outside
103. The doorway of a *mudhif* on the Euphrates, from the inside
104. A *sarifa*

102

103

104

105

105. A boat-load of mats
106. A *mudhif* on the Gharraf
107. Madan on their way
back from market
108. On their way back to
the Gharraf for the
harvesting

106

107

109. Amara bin Thuqub
110. In the Eastern Marshes

109

110

in flourishing cities and towns and had been gradually absorbed into the native population, these new immigrants, with their black tents, their herds of camels and flocks of sheep and goats, divided up the land into grazing grounds. A system of government based on urban life was replaced by the tribal law of the tents. Under these conditions security could only be found in the shelter of a tribe, and in consequence the cowed and disorganized peasantry attached themselves to whatever nomads would have them. Accepting their own social inferiority, they copied the manners and customs of these aristocrats of the desert and sought to emulate their deeds. In time the old distinctions blurred and the two races intermingled. Some tribes settled on the land, others gave up their camels and carried their tents on donkeys.

The desert Arabs who immigrated into Iraq were few compared with the original inhabitants, but theirs were the customs and standards that prevailed. The people of Iraq might proudly have claimed descent from Sumerians or Babylonians, from the Assyrians, whose armies had overrun Egypt, from the Persians who had followed Cyrus or fought under Darius or Xerxes, or from the Parthians who had wiped out the legions of Rome. Instead, they boasted they were of Bedu stock. Alexander too had passed this way, and in Central Asia the magic of his name still lingers in mountain valleys where men swear they are descended from his soldiers. In Iraq, however, he was forgotten. When I heard old men round the fire telling legendary tales of courage and generosity, it was never of two-horned Alexander that they spoke, nor of Caliphs who had ruled in splendour in Baghdad, but of tattered herdsmen in the deserts of Arabia.

The desert Arabs had always been a people born to hardship. For them there was no ease or comfort, only the weariness of long marches and toil at well-heads. 'We are Bedu,' they boasted, and asked only the freedom that was theirs. Stoical in pain, and often very brave, they lived for the raid and counter-raid, which were conducted according to set rules and usually with great chivalry. They took a fierce pride in danger and suffering, and never doubted their superiority over villager and townsman. Thoroughbreds, they called themselves, using the same word 'asil' as they used to describe their bloodstock. They came indeed of the purest race in the world, and for centuries had interbred, cousin marrying cousin as was their custom. They were saved from degeneracy by their environment, where only the best survived and all else was ruthlessly weeded out. Accustomed since childhood to the incessant nag of hunger, they starved when the rains failed, which was often, and discounted thirst as a trivial everyday discomfort. Sometimes, however, they miscalculated and then they died. All through the long months of summer they endured heat that struck like the blast from a furnace door. Then was a grim time for herdsboys; but in winter it was as bad, for icy winds swept across the naked sands, and driving rain soaked them to the skin. During the long winter nights they lay on the ground wrapped only in their rags, and woke too stiff to move. For food they had a bowl of camel's milk morning and evening, if they were lucky. And always there was the threat of raiders, fear of the blood feud and of sudden death.

Their nomad life allowed the Bedu few possessions; everything not a necessity was an encumbrance. The clothes in which they stood, their weapons and saddlery, a few pots and waterskins and goat-hair shelters, were all they owned; those and the animals whose welfare regulated their every move and for whose sake they cheerfully suffered every hardship. Arrogant, individualistic and intensely proud, they never willingly accepted any man as their master, and would rather die than be shamed. The most democratic of people, they yet valued lineage highly, and for centuries had guarded the purity of their blood with the dagger. To their sheikhs they accorded a measure of respect due to their descent, but gave them no more unless they earned it. The head of a tribe was the first among equals. He had no servants and paid retainers to enforce his will, or to effect his judgements. His tribesmen followed him only so long as he commanded their respect, and he ruled them only so long as they obeyed him; if he displeased them they followed another of his family, and his guest tent was left empty. Living crowded together in the open desert, no concealment was possible, every act was noted and every word was overheard. Inveterate gossips, they knew all that passed, and the question, 'What is the news?' succeeded every greeting. If a man distinguished himself, his fellows paraded him through the encampment on a camel shouting, 'God whiten the face of so-and-so!' If he had disgraced himself, they drove him forth with cries of, 'God blacken the face of so-and-so!', and he became an outcast. Avid for acclaim, they went to great lengths to win it, and many of their acts were theatrical in consequence. Though jealous of others, they were staunchly loyal to their fellow tribesmen; to betray a companion was the blackest sin, far worse than murder to people whose disregard for human life enabled them in settlement of a blood feud to knife an unarmed herdsboy with a jest. But while they were callous about their own sufferings, and the sufferings of others, they were never deliberately cruel. Their honour was easily touched and they were quick to repay an insult, real or imagined, but usually they were humorous and light-hearted.

Theirs was a character of opposites. Garrulous by nature, they were always careful of their dignity, and would sit in silence for hours on formal occasions. Indifferent to natural beauty, they had a passionate love for poetry. Often impractically generous, they would give away their only shirt to someone who asked for it. Their hospitality was legendary – a man would think nothing of killing one of his precious camels to feed a stranger who had chanced on his tent; but at heart they were avaricious, with all the Semite's love of money. They were deeply religious and saw the hands of God in everything. It would have been as inconceivable for them to doubt his existence as to blaspheme. Yet they were not naturally fanatical, nor were they passively fatalistic. In their hard lives they fought to the bitter end, and then accepted their fate with dignity, as the will of God.

The Marshes themselves, with their baffling maze of reedbeds where men could move only by boat, must have afforded a refuge to remnants of defeated people, and been a centre for lawlessness and rebellion, from earliest times. Sargon, the great Assyrian king, was defeated by the Chaldeans who lived there. Ten years afterwards, having humbled Egypt and conquered Israel, he returned to win a battle in the Marshes in about 710 B.C., which he recorded in the friezes of his palace at Khorsabad. He exacted a terrible vengeance and finally carried off the Chaldeans to Syria, replacing them with captive Hittites from the mountains of the north.

Sixteen centuries later the Marshes were the stronghold of the Zanj, whose rebellion threatened the very existence of the Abbasid Caliphate. Innumerable slaves, mostly of African descent, had been used to drain the marshes round Basra. Treated with unspeakable brutality, they revolted, killed their guards and terrorized the neighbourhood. They would have been bloodily suppressed had they not found a leader of remarkable skill. Under Ali ibn Muhammad, a Persian, they triumphed for fourteen years, from A.D. 869 to 883, defeating army after army that the Caliph sent against them. They stormed and sacked Basra, and captured Ahwaz in South-western Persia; they pillaged to within twenty miles of Baghdad itself. But in the end the odds were too great. Ali refused to surrender, his army was finally defeated and his head was carried in triumph to Baghdad.

By the seventeenth century the tribal pattern in and around the Marshes was beginning to take its present form. The Muntifiq, that great confederacy of tribes which dominated the lower Euphrates for three hundred years and more, originated there when a refugee from Mecca arbitrated in a dispute and was murdered for his pains. The Bani Malik, with whom he had identified himself, fled into the desert taking with them his infant son. There the boy grew up and in due course led them back to the Euphrates to defeat their enemies. As his fame and influence spread, more and more tribes acknowledged his leadership. Some were aristocratic nomads from the desert, others were shepherds of dubious lineage, while many were despised Madan. At the height of its power the Muntifiq was virtually an independent state, able to fight the Turkish Government on level terms. Still farther down the Euphrates, the Bani Assad established themselves in their present homeland round Kubaish. They too gave the Turks much trouble in their heyday. In the same period the Bani Umair settled west of Qurna and the Kaab were already dominant in the Eastern Marshes. On the Tigris, Muhammad and his two half-Feraigat sons established their rule over a mixture of tribes that now call themselves the Al bu Muhammad. Farther north, the grandson of a certain Lam founded the Bani Lam, or children of Lam, a pastoral tribe of great power, which today numbers a hundred thousand.

The blood of the many races that occupied Iraq for thousands of years may well have survived in the fastness of the Marshes. But the code of the desert Arab was the ideal which governed the Madan's lives and shaped the whole pattern of their behaviour, from their blood feuds to their table manners.

11. Winning Acceptance

Kubaish lay on the north side of the Euphrates, which here was deep, slow-flowing and a hundred yards wide. A dense grove of palms extended for several miles along the same bank, while across the river were reedbeds and swamps. Behind a cement-faced esplanade, complete with lamp-posts, was ranged a row of ugly brick houses – the district office, a police post, a small dispensary, a school, a club house and the officials' quarters. Some were new but all contrived to look derelict. Their incongruous appearance would perhaps have been justified if they had seemed to offer a higher standard of comfort and material prosperity than could be found in the neighbouring villages. Had they been set among lawns and flower-beds, I should have expected a hot bath. As it was, surrounded by tattered reed fences and a litter of broken bottles, rusty tins and pieces of newspaper, they merely looked as if the drains smelt.

The market consisted of a row of shops, little better than booths, at one end of the esplanade. A small concrete bridge embellished the other end, but its purpose was obscure since it led straight into a wide lagoon of deep water. The *Mudir*, who had been a carpenter before becoming a salaried official, had personally supervised its construction. Apart from its waterfront, Kubaish was an attractive place. The façade of government buildings hid a network of small islands, shaded by palms and set among canals carpeted with water-crowfoot, small white yellow-centred flowers that smelt of honey. Sheltering under palms were reed houses and several *mudhifs*, in one of which I stayed.

I had called in at Kubaish a few days after leaving Sadam and the others at Ramla, in order to show the *Mudir* a letter from the Minister of the Interior, allowing me to travel wherever I wished.

In Iraq, each Province, or *Liwa*, was governed by a *Mutasarrif* and divided into two or more *Qadhas*. These were administered by a *Qaimaqam* and divided into *Nahiyas* under a *Mudir*. Kubaish was a *Nahiya* in the *Qadha* of Suq ash Shuyukh in the Muntifiq Province, of which the capital was Nasiriya.

Soon after arriving, I visited the *Mudir*, who invited me to dine with him at the Club. This proved to be the sort of cheap brick building that, in this climate, was bound to be hot in summer, cold and dank in winter. It stood behind a mat fence, under which some zinnias wilted for lack of water. Iron chairs painted green and a few circular iron tables were set on a patch of worn grass. Two or three officials were there already, others arrived later. I had met most of them that morning. We sat round the tables and were served with tea by a harassed old man, in a pair of torn khaki trousers that were too large for him and a jacket that was too tight. One of the schoolteachers fetched a wireless from the building, fixed up the aerial and spent the next four or five hours fiddling with the knobs. Against a background of music, song and recitation from all over the world, and the incidental sounds of atmospherics, the others discussed their allowances, Arab politics and a scandal that had taken place recently in official circles in Nasiriya. Not caring for *araq*, I took endless glasses of sweet black tea, the only other drink available. My hosts, who did not share my prejudice, drank *araq* steadily, argued more heatedly, and seemed to forget that they had invited me to dinner. Behind the mat fence a generator thumped asthmatically, supplying a single naked bulb suspended over our heads; an unpleasant selection of insects, attracted by the light, rained down on the tables. The iron chair on which I sat added physical discomfort to boredom. It was after midnight when the *Mudir* remembered to order dinner, and the *kabab* and rice had not been improved by waiting.

Most of these officials had been born within a hundred miles of Kubaish, but their education had taught them to feel at home only in the towns. Exiled in this uncongenial tribal atmosphere, they dreamed of a transfer and spent much time scheming to bring one about. Meanwhile they confined themselves, for as long as they were here, to the few hundred yards which contained their houses, their offices and the Club. During the years that I was in Iraq, I do not remember meeting an official who had any real interest in, or affection for, the tribal people whom he administered. More than one asked how I could bear to live among the Madan, adding that they were no better than wild beasts.

Nor were they interested in the countryside. In Kurdistan, the previous summer, I had spent a day with a young Iraqi police officer in one of the most beautiful places I had seen. He had been posted there for two months while a large nomad tribe was in the area. Mountains of eight and nine thousand feet rose from the oak woods to the bare green slopes above, and a glittering stream of ice-cold water tumbled down the valley towards further ranges of purple mountains. There were bears in the woods and ibex on the peaks. The weather was perfect. When I called on the young man in his tent, he was sitting beside the wireless and an ashtray full of stubs. 'You are a lucky chap to be living here,' I said enthusiastically, and he burst out, 'Lucky! By God, if it wasn't for my wireless I should go mad. What is there for a civilized person to do in this awful spot? The man who was here before me left after a week. He paid and they moved him. I am poor and can't afford to do that so I just sit and listen to Radio Baghdad.'

Kubaish and the adjoining villages along the Euphrates were inhabited by the Bani Assad, an Arab tribe that, after a chequered history of conquest and defeat, had been driven into the Marshes three centuries earlier. In their heyday they had absorbed many weaker peoples often not of Arab origin, who sought their protection and whose adherence added to their power. From the Marshes they waged intermittent and often successful war with the Turks, and, even after the First World War, continued to give trouble, until the British defeated them and removed their sheikhs in 1924. Since then the tribal structure had disintegrated. Agriculture at Kubaish was always unpredictable, and in recent years the tribe, now numbering some ten thousand, relied increasingly on weaving mats (Plate 19). But even after three centuries in the Marshes, they regarded themselves as distinct from the Madan. They kept cows but scorned to keep buffaloes.

There was a corner-boy atmosphere about Kubaish and I was glad to leave, wandering eastward until I came to the edge of the desert at Khamisiya, where I turned back again. I would arrive in one village during the morning, be given lunch, and then be taken on in the afternoon by my host, to the next. However poor the household, and some were very poor indeed, I was everywhere hospitably received, but for a month I was met with the same constraint and watched by silent, staring faces. There was no privacy anywhere, my every move was observed, and even when I went to relieve myself I was followed by a boy to guard me from the dogs. I could imagine the speculation that started as soon as I left a room. 'What does he want? Why has he come? Obviously no townsman would wish to be bitten by mosquitoes and to eat our food unless he had a good reason. The Government must have sent him to spy on us, to count our young men or to inspect our buffaloes.'

My hosts were courteous enough but clearly anxious to get rid of me, and treated me as unclean. Shias regard ritual purity as a religious duty, and the stricter ones will not drink from the same cup as an infidel. Since these people were notably lax in their other religious observances, this particular differentiation seemed a deliberate slight. I began to wonder whether, as a Christian and a European, I would ever get on terms with them at all, as I longed to do.

Until, on my way north to the Fartus, I happened to stop at a *raba* in a large village in the Amaira country.

The owner was not at home, but a tall, good-looking youth welcomed us. The men who had brought me returned to their village as soon as they had drunk tea. My host himself, whose name was Abid, short for 'the Slave of God', arrived at sunset.

'What have you got in those boxes?' he asked after dinner.

'Medicines.'

'Are you a doctor?'

'I know about medicine.'

'Can you circumcise?'

I had never done this operation but had watched many in hospitals and among the tribes, so I took a chance and answered: 'Yes.'

'Will you circumcise my son Kharaibid? It is years since someone came here who knew how to circumcise and I want him done so that he can marry.' He pointed to the lad who had received me and who, at this moment, was busy pouring out coffee. Rather apprehensively, I agreed to operate in the morning.

Circumcision, although nowhere mentioned in the Koran, is generally regarded as obligatory for Moslems, following the example of the Prophet himself who was circumcised in accordance with Arab custom. No uncircumcised person may lawfully make the pilgrimage to Mecca. Among the tribes in southern Iraq, whether Madan or shepherds, the operation was often deferred till manhood, as in the present case, and was seldom performed before puberty. It was done by specialists who travelled round from village to village in the summer. Their traditional fee was a cock, but more often they charged five shillings. The examples of their work which I saw later were terrifying. They used a dirty razor, a piece of string and no antiseptics. Having finished, they sprinkled the wound with a special powder, made from the dried foreskins of their previous victims, and then bound it up tight with a rag. People living under these conditions acquire a remarkable resistance to infection, but they could not resist this, and boys sometimes took two months to recover, suffering great pain in the meanwhile. One young man came to me for treatment ten days after his circumcision, and although I am fairly inured to unpleasant sights and smells, the stench made me retch. His entire penis, his scrotum and the inside of his thighs were a suppurating mess from which the skin was sloughing away, the pus trickling down his legs. I cured him eventually with antibiotics. In spite of the social stigma of being uncircumcised, some boys not unnaturally refused. In other cases the fathers would not allow their sons to be operated on, because there was no one else to look after the buffaloes. A few maintained that they had been circumcised by an angel at birth, a superstition that is also current in Egypt. Later I visited villages, among the Suaid and Kaulaba in particular, where I heard that hardly anyone was circumcised – almost incredible among Moslems.

In the morning, Abid suggested I should do the operation out of doors, in order not to defile the house with blood. A small crowd waited among the buffaloes in the yard, which was not the ideal surgery. A number of Kharaibid's contemporaries had turned up, to give him moral support as I presumed. I selected an intelligent-looking boy as my assistant. Kharaibid produced a large wooden mortar, turned it upside down and sat on it.

I could have wished for a simpler first operation. Examination showed that he had an 'attached foreskin'. I prepared a syringe with local anaesthetic, but Kharaibid said immediately, 'What is that for?' I explained that an injection would stop him feeling any pain. 'No, no, I don't want any needles stuck into me; just cut it off,' and nothing I could say would change his mind. By then I was wondering if he was as nervous as I was, though he showed no signs of it. While I operated, which in this case took some time, he sat absolutely motionless, and after I had finished said, 'Thank you,' and stood up. My assistant, who had been holding the various forceps, dropped them in the manure and pushing another boy aside, sat down on the mortar and said, 'Now it's my turn.' I realized with a shock that Kharaibid's nine friends had all come to be circumcised. The youngest was about fifteen, the eldest twenty-four, and I learnt later that they all recovered in a few days. Evidently sulphonamide powder and penicillin were more efficacious than powdered foreskins. The news had reached the next village by the time I got there and I found a score of boys waiting for me.

In time few of these people were prepared to let the local specialists circumcise them; they preferred to wait until I visited their village or to come and find me somewhere else. On one exhausting occasion, a hundred and fifteen turned up, and I was hard at work from dawn till midnight. They believed that, after circumcision, the smell of baking bread, or of scent, would inflame the wound. Consequently their custom was to stuff their nostrils with pieces of cloth (Plate 38) and hang onions round their necks, if they could find any in the local shop. Nor might they eat fish, curds or water melons, or drink more than a few sips of water till they were healed. The local practitioners seized on these superstitions as a ready-made excuse for their incompetence. When some wretched youth hobbled past in agony with legs wide apart, they would explain sententiously, 'Of course, the stupid fool hasn't taken enough care to block his nostrils. He must have smelt baking bread, or perhaps has drunk too much water.'

The Madan were never visited by a doctor, and if they went to the local dispensary at Kubaish would be made to pay for drugs which, they maintained, did them no good. Wherever I happened to be, my surgery grew daily in numbers, and from now on I spent hardly a day in the Marshes without treating someone. Sometimes half a dozen turned up, sometimes a hundred or more. Often I was still asleep when the first patients arrived, and I would be shaken awake, perhaps by an old man who would lean over me and explain wheezingly that he had a cough. Many of them suffered from nothing worse than colds, headaches, constipation, or minor cuts and bruises. These were easily dealt with, although even they took time. Others, however, were seriously, and perhaps fatally ill. Some I could help; others I could do nothing for. On such occasions I would have given much for a proper medical training.

They suffered from trachoma, and other eye troubles, from scabies and piles, from stones, from intestinal worms of many varieties, from dysentery, both amoebic and bacillary, from bilharzia and from bajal, to name only a few of their complaints. Bajal was one of the commonest diseases and perhaps the most unpleasant. Resembling syphilis, but non-venereal, it is a form of yaws and highly contagious. The sores, which might occur anywhere on the body, were often extensive and sometimes stank horribly. I usually felt sick when there were several such patients in the room. No doubt some of the cases which I thought were bajal were really syphilis, but penicillin injections were effective for both. Gonorrhoea was almost unknown; in seven years, I only treated three cases, all infected in Amara. I could do nothing about the bilharzia from which everyone suffered. The course of injections lasted a month and I was never that long in one place. I treated my own canoeboys, but they always got reinfected. There were also epidemics of measles, chickenpox, mumps and whooping cough, and there was the 1958 epidemic of Asiatic 'flu which most of the Madan caught. My drugs saved many who developed pneumonia as a consequence of the 'flu. Although we were surrounded day after day by the sufferers demanding medicines, my canoeboys and I somehow escaped; to my relief, for I dreaded catching it in summer under these conditions.

Surprisingly, I met few typical cases of malaria, and most of those were probably contracted outside the Marshes. On the other hand, many of the Madan suffered from recurrent low fevers, and a large number of children had enlarged spleens. The dominant mosquito there, *Anopheles pulcherrimus*, was a poor carrier of malaria. The more malignant variety, *Anopheles stephensi*, was comparatively rare in the Marshes themselves.

Then there were the accidents. Some of the victims had been appallingly burnt when their houses caught fire, and all too often small children upset pots of boiling water over themselves. Men were brought to me who had been gored by wild boars. Sometimes they were out hunting when attacked, but more often cutting reeds, or harvesting their crops. One had wounds in his arms and thighs and a three-inch gash in his stomach through which his intestines protruded. Luckily they were not perforated and I managed to put them back and sew him up. Surprisingly, he survived. On one occasion, I was taken to a house to see a boy whose home-made gun had burst and blown off half his hand. All I could do was to amputate three of his shattered fingers. On another, two boys woke me during the night and paddled me for three hours to their village. We arrived at dawn and found their father writhing on the floor with his hands over his eyes. They told me he had been blinded in one eye by a blow two years earlier. Now some internal pressure seemed to be forcing the dead eyeball out of its socket, and the only thing was to try and remove it. I had some knowledge of the eye structure from skinning animals for trophies. I gave the old man morphia, and managed to get the eye out while they held him down. In spite of the morphia, he had writhed and groaned and I felt pretty shaken. When he came round, he declared that the pain was much better. I stayed with him for two days, and when I saw him six months later he had recovered.

But there was much that I could not even attempt to do and I had many failures. I am still haunted by the face of a small boy dying of dysentery. Often, too, it was very difficult to convince them that I could do nothing. They would bring me, perhaps from a great distance, an old man dying in agony of cancer, or a girl coughing up her lungs from tuberculosis, confident that I could cure them, and would go on begging pathetically, 'Just give us medicine, Sahib, give us medicine.' Others could have been cured if only they would have gone to hospital in Amara or

Nasiriya, but they were terrified of hospitals and would seldom consent.

The doctors in Majar, Kubaish and Amara might well have resented my lack of qualifications, but they never appeared to. On the contrary, several helped me with advice and medicines. The Minister of the Interior in Baghdad agreed to my doing medical work in the Marshes, but warned me that if anyone died as a result of my ministrations, and the family made trouble, nothing could save me from criminal prosecution. This was a risk I was willing to take. I treated many people who were already dying; no one afterwards suggested that I had killed them.

12. Among the Fartus

After leaving Abid's village, I stayed in a small house on a *kibasha*, and the weight of my patients submerged the floor. I finished treating them ankle-deep in water. My host assured me that it did not matter, but nevertheless he seemed relieved when I moved on.

At the next village, Mabrad, forty or fifty houses, each on its own *dibin*, were built on both sides of a canal, with lanes of shallow water between them. Again, a large and particularly vociferous crowd collected, and I struggled with them for three hours until dark. I was staying with the village headman, an unattractive old man called Mahsin. I asked his sons to help me but they preferred to play the fool and pester me for medicines they did not need. They were younger replicas of their father with the same long nose, close-set eyes and whining voice. In the end, thoroughly fed-up, I gave the most persistent two quinine tablets to chew and soon I heard him retching behind the house. My temper was not improved by having to wait hours for dinner, which, when it came, consisted of a dish of cold, lumpy rice and a bowl of dirty buttermilk. Afterwards I waited again, this time for Mahsin to make tea, which he showed no sign of doing. One of his sons suddenly turned his head and exclaimed, 'Hullo! What is that?' He dived through the door and I heard him shout. 'Fire! Fire!' We crowded after him pushing our way past the buffaloes.

The second house downwind of us was alight. As I watched, the whole roof caught and went up in a roaring sheet of orange flame, showering sparks into the darkness. We piled into canoes and poled towards it. Before we got there, the house beyond had also caught, and the sparks from both, carried by a strong wind, were landing on others. A variety of boats came and went across water lit by the blaze. The owners rushed in and out of their homes, threw anything they could lay hands on into waiting canoes, and then hurried back to save something else. A woman wailed, men shouted, dogs barked, buffaloes took fright and splashed away into the dark, and over the general din sounded the frightening roar and crackle of the fires. A third house caught as we landed at the one beyond. A distraught woman pushed past me with a baby in her arms; a small boy clung to her dress and screamed. She handed the baby to a girl in a canoe and shoved the yelling child in beside her, before rushing back, to reappear a few seconds later with a bundle of quilts.

In the doorway I collided with an old man and a boy struggling with a sack of grain. I helped to drag it to a boat; then we fetched another sack. There were several more, all very heavy. By now the house next door was afire from end to end. Silhouetted against the light, a woman stared at the blazing roof and beat her breast. The roof caved in, sparks poured upwards and several people splashed through the intervening water. We were heaving another sack outside, when someone shouted: 'It is on fire,' and we saw that the roof above us was alight. The heat was soon terrific, the flames licking their way towards us. There was only one sack left but we could not stay. 'Come on,' the old man shouted. We jumped into the ditch and waded across to the next house. To prevent it catching people were throwing water on to the roof, but obviously they could not save it.

Twelve houses were burnt that night in Mabrad. The last in the row blazed like a pyre, lighting the black water with red and gold. We crossed to the other side, and watched it burn. The night was dark, the stars cold and clear, and the wind chilly after the heat of the flames. Elsewhere heaps of ashes glowed, stirred to flickering life by the wind. Men, excited by their battle, talked noisily of their deeds. In the distance, women keened, wailing for their lost homes and possessions.

A stranger came up and said, 'Come and drink tea with us, Sahib.' When I got back to Mahsin's, I found the family from the first house that had been burnt. The father had lost his headcloth and his white shirt was badly singed. A small, sinewy, grey-haired man, with a seamed face and a broken front tooth, he squatted by the hearth with his two boys. The elder, about seventeen, had a nasty burn on his shoulder. At the other end of the room an old crone, probably the grandmother, lamented noisily, and a younger woman sat in silence, with a child on her ap and two others beside her. Mahsin, who had at last produced some tea, said, 'It is lucky the fire did not start when everyone was asleep. That is what happened at Sada last month when the *Sayid*'s wife and child were burnt to death.'

The father told us that he and his boys had been in the house next door when the fire started. 'We rescued the children and then I tried to fetch my rifle. It was under the bedding and I could not find it. That was when Ali got burnt. Everything gone, rifle, eight dinars in a box, bedding, clothes, everything; all the grain – everything. Well, it is not the first time I have had my house burnt. Tonight – twelve houses gone, just like that! The praise be to God,' he added resignedly.

All night the old grandmother wept and no one heeded her. The man and his two boys slept beside me, one of them sharing my blankets. At least their buffaloes and canoe were safe; it was those that really mattered. The family would build a new house as soon as the ground cooled; there was plenty of suitable *qasab* near by. Others in the village would help with grain and bedding, and they could salvage their cooking pots. The one serious loss was the rifle. In the morning I gave them a few dinars to help towards that.

We took two hours to reach Awaidiya, a small Fartus village where Dugald Stewart and I had been the year before. To get there we paddled across a small lake encircled by high reeds, and then punted along a wide, shallow waterway. For some time before the first house appeared above the reeds, the unmistakable sounds of a Marsh village came to us across the water; the hum of many voices, the dull beat of women pounding corn, the grunts of buffaloes, the barking of dogs, and, sharply distinct, the crowing of a cock. The village straggled between reedbeds. Jasim al Faris's small *mudhif* was at the far end. Raised on a *dibin* a little above the water, the whole structure listed to port. Jasim himself, a tall gaunt man in a white shirt, stood in the entrance, and I liked him on sight. He had a deeply lined face, a straight nose, a firm mouth and kindly eyes (Plate 26). Falih, his younger son, who had entertained us the year before, hurried in with carpets and cushions. He was now fifteen, handsome but with a rather petulant expression, and suffered from a fungus infection of the head, his whole scalp a nasty mass of dry scabs. However, he always kept it carefully covered and I only saw it later when he asked me to treat it. This infection was fairly common among children. It seemed gradually to clear up when they were about fourteen, but many of them remained permanently bald in consequence.

I stayed with Jasim for a week, and soon felt at home with the Fartus, who treated me as one of themselves. Here, from the start, we drank from the same cup. In the mornings and evenings Falih paddled me to the nearby lake to look for duck, but they were always too wary, and we had to be content with coots, herons and cormorants, all of which the Madan ate. I tried a cormorant, which they assured me was delicious, just like fish. I only took a mouthful and could not get the taste out of my mouth for hours.

One morning Falih and a cousin of his called Daud punted me towards the mainland. We soon left the *qasab* and emerged on to a waste of fallen bulrushes covering many square miles. The new growth was rising through the tumbled grey of last year's flags, but was not yet high enough to obstruct my view, even from the bottom of the canoe. The place was alive with birds. Snipe sprang into the air beside us and zigzagged away, and flocks of small waders swept past. Ruffs and godwits, curlews, redshanks and avocets, among other waders that I could not identify, fed on patches of open mud. There were spoonbills, ibises and egrets, and grey and purple herons. Once we heard the far-off crying of geese. Harriers hunted low over the rushes, and the usual eagles circled overhead. Falih and Daud poled as far as possible, then tucked their shirts round their waists and ran the small canoe through the slush.

We had hoped to reach the mainland, but several miles of drying mud separated us from the great open plains, where the shepherd tribes of the Muntifiq lived in their black tents. 'The Arabs,' Falih called them, and promised to take me there another time. 'We shall visit Mahsin the son of Badr,' he said. 'He is the greatest of them. He is my father's friend. My father hid him in the days when the English were looking for him. Have you not heard of Badr? "Generous like Badr," the Arabs still say, and his son is like him. Come back when the floods are high and we will go to him.'

On the return journey I shot several purple gallinule which Falih insisted were good eating. Rather like coots in shape and size, they rose from the reeds with their long legs swinging beneath them. In summer they, and the marbled duck that arrived in the spring, were the only birds fit to eat.

Daud, who had spoken little, asked me shyly if I would take him with me to Amara, where his father was in prison. 'He served the Al Essa sheikh, at Saigal,' he told me. 'One day the sheikh sent him to arrest three of the Azairij who were causing trouble. My father brought them to the sheikh who flogged them. Later they attacked my father and one hit him on the head with a club and knocked him unconscious. When my father recovered he fetched his rifle and shot the man. The man died. Instead of protecting my father, the sheikh, God curse him, handed him over to the Government and they sentenced him to ten years. My mother and I came here to live with my uncle Jasim. That was six years ago. Now I wish to see my father.'

Daud was a strange boy. Usually cheerful and full of chatter, he occasionally lapsed into brooding silence. When Jasim heard he was coming with me to Amara, he said he was glad. 'He's devoted to his father and hasn't seen him since he was imprisoned. When that happened he wouldn't speak or eat for days. Again last year he went all strange and no one knew what had upset him. He wandered round saying, "Daud is dead." We had to take him to the shrine of Fuwada before he was cured.'

Every evening, men and boys paddled across to Jasim's *mudhif*, left their canoes at the entrance and ranged themselves round the walls. The first few times we just chatted, but one day Jasim suggested that we should have some singing. 'Yes, by God, song and dance,' the others agreed, all talking together. 'Let us enjoy ourselves; where is Khayal? He came back today from Mabrad. Where are the drums? We will show the Englishman how the Madan entertain themselves. Go, Falih, fetch the drums and tambourines. Daud, go and get Khayal.'

Falih returned with two drums, and someone else brought two tambourines. The drums were of earthenware and shaped like tapering vases, about eighteen inches long and eight inches across at the wide end, which was covered with a thin skin. The other end was open. Khayal, who now arrived, was the same age as Falih and Daud. He sang several songs, accompanied by Falih on a drum. Drawn by the sounds, others paddled across to the *mudhif*, and the room, already fairly full, was soon crowded. Khayal had an attractive voice and a large repertoire of songs, some lilting and gay, others mournful. Later, he, Falih, Daud and half a dozen other lads formed a small circle, and two thin, impish-looking boys were dragged into it protesting and told to dance. They were brothers, the elder about thirteen. Khayal took one drum, Falih the other, and they began to play, using only the tips of their fingers to beat out a quick, broken rhythm. Two boys banged the tambourines. Each of the others joined his hands together and kept time by clicking the two middle fingers and by thumping the floor with the heel of his right foot.

At first the two brothers circled slowly and languidly, their bodies swaying and their arms raised, elbows level with the shoulders. As the rhythm quickened, their arms swung lower, their bodies twisted and squirmed, and their feet moved faster, forwards, sideways and backwards. The others were singing now, without restraint. The dance had reached its climax. Suddenly the boys stood, feet apart, their bodies jerking forwards and backwards in ever quickening thrusts from their hips. The thrusts slowed, their bodies shuddered, as each twitching muscle passed the spasm on to the next. Then, quite casually, the boys stopped, grinned at their audience and sat down.

But they were not allowed to remain seated. Again and again they repeated their performance, varying it a little. As a parody of the sexual act by children it was remarkable, but did not strike me as obscene. Later in the evening, while the audience intoned a religious chant, they performed a blasphemous and indecent parody of Moslem prayer, with one boy making suggestive gestures behind the other's upthrust bottom. Used to more conventional behaviour among Moslems, I looked anxiously at a venerable *Sayid* who had brought his two grown-up sons for me to circumcise in the morning. All three were chanting with the best.

13. Feuds in the Marshes

The following evening, as darkness fell, Daud and I sat in the *mudhif* with half a dozen patients who had come for medicine and were not staying the night. Through the entrance I could see the fires, lit to protect the buffaloes from mosquitoes, and the thickening pall of smoke drifting low over the water. The mosquitoes were beginning to appear and I could imagine that, with the reedbeds so close, they would make this place uninhabitable in the summer, even for the Madan. The background rhythm of croaking frogs, to which by now I hardly listened, was suddenly altered by the repetition of a single intrusive note. The others remarked on it too. 'A snake has grabbed that one,' said Daud. 'There are a lot about and we killed one in the roof recently.' The pitiful, disturbing sound continued for a long time.

Two years later I was in the same *mudhif* during summer, trying to stir a little movement into the air with a reed fan, when I felt something behind me. I was about to put down my hand, but some instinct warned me not to. I shifted my body forward, glanced down, and saw a light-coloured snake two feet long. I hit it on the head with the handle of the fan and killed it.

Snakes were common, especially in summer. The Madan maintained that the most poisonous species was the *arbid*, usually about four feet long with a thick body, and in colour black blending into a dull red. Even so, I only came across one case of snake-bite in Southern Iraq. It was during the feast of Ramadhan, which that year fell in summer. A man and his fourteen-year-old daughter had intended to visit Kubaish to sell some homemade cheese. To avoid the heat they went down to their canoe in the dark. Getting into it the girl trod on a snake and was bitten in the foot. She died within half an hour. Her face went almost black, and when they moved the body, dark blood poured from the mouth and nose. I arrived in their village just afterwards. As if there were not enough real snakes, the Madan firmly believed in two monsters, the *anfish* and the *afa*. The first was reputed to have a hairy skin and the other to have legs. Both were said to inhabit the heart of the Marshes and to be very deadly.

After Falih had cleared away the dinner, a tall thin-faced man entered the *mudhif*, his left hand wrapped in a blood-soaked rag. He had cut it deeply while gathering reeds. His eyes were the colour of dark amber, and a cast in one gave him a sinister appearance. He came from Qabiba, a large Fartus village two hours distant on the way to Saigal.

Years earlier the Al Essa, the same shepherd tribe in whose encampment Dugald Stewart and I stayed on the edge of the desert, had gained control of the large Marsh village of Saigal and the rich rice-fields round it. From there they had occupied Qabiba, and built and garrisoned a small mud fort, until the Fartus of Qabiba revolted and regained their independence. Dugald and I passed hurriedly through this village the year after the revolt. Our canoemen, who were Al Essa, kept their rifles ready and exchanged no greetings with the villagers for there was blood between them.

The man whose hand I dressed in Jasim's *mudhif* turned out to have been one of the leaders of this revolt, and I questioned him about the fighting. 'The Al Essa had no right there,' he declared vehemently. 'They are not Madan. They are shepherds from the desert. Qabiba is in the Marshes, it belongs to the Fartus and our fathers built the *dibins*. Ever since their sheikhs seized Qabiba there was trouble, and most of us left the village and built our houses elsewhere. Why should we be driven from our homes?'

'Yes, why indeed? God's curse on the Al Essa!' someone else exclaimed.

'So we decided to fight. We surrounded the fort on the twelfth night of the month of Qusair. It was three hours after sunset and the moon was bright. We knew there were six men there and that Falaij was their leader. We sent old Zair Ali to the fort to tell them to surrender, but they shouted back that we were Madan, dogs and sons of dogs, and that if we came near, they would kill us. Then we attacked from all sides in our canoes, giving our battle cry, "I am the brother of Alia." '

By now all his listeners were leaning forward, enthralled by a tale of tribal war which most of them must have heard a score of times.

'They had a machine-gun; its bullets cut down the reeds behind us like hail. Praise be to God, the slave who fired it did not know how to shoot, or many more of us would have died that night. We jumped out of our canoes and rushed the fort. Before we got there we killed two of them with our bullets and then we killed two more with our knives. We were crowded into the room downstairs when one of the two remaining Al Essa fired down through the floor and shot off a man's nose. The wounded man cried, "I have been shot from above." So we fired volleys back through the ceiling and killed another. Only Falaij was left. We called on him to surrender, but he refused. Truly he was brave. Some Fartus climbed the stairs and he shot two of them; they were brothers. Then, shouting his war-cry, he jumped off the roof and fell riddled with our bullets. His small son had been with him. He asked for mercy and we spared him. He wasn't worth killing. He is now at Saigal with the Al Essa sheikhs. Twelve Fartus died in the battle.'

As soon as he stopped speaking, Falih sprang up and, stamping his feet, chanted:

> 'Oh mother of Karaim do not lament
> For Karaim fell on the full flood of war.

In a second, the rest were on their feet shouting back the words, as they stamped round in a circle.

Falih ran out and came back with a rifle which he fired at intervals through the roof. I joined in and fired ten shots with mine. More people pushed into the room, the roaring deepened and grew louder. At last they stopped exhausted, and Jasim sent Daud to get more sugar and tea from the merchant. I asked who Karaim was and they told me that he had been killed leading the attack on the fort.

Three years afterwards, I went to stay with the Al Essa on the mainland. At sunset I saw the new moon that terminates the month-long fast of Ramadhan. The following day the scattered tribe gathered to pay homage to their sheikh, and feast in his great guest tent. At dawn they started to come in across the plain,

some on horseback, others on foot, each contingent under its
own crimson banner. When at length they were assembled, they
charged and counter-charged on their horses, while those on foot
stamped round (Plate 40), firing off their rifles and chanting:

> 'We will go back to the open water,
> We will go and bring back Falaij.'

– and I remembered the night when I first heard how Falaij died,
from one of the men who killed him.

I left Jasim early next morning. Daud came with me, and two
of Jasim's retainers armed with Lee-Enfield rifles. We followed a
narrow way between high reeds, where the water was so clogged
with hornwort and other weeds that it looked like a path overgrown with moss. The canoemen were hard put to it to force the
boat through this mass of vegetation. On this occasion we passed
by Qabiba, a large village of three hundred houses, and reached a
string of small lagoons. Beyond them lay the rice-fields on the
western outskirts of Saigal. To the east of the village a lake, three
or four miles wide, divided the Marshes from the mainland. At
this time of year it only extended for about fifteen miles into the
Azairij country. Later, however, at the height of the floods, it
would link up with the inundations that covered so much of the
desert.

Saigal was the largest village I had yet seen. It was divided by
a broad waterway, on either side of which a narrow strip of dry
ground carried a number of *mudhifs* and shops. Otherwise most of
the four or five hundred houses were built, Madan fashion, on
dibins. Commanding the eastern entrance to the village was a
brick fort. Put up hurriedly by the Al Essa when the village had
been threatened by the Al bu Muhammad, its walls already
showed deep cracks. Opposite, on the southern bank, was a flat-
roofed brick building, also intended for defence in case of war,
with its rooms constructed round a small court. Thirty yards
away, on a tongue of dry ground running into the lake, stood a
splendid *mudhif* with eleven arches. Both belonged to Abdullah,
Maziad's uncle and representative in Saigal. Sheikh Maziad
himself lived on the mainland with his tribe, the only Al Essa
in Saigal being some of his family and their retainers. Otherwise

the village was inhabited by Fartus and Shaghanba, and by a few Al bu Muhammad and Azairij.

Abdullah was away at present, but his son Tahir was at home, a friendly boy of sixteen, with the careful good manners of the desert Arab. He took me over to the *mudhif*, where several armed men sat, wrapped in dark cloaks. These were Al Essa on a visit from their tents on the mainland. Jasim's two Fartus, who bore the Al Essa no love, returned to Awaidiya as soon as they had drunk the formal cups of coffee. Daud was safe enough in Saigal, since his father, Hashim, belonged not to the Fartus but to the Jara, a small, broken tribe scattered in twos and threes among the Marsh villages. He could be in danger if he went among the Azairij across the lake, for it was one of them whom Hashim had killed. Now, feeling that Abdullah had betrayed his father, he sat in silence, playing with a string of beads, and would make no response to Tahir's attempts to be friendly.

Hashim was eventually released from prison and went to live in Awaidiya where I came to know him. He was one of the most attractive characters I met among the Madan. He looked more than his forty years, for ten years in prison had grizzled his hair and lined his face. Although poor, he always insisted on entertaining me, and taught me much about the Madan and their customs. He was still involved in the feud with the Azairij, because no tribesman considers that imprisonment nullifies a killing, which in their eyes can only be settled by another death or the payment of blood money. Hashim's tribe were too few and scattered to raise blood money, even if the Azairij had been willing to accept it. However, he was fairly safe from vengeance so long as he remained among the Fartus at Awaidiya. Unfortunately he was induced to leave it.

While Hashim was still in prison, his brother-in-law, Jasim, had given his daughter to one of the Al bu Muhammad, exacting seventy-five dinars as the bride price. As was customary, Jasim spent part of the money on quilts, cushions and other household furnishings for the bride to take to her new home. After his release, Hashim demanded the balance of the money for himself, but Jasim declared that he had spent it on supporting Hashim's family. By tribal custom, a father could take back his married daughter, even against her wish and even if she had bred children, but would have to return the bride price in full. This right Hashim now exercised, although his daughter had borne a child. When her husband demanded the bride price, Hashim told him to recover it from Jasim. Getting no satisfaction from the latter, the husband appealed to the Government, who sent two policemen to conduct Hashim to Amara for questioning. Whether by ill luck or design, the policemen were Azairij and the family with whom he had a blood feud contrived for them to bring him through their country. When he heard of the proposed route, Hashim protested vigorously, but gave in when they assured him they had work to do on the way and that he would be quite safe with them.

They landed for lunch at the police post at Suq at Tawil and, as they came out to continue their journey, a crowd was waiting for them. The dead man's brother stepped forward and shot Hashim in the chest with a revolver he had borrowed from the sheikh. Hashim drew his dagger but collapsed. After his assailant had fired twice more and fled, the police feigned pursuit. Hashim lay where he had fallen, bleeding to death, and no one went near him. An hour later the police returned and carried him into the post. Still conscious, he accused them of murdering him, and then died.

I saw Daud six months after his father's murder. He had bought himself a revolver and was setting off alone for the Azairij country to find the man who had killed him. Never a stable character, the shock seemed to have unhinged him. When I tried to dissuade him from going there by himself, he merely reiterated, meaninglessly, 'Daud died ten years ago.' I never saw him again.

14. Return to Qabab

In the evening Tahir took me on the lake in his *tarada*. We drifted about in pleasant surroundings and he proved an agreeable companion. With him was a silent well-mannered little boy dressed in a gold-embroidered cloak. I thought he must be a relation of Tahir but learnt later that he was Falaij's son, the same who had been with his father when he was killed in the battle at Qabiba. When we got back to the *mudhif* at dusk, swarms of small bats were flighting out from the village towards the Marshes. Quantities of these bats hid up in the roof of *mudhifs*, fouling the room with their droppings. Sparrows could also be a nuisance in a *mudhif* by severing the *qasab* bindings round the arches, though how and why they did this I never discovered. The next year I brought an air rifle with me from England, which proved a useful gambit among strangers who were being formal. As soon as I produced it, even the dourest greybeards clamoured to have a shot. You can usually get on terms with people by helping them to kill something.

Early next morning, Daud and I were taken on to Al Aggar. As we paddled across the silvery lake, grey terns, airy as swallows, skimmed the shining water, and numbers of duck, collected for the spring migration, took wing at our approach. Behind us, in Saigal, the traffic of canoes moved slowly and without noise among the awakening houses. Gradually the village sank below the horizon, until only Abdullah's *mudhif* showed where it lay. Then we were back in the enclosed world of the Marshes where the new growth of reeds, shooting up in the last few days, was already high among the old. Two hours later we came unexpectedly on open water and, in the middle of it, the two islands of Al Aggar. The larger belonged to the Shaghanba, with two hundred and fifty houses crowded so close together that almost no part of the island was visible. The smaller was a hundred yards away, with just enough space for thirty houses belonging to some Al bu Muhammad. Both villages owed allegiance to Majid al Khalifa. We stepped ashore over a low fence on to a soggy heap of rushes, and at a large *raba* were welcomed by Yunis, a slightly built man with an intelligent, refined face. Although reserved by nature he seemed friendly.

The room was packed. A young *Sayid* from Qurna sat in the place of honour. While collecting money, ostensibly to build a mosque at Qurna, he took the opportunity to warn his audience that the Day of Judgement was at hand. I was aware that he resented my intrusion, and soon afterwards he asked how his listeners could hope to be saved if they allowed infidels to defile their houses. Yunis, who was brewing coffee, kept silent. When the coffee was ready, he stood up with the pot in his hand, turned to the *Sayid* and said, 'I am a simple Madan, not a theologian, but it has always seemed to me that the English are purer than we are. Some of us have met them, all of us have heard of them from the time when they ruled this land after driving out the Turks. They did not lie, they did not take bribes and they did not oppress the poor. We Moslems, as you well know, do all these things. But that is beside the point. This Englishman is my guest. Welcome, Sahib,' he said to me and went on, 'In my house, guests drink from the same cup. That is my custom. Those who won't do so, must go without.' He came across to where I was sitting a little apart, and gave me coffee from the only cup he held. When I had finished, he poured out again and handed it to the next man. All drank except the *Sayid*.

Later on, a *Sayid* from Al Aggar itself came in. A poor man, who spent most of his life cutting fodder for his few buffaloes, he looked like any other indigent Madan except for his green headcloth. Sitting down beside me, he inquired several times after my health. I suspected that he had heard of his colleague's behaviour and was anxious to make amends. After dinner he said to Yunis, 'I hear the Sahib likes singing and dancing; let me show him how they dance in the Hejaz, the land of my ancestors'; and he performed a stately pirouette, very different from the uninhibited caperings of the Madan. I appreciated the gesture. The other *Sayid* had withdrawn into a corner where he sat muttering and counting his beads. He was the only *Sayid* who was ever rude to me. Many were aloof when they first met me, but they thawed in time, and several became my close friends. Some of the most distinguished brought their womenfolk to be treated and their sons to be circumcised, a religious rite which, after all, they might well have preferred a fellow Moslem to perform.

Next morning Yunis suggested that we should watch a wedding celebration in a large *raba* at the far end of the village, for which they had engaged a famous *dhakar binta* from Majar. For some time we had heard the distant sounds of singing and drumming. The boy wore a scarlet gown with ropes of imitation pearls and heavy gold ear-rings. His hair, combed and scented, hung round his shoulders; his breasts were padded and his face was made up. He looked like an affected girl and behaved with the mincing mannerisms of a female prostitute, but he certainly could dance. He used a pair of castanets in each hand, the mark of the professional since no village lad used them. Strangely enough, his gestures were far less erotic than those of the boys I had watched at Awaidiya. Much of his dancing was a gymnastic display of a high order. The comments I overheard, however, left no doubt about his other proclivities.

Among the tribes there were no loose women, prostitutes or otherwise. Little proof was needed to convict a girl of immorality, rumour being usually enough. Then her family killed her mercilessly to redeem their honour. The duty of executioner devolved on her brother, who could not spare her and hope to remain within his tribe. As a consequence, a lad could not sleep with, or even fondle, a girl until he had married her. Young men found sexual satisfaction with one another, but were discreet, and careful to show no signs of abnormality in their outward behaviour. A *dhakar binta* was a professional prostitute of the towns, and the Madan spoke of him as such, but I never heard them discuss homosexuality, either in theory or with specific reference to any man or boy in their society. In further contrast to ourselves, they sometimes referred quite openly to masturbation, and would even joke about donkeys.

After the dance, Yunis took me to a yard where his canoe was being recoated. The bitumen never lasted more than a year, after which it began to crack and let in water. These cracks could be temporarily sealed by heating the bitumen with a torch of reeds. The Madan always maintained that a coating put on in cold weather did not last as long as one put on in the summer. Inside the reed fence, several canoes were drawn up out of the water. One was upturned, and four small boys had nearly finished chipping the bitumen off its bottom and sides. An older boy melted chunks of fresh bitumen on a metal sheet over a small fire. The whole yard, littered with bits of plank and broken-up canoes, smelt pleasantly of warm tar. The boy shouted, 'Ali, Yunis is here.' An old man in a filthy shirt appeared from one of the houses. Yunis asked, 'Have you done my canoe yet?' and Ali answered, 'No, not yet; but it won't be long now. The chicks have just about stripped it.' Chicks was the usual expression in the Marshes for small children. He spread a reed mat against the wall of his house and said, 'Sit down; make yourselves comfortable while we finish.' He called to one of the boys, 'Hasan, my son, go and tell them to make tea.' I said we had already drunk tea at Yunis' house and again several times at the dance, but he insisted, 'No matter. Have some more,' and went over to inspect the canoe.

The exposed planks were full of gaping holes and cracks. Choosing small pieces of wood from those on the ground, he thinned and shaped them with an adze and then nailed them over the worst holes. Next, the eldest boy scooped up some of the boiling pitch in a shovel and dolloped it on the bottom of the canoe; then Ali spread it a quarter of an inch thick. When he had finished, the canoe looked as good as new, black, smooth and shining.

Ali came and sat beside us and lit a cigarette. 'Wait a little longer and you can take your canoe back,' and he sent Hasan for the paddles. I had noticed that at night all canoes were moored away from the houses, about a hundred yards out on the lagoon. Yunis explained that this was to put them out of reach of the buffaloes that would otherwise eat the pitch – a habit they had in some villages but not in others. When arriving in a strange village, the Madan generally inquired whether the local buffaloes ate pitch. Those in Al Aggar were notoriously bad.

They also told me that the pitch came from Hit on the Euphrates near Baghdad. I had been there and seen the small pools where the molten bitumen bubbled out of the ground. After cooling it was sent away in small, hard chunks like the broken-up surface of a macadam road. There was no wood suitable for canoes in Southern Iraq. The boat-builders favoured mulberry from Kurdistan for the ribs, and for the planks they used woods imported from abroad. There were craftsmen, like Ali, in many of the larger villages in and around the Marshes. At Huwair on the Euphrates, a few miles below Kubaish, the whole of a large village was given over to this industry, where they not only made canoes, but also large two-masted sailing boats. Haji Hamaid, who lived there, was the most renowned of these craftsmen (Plate 74), and his *taradas* were famed throughout this part of Southern Iraq, but the work of several others was nearly as well known. The Marshmen could tell which craftsman had built a *tarada* by glancing at it.

The people of Huwair itself were Moslems, but elsewhere most of the boat-builders were Sabaeans (Plate 50). Although they are mentioned three times in the Koran, with Christians and Jews, as 'People of the Book', the Sabaeans, known as Subba, were generally despised and no Moslem would eat or drink with them. Their religion forbade mutilation, and in consequence they did not circumcise. The Moslems therefore used Subba as a term of contempt for any grown man who had not undergone the operation. Distinguished by their large beards and by red-and-white check headcloths, there were a few thousand Sabaeans all told, most of them in Baghdad, Basra, Suq ash Shuyukh and Amara where they were famous for their silver work. Isolated families lived in Moslem villages round the Marshes and farmyard ducks were a sign of their presence since, for some unaccountable reason, the Moslems would eat wild but not tame duck. The Sabaeans practised baptism by immersion every Sunday, and every time that they incurred pollution or otherwise infringed their code of ritual purity. For this reason they were known by ill-informed Europeans as Christians of St John. In fact they were pagans, though they worshipped a Supreme Being. Their religion, so I understood, contained elements of Manichaeism but not of Islam, and their ceremonial language was Aramaic.

In the Marshes children often fashioned small rafts from bundles of bulrushes, sometimes turning up the end for a prow, and paddled about the villages on these primitive craft (Plates 46–49). I once saw an interesting type of coracle, called a *zaima* (Plate 45), on a branch of the Euphrates below Suq ash Shuyukh. Made of *qasab* and coated outside with bitumen, it was ten feet long and two and a half feet at its widest. The owner told me that a *zaima* would only last a year, as the bitumen could not be renewed. He demonstrated how to construct one. First he made half a dozen tight bundles of five or six *qasab* reeds rather longer than the length of the proposed boat, and fastened them securely together side by side to form the keel, leaving eighteen inches free at both ends, which he bent upwards. He next bent five long reeds into the shape of a U, passed the middle among the loose ends of the keel, and laced them back to the keel itself. He repeated the process at either end alternately, until he had built up the sides and ends of the hull. This framework he stiffened by tying into it a number of ribs made from two or three willow wands. Bundles of a few reeds, fastened one below the other along the inside of the boat, covered the top half of the ribs and formed the inner planking. Finally, he wedged three stout sticks across the boat as thwarts and secured their ends in place with lumps of bitumen. The *zaima* was now ready to be coated outside with bitumen. Nowadays even the poorest of the Madan possess wooden boats, but in the past, when communications were precarious and wood difficult to obtain, many probably used just this type of coracle. A circular coracle, called the *quffa*, used to be common around Baghdad. The farthest south I saw one was below Kut, near Sheikh Saad.

From Al Aggar, I decided to return to Qabab, where I could easily send Daud on to Amara. Two cousins of Yunis accompanied us. One of them tipped the canoe clumsily as he pushed off and water came over the side. I was amused to hear the other ask him scornfully, 'Are you an Arab? Are you a Kurd?' implying that he certainly could not be a Madan. All the way to Bu Mughaifat our route lay through dense reedbeds. Soon after we started we passed a whole family on the move. Two boys in a canoe urged on half a dozen buffaloes, following behind a *balam* that was paddled by an elderly man and another boy, who made yodelling cries to encourage the swimming animals. A woman and three small children, one of them wearing nothing but a silver collar round his neck, shared the back of the boat with two buffalo calves, a kitten, and a lot of hens. The front was piled high with their belongings, including the dismantled framework of their house, reed mats, water jars, cooking pots, sacks of grain and a pile of quilts. A dog stood on top of all this between the wooden legs of a churn, and barked at us as we edged past.

Sadam, having heard that I had reached Al Aggar, was waiting to welcome me back to Qabab. I asked after young Auda, his son, and he replied, 'He kisses your hand. He has gone over to the merchant's shop and will be here in a minute.' Almost as soon as I landed, the first of my patients arrived, a young man moaning and writhing in the bottom of a canoe. The pain was over his kidneys and came in agonizing spasms. I suspected that it was caused by a stone. To try and give him relief, I gently rubbed his side with capsicum vaseline. When the spasms passed, he declared that I had cured him, and I felt more of a quack than usual. However my 'burning medicine' became very popular, for nearly all the Marshmen, even quite small children, suffered at one time or other from these pains which they called *khasara*. A boy about twelve once showed me some stones, the largest the size of a pea, that he had just passed. On another occasion, a consequential young *Sayid* asked for the burning medicine, declaring that he suffered periodically from *khasara*. I gave him a little in an empty matchbox, warned him not to get it near his eyes and to wash his hands after using it. Ten minutes later he was back, raving and almost unintelligible. For some reason best known to himself he had rubbed the capsicum vaseline on his penis. Grimacing and dancing about, he swore the pain was killing him. I could only suggest he washed himself thoroughly with soap and water. One of my canoeboys, who found the *Sayid*'s predicament irresistibly funny, recommended that he should go and cool himself in his wife.

The following morning, before it was properly light, Daud shook me awake, saying that some people had brought a wounded boy. A man and a woman helped their twelve-year-old child into the room. His blue-and-white striped shirt was torn and soaked in blood, and the lower half of his face was covered with a bloody rag. Large black eyes stared at me from a very white face. I asked what had happened and they said, 'Our dog bit him.' The child was shivering and I wrapped him in some of my blankets, while we lit a fire and warmed some water. Then I soaked the bandage off his face. His cheek was torn and a flap hung down exposing his back teeth. There were other bites in his arm and shoulder. He never spoke, but watched me with un-blinking eyes. I cleaned and disinfected the wounds, sprinkling them with sulphonamide powder, and then, as carefully as possible, sewed the flap back into position. He screwed his eyes but never even whimpered. When I had finished he murmured, 'Thank you, Sahib,' the first words he had uttered. I gave him a penicillin injection and made him comfortable by the fire.

Sadam joined us and while we drank tea, the father, who came from Daub, a village in the Marshes to the east, told us that his son had gone outside before lying down to sleep. 'Our dog – you know it, Sadam, a great big brute – sprang at him and seized him by the arm. Those are the toothmarks. It pulled him to the ground and then went for his throat. Thanks be to God it missed or it would have killed him, but it got him by the cheek. The chick never cried out. Truly, Sadam, I only went outside to see what was disturbing the buffaloes and found my son fighting for his life. God is merciful. We had heard that the Englishman was at Qabab so we brought the boy here at first light. I shot the dog before we left.'

I was worried that the dog might have had rabies, but the father assured me that it never left their isolated *dibin*. They took the child back in the afternoon, clutching in his small hand a dinar note I gave him for a new shirt. The wound healed well, and, though it left a large crescent-shaped scar on his cheek, did not pull his mouth out of shape. The Madan maintained that dogs never bit women and girls and certainly I never came across a case.

Having heard that I enjoyed their dancing, Sadam was deter-mined to give me an evening to remember. As soon as we had fed, he produced drums and tambourines, which were warmed over the fire to tighten the skins. Hearing the first few taps – to test their resonance – people came over from the village. Ajram turned up with his father, and young Helu with two brothers, smaller and skinnier than himself. They had even shriller voices, that were soon accompanying him in 'A tyrant from your earliest days'. Sahain, the headman of Bu Mughaifat, also arrived with his brother Hafadh and a large party from their village, including two lads called Yasin and Hasan who later became my canoeboys.

There was also a Fartus boy called Dakhil. An orphan and completely destitute, he quarrelled with everyone in turn and in consequence moved from one village to the next looking for employment as a herdsboy, but he had a curious charm, so that people spoke of him with exasperated affection. He was very much in love with the sister of Wadi, the cheerful fourteen-year-old boy sitting beside him. With a little encouragement, Dakhil now got up and danced, his face and movements conveying a comic impression of being aggrieved and rather indignant. He was the success of the evening. Several other boys also danced, among them Ajram, but it was Dakhil for whom the crowd shouted again and again. Then Ajram's father, Husain, insisted on dancing. He had been famous as a boy, but now was merely ludicrous and capered about like a performing elephant, until Sadam called, 'Sit down, Husain, let Dakhil dance again.'

During the evening several people I did not recognize sat beside me and said how glad they were I was back. I had only spent two days here, more than two months before, but they now made me feel I had lived with them for years. The party broke up just before dawn and when I went outside a faint light already showed in the east. In the darkness just below I could hear the splash of paddles, and voices calling to each other as they returned to their houses. It was impossible not to respond to such a friendly people.

15. Falih Bin Majid

Majid al Khalifa was sheikh of the Al bu Muhammad in all the Majar area, and overlord of much of the Marsh country as well. A deputy in the Iraqi parliament, he spent much time in Baghdad, leaving his vast estate to be run by his eldest son Falih. I had been in the Marshes a further year before I met him. Passing through Qabab, I heard that he had recently arrived from Baghdad, and that Sadam and the village elders had called on him to pay their respects. I thought I should do the same and therefore left early one morning, paddled by Yasin and Hasan, the two boys from Bu Mughaifat who by now had been with me six months. Our canoe belonged to Yasin (Plate 50). About sixteen, tall and gracefully built and with the body of an athlete, he had an attractive open face with a hint of Mongol blood. Hasan, the same age, but shorter and stockier, was a keen wildfowler, and owned a fearsome muzzle-loader of local make, the barrel bound with copper wire. I persuaded him to leave this gun behind, saying he could use mine. Of these two, Yasin was the more dominant character and the better waterman. Although only a boy, he was already deemed exceptionally skilful, even by Madan standards.

The Majar river, a branch of the Tigris, divided below Majar al Kabir into the Adil and the Wadiya, both of which dispersed into the Marshes about eight miles farther down, having by then lost much of their water in irrigation channels. We followed one of these channels until we joined the Adil, on which Majid's village lay, when Hasan tied a rope to the front thwart and towed the canoe upstream while Yasin steered with a paddle from the stern. We passed a succession of villages and at about ten o'clock came to one dominated by a large, square, flat-topped brick building, its walls cracked and weathered, which was Majid's private house. Beyond it stood a dilapidated old *mudhif*, leaning over to one side. He had evidently not yet built his new *mudhif* although bundles of *qasab* were stacked nearby. A crowd hung about outside the *mudhif* where Majid was giving audience. A man came forward and led us in. Majid got up from his carpet and we shook hands. He appeared less than his medium height for he was heavily built with very broad shoulders. Immensely powerful in his youth, he had run to seed in his old age and now his belly sagged in folds and he waddled as he walked. Above a short thick neck, his face was veined and covered with silver bristles; his eyes, small and red-rimmed, were hot and arrogant. He looked as if he had just been roused from his lair and his temper might be unpredictable. He ordered two box-like arm-chairs, made of deal and covered with blue velvet, to be carried in and placed facing each other across the room. Inviting me to sit on one, he took the other. The *mudhif* was crowded and I would have felt less conspicuous on the floor.

After a few inquiries about my health, Majid concerned himself once more with the business of the day. He dealt ably and speedily with each case, but he showed little regard for the feelings of others. If anyone tried to protest he silenced him with a glare. His scribe, pockmarked and middle-aged with a subservient manner, sat beside him recording his decisions. Like Majid he wore a surcoat of heavy dark material and a brown cloak. Majid's cloak, however, was of far finer weave and as light as gossamer. All the land belonged to Majid and consequently he was impartial in his judgement, being only anxious to secure the highest possible yield. Notoriously avaricious, he was also an efficient landlord, who knew every corner of his estate and had half a century's experience of judging the water-level on which its prosperity depended. He knew exactly when and where to build a dam, when to reduce its waters and by how much.

I was always amazed to see the way that deep rivers, fifty yards wide and tearing along in flood, could be damned with nothing more than brushwood, reeds and earth. A great deal of labour was required not only to build such dams but also to clean out the canals and strengthen the banks. Like all Arabs, these cultivators possessed little communal sense. Left to themselves, they would talk for hours before agreeing to do any work, however vital.

Then, on the appointed day, only a handful of them would turn up and these would soon go away discouraged. Majid knew what required doing, gave his orders accordingly, and enforced them. If a man avoided or skimped his task, he was put down on the ground and flogged.

In general the official class, and the intelligentsia of the towns, were hostile to the sheikhs, envying their wealth, and being anxious to destroy their political power. When they talked glibly of confiscating the sheikhs' land and distributing it among the peasants, they overlooked the fact that Iraq did not possess an Irrigation Service capable of taking their place. The larger sheikhs of Amara Province were usually extortionate and tyrannical, but most of them, like Majid, were first-rate farmers, with a knowledge of their estates acquired since childhood. The best felt a love for the land that went deeper than self-interest. If they were replaced, officials, brought perhaps from Baghdad or Mosul, would take years to acquire the same local knowledge, even if they could be induced to remain. The success or failure of the harvest would not affect them personally, and inevitably they would be tempted to grant water, not to the farmer who needed it most, but to the one who would pay most for it. 'You want water? What will you give me? Half a dinar! Why come here and waste my time? Get out.' It was easy to imagine the scene. The answer was not to dispossess the sheikhs but to ensure that they allowed their labourers a larger share of the crop and some security of tenure.

After three hours in the *mudhif*, and by the time the audience began to thin out, I was bored and hungry. The room was more than half empty when a servant brought in a tray with a roast chicken, a grilled fish, rice, bread and soup. On Majid's orders, a small rickety table was placed in front of me and the tray on it. After I had washed, he invited me to start. I had expected him to eat with me, but, as he showed no signs of joining me, I asked for the tray to be put on the ground so that I could feed with Yasin and Hasan. 'No, no, eat where you are. They don't matter, they can have theirs later,' he answered brusquely. I insisted that I would prefer to be on the ground as it was my custom to eat with my companions. 'No, no, go on, eat where you are,' he told me, and turned to speak with someone else. This was no way to treat a guest and by now I was thoroughly angry, so I took one mouthful of his rice, stood up and called for water to wash. Everyone looked at Majid, who asked me what was wrong. I answered:

'Nothing. Thank you very much, I have finished.'

'Oh, let him eat on the ground if he wants to,' he exclaimed.

I thanked him again, assured him that I had had enough and went back to my seat. Yasin and Hasan, benefiting by my abstinence, did themselves well. We departed shortly afterwards.

I did not go near Majid again for more than a year. Next time he received me very differently. He insisted that I should stay the night, fed with me, and was as attentive as Arabs generally are to their guests. After that I stopped at his *mudhif* on a number of occasions and, although I never liked him, I came to respect him.

On our way from Qabab that morning we had agreed to spend the night with Falih in his *mudhif* on the Wadiya. He had been hospitable to me the previous year and had pressed me to return. I had not done so, being in fact prejudiced against the sheikhs as a whole by those I had met when I stayed with Dugald Stewart in Amara. Amid the pretentious vulgarity of their town houses they had not shown up well. After my reception by Majid, I felt still less inclination to call on his son and suggested we should go straight back to Qabab, but Yasin said, 'No, let us spend the night with Falih, he is different.'

Two hours later, Falih made me comfortable in his *mudhif*. 'I hoped you would eventually come back,' he said. 'I have been hearing a lot about your doings from the Madan. They always refer to you as their doctor, and I am sure my villagers will all be along for medicine. You have seen the Marshes. Now let *us* see something of you. Have you shot any pig lately? What! Not even one? Just wait till the floods rise and then we will go after them together.'

He was busy supervising the cleaning out of the canals and the strengthening of banks before the floods. I stayed a week on that occasion, glad of the chance to get to know the cultivators as opposed to the Madan. We set off each morning in his *tarada* and came back in the afternoon, having lunched in some village on the way. As he had predicted, many patients turned up at his *mudhif* each day and I dealt with them before leaving or when we got back. At Zair Mahaisin's village we met Manati, the man who had been bitten by the pig. I was shocked to see how frail and bent he looked and recalled the old man's words: 'That sow has finished Manati.'

'That's a good lad,' said Falih, pointing to one of two boys who were helping Zair Mahaisin to serve lunch. 'Thuqub, his old father, can't work now and Amara keeps the family; they are very poor.' He asked the boy: 'It is true, isn't it, that you're called Amara because your mother gave birth to you there in the market?' Amara smiled and answered: 'Yes, it is true, but I've never been there since.' Slightly built and remarkably handsome, he was deft and self-possessed, a natural aristocrat (Plate 53). In contrast, the other boy was rather clumsy and far from handsome, but obviously good-natured. Falih called him Sabaiti and told me that his father kept the village shop, adding that they were well off and very hospitable. Sabaiti looked pleased. Next morning I found both boys, and several others from their village which was about five miles away, waiting outside Falih's *mudhif* for me to circumcise them. When I asked Amara how they proposed to get home afterwards, he said, 'We will stay here until the pain wears off a bit and the bleeding has stopped, then we will walk back,' which they did.

In his own *mudhif*, Falih kept up the state becoming to a sheikh of his importance, but in the villages he was friendly and informal. The warmth with which all the villagers greeted him was rather moving. Children would scamper ahead of us, shouting 'Falih is coming!' and when we arrived their parents would press round urging him to honour their house. On occasion he could be hard, even merciless, but they respected him the more for it and I never heard his judgement called other than just. He fulfilled their ideal of a sheikh; nobly born, he was a leader whom they admired, trusted and feared. All envied him his skill with a gun and on a horse and were pleased that, unlike so many sheikhs, he could handle a canoe with ease. Of the other sheikhs, Majid and Muhammad al Araibi were still impressive in their old age, survivors from harder and more vigorous times. Most of the rest, and especially the younger ones, were fat, slack-bodied and indolent; they worried perpetually about their health and were for

ever experimenting with patent medicines. Jasim, Muhammad al
Araibi's son, was alone reputed to have been Falih's equal, but he
had died and men now said, 'There is only Falih left.'

When I got back to Qabab a week later, I bought myself a
canoe, a roomy craft more stable than most, for which I paid ten
pounds. It was nearly new and in good condition. Yasin said,
'Now you are one of us: in this boat we will take you wherever
you wish to go, to Suq ash Shuyukh, to Kut, to Basra, anywhere.'
We returned in it to Falih's village after a further six weeks, and
as we landed I asked him with pride, 'What do you think of my
new boat?'

'Not bad, but wait until you see what I have waiting for you.'

He gave an order to one of his servants who went off and came
back poling a brand new *tarada*. Dark and glistening, slim and
high-prowed, she glided towards us through the water. 'She
arrived yesterday from Huwair. She is yours; I had her built for
you,' Falih said. 'You may like to think you are one of the Madan,
but in fact you are a sheikh. This *tarada* is worthy of you'
(Plate 58).

Yasin exclaimed, 'God she is beautiful! One of Haji Hamaid's
and the best he ever built. There is not another like her.'

Much moved, I tried to express my thanks, but Falih put his
hand on my shoulder, saying, '*Sahib inta sahibi*' (Friend, you are
my friend).

That evening Falih suggested that I needed two more lads like
Yasin and Hasan to complete my crew. Anyone older and married would not wish to leave his family for months on end.
Amara and Sabaiti, having heard of this, turned up next morning
to offer their services. I asked them how long they had taken to
recover and Amara said, 'As done by you, there was nothing to
it. I was cutting reeds three days later, and the others were the
same.'

Amara had a quiet charm that was very engaging, but I
doubted if he was strong enough to paddle a *tarada* on long
journeys. However, Hasan, who was also from the Feraigat,
assured me that he was stronger than he looked. Yasin belonged
to the Shaghanba, and Sabaiti to an obscure tribe I had never
heard of. I told Amara and Sabaiti they could join us, and both
remained with me until I left Iraq. Although considerably younger

than the others Amara had the strongest character. Sabaiti followed him without question and Hasan seldom demurred from his decisions. Only Yasin was sometimes resentful of his leadership and apt to find himself the odd man out in consequence. Amara and Sabaiti soon learnt to assist me with my medicines, and Amara generally gave the injections. I never paid my canoeboys a regular wage, saying that I wanted companions not hired servants. I clothed them and in fact gave them more money than they could have hoped to earn. Later, when they married, I helped them with their bride price. When asked what the Englishman paid them they took a pride in answering, 'We have no wages, we accompany our Sahib for our pleasure. He is generous and takes care of us.'

That year, in our *tarada*, we crossed the Central Marshes and travelled down the Euphrates to Qurna: we went back to Saigal and stayed once more with the Al Essa on the mainland, and we visited the Azairij, liking neither them nor their sheikhs. We revisited Jasim and his Fartus, where we found Dakhil, the boy who had danced so amusingly at Qabab. He was still destitute but now he was wasting away, evidently dying of bilharzia and various complications. After endless argument, I persuaded him to go to Basra for treatment, but he was in tears when he left. I sent him there with a letter to my friend, Frank Steele, who was the Vice-Consul.

By then it was summer, and in the Marshes clouds of mosquitoes hung around our heads even in the daytime, as we moved along the silent passages between dark towering reedbeds (Plate 77). At night they gorged on our naked bodies, for it was too hot to bear even the lightest covering. We were glad to leave the Marshes and to travel instead among the villages in the Majar area, making new friends among the cultivators. But, whether our journey had been long or short, we always came back in the end to Falih's *mudhif*. Someone would see our *tarada* and Falih himself would be waiting on the bank to welcome us. Occasionally we returned late at night or in the early hours of morning, and then we would bed down in the empty *mudhif*. Old Abd ar Ridha, the coffee-man, would find us when he came in at dawn, and would hurry off to tell Falih his friend was there.

Unlike most of the sheikhs, Falih disliked town life and seldom visited Baghdad or Amara. Sometimes he stayed away for a night or two with relations near Majar, most often with his uncle Muhammad, Majid's youngest brother, who, though poor, was the most open-handed of his family and one of the most likeable. Muhammad's ill-fated son Abbas, a thick-set youth of twenty, was Falih's favourite cousin. Accompanying Falih, I spent several amusing evenings with Muhammad. After dinner in the *mudhif* we would retire to a private room in his house. His retainers included several boys exceptionally gifted at singing and dancing. One lad in particular used to mime, with what, I hope, was startling exaggeration, local officials enjoying themselves in their leisure hours.

A marsh near Muhammad's house was at certain seasons a favourite haunt of pig, which devastated the rice-fields at night. Falih and I stalked them in small canoes along the ditches intersecting the reedbeds. One day I shot forty-seven and on another forty-two. These pigs were of the same species as the European and Indian wild boar, but ran to an exceptional size. I measured two that were average, and both were thirty-seven inches at the shoulder. I regret that I never measured a really big one. By day they lay up on sodden nests, usually built on the low banks that bordered these ditches. The nests, sometimes six feet across, were great heaps of rushes which they must have bitten off and carried in their mouths, often for yards. When the floods were high the pig moved out of the marshes and lay up in the date gardens, mostly jungles of untended palms and close-growing thorn scrub, in one of which I also saw a wolf and three cubs. Falih and I either walked the pig up, which was exciting, but usually unrewarding, or we had them driven out into the open, when we rode them down on horses and shot them from the saddle.

At length I had to leave, as I planned to travel that autumn in the mountains of northern Pakistan. Amara, Sabaiti, Yasin and Hasan, who now called themselves my men, were with me on my last night with Falih in his village. In the evening we all moved outside the *mudhif* for coolness and sat on the grass. The forty days' wind that blew throughout June was over some time past, and now no breath of air stirred. As the sun set jackals yapped their brief unearthly chorus from beyond the falling river. The moon rose, and bats dipped and wheeled above our heads. We

ate melons and grapes from a *Sayid*'s garden, and drank lime tea.
Abd ar Ridha came out of the *mudhif* with his pot of coffee and
said to me, 'You won't be getting coffee like this where you are
going. Have some more while you can.' And Falih said, 'Don't
stay away from us for long.'

16. Falih's Death

'Welcome Sahib; welcome!' Abd ar Ridha's young son scrambled to his feet and shook another sleeper. 'Come on, wake up; the Englishman is back. Go and tell Falih. I go to fetch my father.' Several shrouded figures lay on the mats in the *mudhif*. One by one they sat up, straightening headcloths and adjusting cloaks. As they came forward to greet me I recognized them all as Falih's retainers. 'Welcome, Sahib, welcome. This is a happy day. You have been away from us too long.'

I had left in the last week of July 1952 and it was now an early afternoon in February. Seven months later; it seemed longer. In that time I had crossed high passes through the snows of the Hindu Kush to the cold blue lake of Korombar where the Chitral river rises; I had looked out over Wakand from the Borogil Pass and seen in the distance a glint that was the Oxus; I had slept on the glaciers at the foot of Tirich Mir, and in dark, verminous houses among mulberry orchards, where the last of the Black Kafirs lived on the borders of Nuristan. Now, back once more in Falih's *mudhif* on the edge of the Marshes, I felt that I had come home.

Abd ar Ridha himself bustled in, gap-toothed and rather bent. 'Falih was talking about you only last night, wondering when you would be back. Sadam was here the other day from Qabab, and he too inquired after you. Welcome, welcome. Today is a feast day.' We sat down round the hearth to coffee. Then everyone rose as Falih came in. He embraced me, kissed me on the cheek and asked how I was. 'Why have you been so long? We have been expecting you for the past month. Is that not so, Abd ar Ridha? Anyway it is good to see you back now. The Madan will be glad when they get the news. Amara and Sabaiti are always asking when you are coming. They will be here as soon as they know you've arrived.' After the coffee he said: 'Sahib, you are no longer a guest, and you cannot go on staying in the *mudhif* as if you were. You are one of the family and must come and live in our home.' Turning to one of his men he said, 'You, Jasim, take the Sahib's things over there.'

His house was single-storied, built of bricks that had been baked on the spot. As we reached it he said, '*This* is your home. Welcome. Enter.' We went into one of the rooms. On the walls hung garish equestrian portraits of Ali and Husain, the Shia saints, cleaving their adversaries asunder amid pools of gore; also one large photograph of Majid in a gilt frame. Mattresses covered in red or green silk, with cushions and bolsters of different colours, were spread round the room. The effect was spacious and comfortable, very different from the *diwaniyas*, in which I had sometimes been incarcerated, uncomfortable brick guest houses that the richer sheikhs had built in the last twenty or thirty years to accommodate Iraqi officials and visiting Europeans. Locked and shuttered when not in use, their rooms were generally thick in dust and the floors littered with cigarette butts. Square heavy armchairs of a standard Iraqi pattern, upholstered in dark velvet, were invariably dressed round the walls, each pair separated from the next by a small table squeezed in between. There, behind barred windows, the sheikh would make laborious conversation to visitors, while everyone else was kept at a respectful distance.

Abbas, Falih's favourite cousin, was staying with him and was anxious to get back to his father's house near Majar. Falih turned to me. 'You will come shooting tomorrow, won't you? We will try the edge of the Marshes for duck. We may even find some pig. Now, Abbas, you can't go home when the Englishman has just arrived and wants to shoot with us tomorrow. Let me send someone at once to fetch your gun. You can go back tomorrow evening. What is the hurry? You are not getting married.' Unfortunately, Abbas allowed himself to be persuaded.

We breakfasted on fried eggs, rice pancakes and hot sweetened buffalo's milk, and walked out into the bright chilly morning. We inspected Falih's horses, three grey, pedigree Arab mares, each wrapped in a blanket and with her fore-feet shackled. After the customary visit to the *mudhif*, we went to where the canoe-men waited beside Falih's *tarada*. 'Well, Dair, are we going to find any duck at the mouth of the Khirr?' Dair, an elderly grizzled man, the most trusted of his retainers, grinned.

'God knows. We may find a few, but they seem to have moved recently – the result of the high water. There should be plenty of coot.'

Falih, Abbas and I stepped into the *tarada*, while Abd al Wahid, Falih's son, got into a canoe, and we all set off together down the side-stream. Abbas was seated in the middle of the boat between Falih and myself. He had dropped his cartridge belt on the rug in front of me and I noticed several cartridges marked L.G., interspersed at random among the others. He explained that Abd al Wahid had given them to him to fill up his belt. I said, 'They are only for pig; for God's sake don't use them to shoot at duck or you will kill somebody.' To prove my point I cut one open and showed him the seven large pellets, which I dropped into my pocket. I suggested to Falih that he should warn his son, and he did so.

At the edge of the Marshes each of us transferred into a small canoe with a man to paddle and started off into the reeds. The others went in one direction to look for duck, I went in another to hunt for pig. But the water was high and the pig had evidently left the marsh for dry land. I could hear the others shooting, and when I returned to our rendezvous they were already there. They had seen no duck, but had shot a number of coot. Falih asked if I would like to go on or wait for lunch. I said I didn't mind. He said, 'I have nine coots; I would like to make it ten. Lunch won't be ready for another hour so let's go on.' This time I accompanied them.

We spread out in line, our canoes seventy yards apart, and paddled, parallel with the shore, through scattered clumps of bulrushes. Falih and Abbas were on my right, Abd al Wahid on my left. Occasional coot rose and swung back down-wind over our heads. I had got one and stopped to pick it up when I heard the unmistakable sound of a shot fired in my direction. It came from my right. I shouted, 'For God's sake look out where you are shooting!' A little farther and we saw Falih's canoe stationary in the middle of some open water, fifty yards from a reedbed. My canoeman took one look, cried 'Falih is hurt,' and paddled frantically towards him.

Falih was slumped forward, held up by Dair. His eyes were shut and he seemed unconscious. Two spots of blood marked the front of his white shirt. Telling my canoeman to keep me alongside, I leant across and took hold of his wrist. I could just feel the pulse. Then I unfastened his shirt. Over his left nipple, blood dribbled from a round blue mark that had obviously been made by a single large pellet. Abd al Wahid arrived and asked what had happened. 'It was Abbas,' Dair said, speaking for the first time and nodding towards the nearby reedbed. I looked round but could see no sign of anyone.

The other four broke suddenly into wild lamentations, repeating over and over again, 'My father, oh my father,' while the three canoes, like a small raft, rocked on the waves. I turned on them angrily. 'Shut up! It is no good sitting here, wailing. We must get him ashore. Dair, you hold him and we will paddle on each side and pull your canoe.' They stopped wailing abruptly and we started off.

The shore was three hundred yards away and in the distance I could see a small village. Dair told us what had happened. 'We were trying to get near some coot. No one was in sight. Then a heron flew out of those reeds. Abbas was on the other side of the reeds and fired straight at us. I heard the shot strike Falih. He cried out, "Abbas, you have killed me." Then Abbas stood up; I could just see him above the reeds. He shouted back, "God, I did not know you were there." I have not seen him since.'

The water was deep and Falih would certainly have drowned when he was hit if Dair had not somehow managed to keep the canoe upright. As we reached the shore we met Abbas's canoeman. He was alone.

'Where is Abbas?'

'He ordered me to land him. Then he ran off.'

Falih was still unconscious and I could barely feel his pulse. We had to get him back as quickly as possible to his house, then to Majar, and from there by car to Basra or Amara for a blood transfusion. I sent Abbas's canoeman racing to the village to fetch a larger canoe. It occurred to me that Falih should be kept warm, so I sent another man to the village for bedding. Abd al Wahid just stood staring in a daze at his father and asked again and again, 'Will he die, Sahib? Will he die?'

'God willing he will live, but he is very badly wounded.'

Abd al Wahid broke out hysterically, 'Where is Abbas? Where has he got to? By God, if Falih dies I will kill him. Sahib, you are Falih's friend, you must help me find him and kill him. Where has he got to, the accursed one?' and he started to weep, sobbing convulsively.

Two small boys appeared from nowhere, obviously frightened. They stood together a little way off, watching us. I called to the bigger one and told him to go to the village and hurry up the canoe. They both ran off. I could think of nothing else that needed doing and looked helplessly at Falih, and at Dair, who still held him. Tears streamed down the old man's face.

Men and women began to arrive, running across the fields. They stood about in little groups. Someone told me the large canoe was coming down the stream from the village. To save time he suggested taking the canoe in which Falih lay to the stream's mouth. Two of them pulled it along, wading through the shallow water. At last we met the other canoe which, I was relieved to see, had rugs and cushions, as well as a carpet spread on the floor. When we started to lift Falih, he opened his eyes and said distinctly, 'Look out, the gun is loaded.' Then he shut his eyes again and lay very still. We transferred him carefully. Dair sat behind to support his head, and we wrapped the rugs round him. Several people offered their cloaks.

A man climbed into the stern to steer, another fastened a rope to the bows, while two more towed the boat upstream. Abd al Wahid and I followed, walking along the bank which was covered with dead thistles and low thorn scrub. We had left our shoes in the *tarada*. My feet were still hard after years barefooted in the desert, but Abd al Wahid, who had probably never gone without shoes in his life, was soon limping, and dropped behind. Falih opened his eyes and tried to speak. Ordering the men to stop, I knelt beside him.

'Where is Abd al Wahid?' he whispered.

'He is coming.'

'Tell him ... tell him from me, Sahib, that he is to take Abbas to his father. He is not to leave him until he is safe with

Muhammad. Whatever happens to me, he is to see that nothing happens to Abbas. That is my command. Tell him to go there now.'

He shut his eyes again and I signalled to the men to go on. Abbas was presumably ahead of us, running desperately for home.

News of the accident had spread across the countryside while we moved slowly upstream. Small groups of silent people hurried towards us from different villages. As soon as they reached us, they flung themselves shrieking into the water and, standing in it, plastered mud on their heads and dripping clothes, the women tearing their garments and beating their breasts. 'Falih, my father, my father,' they wailed and followed behind us.

Falih lay in the bottom of the canoe, his face very white against Dair's dark shirt. Less than twenty-four hours before he had welcomed me back to his house. Till now my mind had been too numbed to take in fully what had happened. That there had been an accident and Falih was badly hurt, I realized, but now I was convinced that he was dying. To the others it would have been more understandable if I had wept like them, but some deep-seated inhibition denied me this relief. I, who shared so much with them from choice, could not share in this expression of their grief.

At last, in the late afternoon, we reached Falih's village. They fetched a bedstead, lifted him on to it, and, amid a demented throng, carried him into his house. As many as could pushed their way into the room and remained quiet. Outside, however, the keening rose and fell against a dull steady throb, which sounded like the beat of muffled drums but was the women beating in unison on their bared breasts. Falih opened his eyes and stared at the ceiling, the only sign of life in a face which, drained of blood, looked as waxen and insentient as a mask. People begged me to give him medicine and refused to believe there was nothing I could do. Leading Abd al Wahid aside, I urged that the only hope was to take Falih where he could be given a blood trans-fusion, and that every moment's delay lessened his chances. He agreed with me, but did nothing. The others stood round the bed saying, without lowering their voices, 'He is clearly dying.'

'Yes, he is almost dead.'

'By God, Falih did not deserve to die like this.'

In a whisper Falih asked for water, but when they fetched it, he could not swallow, and the water ran down his chin and wetted his shirt.

Another of his cousins, called Hatab, arrived. Luckily, he was a decisive character and accustomed to obedience. He immediately took charge, had Falih carried outside to his own *tarada*, and set off with him for his father Hamud's village at Majar. I followed in another boat but it was heavy and slow and we were soon outdistanced. When I arrived at Majar, Falih had already been carried into a *diwaniya* belonging to Hamud, who had gone to telephone to Majid in Baghdad. The local doctor was among the crowd in the passage and I asked him what he thought. He shook his head and said he was afraid Falih was dying. He agreed that the only hope was to take him straight to Basra, the nearest place for a blood transfusion.

Someone called, 'Where is the Englishman?' Entering the room, I was told Falih had asked for me and I went over to where he lay. He moved his eyes and looked at me, but did not speak. Only his family were there and, though I hesitated to intrude, I remained standing beside his bed. We waited for what seemed a long time. It had grown dark outside and they brought in a Petromax lamp that hissed in a corner and lit the room with a harsh glare.

Hamud came back. It must have been unnerving to break the news to Majid and he looked distraught. 'Falih is to be taken to Baghdad at once. Those are Majid's orders. I have sent for three cars.'

I knew that Falih would never survive a journey on that awful bumpy road, two hundred and fifty miles in the dark. 'Take him to Basra,' I pleaded with Hamud, 'you can fly him on from there in the morning, if Majid insists. I implore you to take him to Basra; it is only three hours, and there you can get him the medicine he needs. Don't even go to Amara; go straight to Basra.'

But Hamud simply said, 'We will go to Amara first and then we will see.'

The cars arrived. Falih was moved again and lifted into the back of one. All his family, who could find a place, women as well as men, squeezed into the other cars and drove off. Dair and I paddled back down the river in the dark to Falih's village. We spoke little, but I can remember him saying, 'That this should have happened simply because he wanted to shoot another water-hen. Falih's life for a water-hen.' He paused, then said, 'It is written, Sahib.'

To me, also, it seemed that Fate, not chance, had ordained the accident. Why, otherwise, should Abbas have mixed up his cartridges and loaded with buckshot on the single occasion he fired in Falih's direction? Why, otherwise, should the one pellet have struck him where it did at seventy yards range? When I undressed in Falih's house, in the same room I had slept in the night before, I found in my pocket the seven L.G. pellets from the cartridge I had cut open that same morning.

Early next day I returned to Majar and hired a car to Basra. There I heard that Falih had been flown to Baghdad. People said he was better and I began to hope. I wired to a friend, caught the evening train and reached Baghdad the following morning. My friend met me at the station and we drove into the town to look for Majid's house. A policeman explained where it was, adding as an afterthought, 'but Majid has gone to Najaf to bury his son who died yesterday.'

That was how I heard of Falih's death.

17. The Mourning Ceremony

We found the house quite easily, a villa on the outskirts of the town. I rang the bell and was taken inside. Abd al Wahid and Khalaf, Falih's younger brother, were sitting in a small room. I greeted them and we waited for Majid. He came in almost immediately. His eyes were red with weeping and his face heavy with grief. After the formal salutations, he invited me to sit beside him on a couch; then he asked how I was and when I had arrived, conventional questions that Arab manners demand. I expressed my condolence, but he turned and said quite simply, 'Sahib, I know you were his friend.' We sat in silence. After a while a servant brought in coffee and when I had drunk Majid again asked how I was. Once more we fell silent. To be beside this stricken old man, whose hopes and ambitions had ended with his son's death, was almost more than I could bear. I waited a little longer and asked his permission to leave. He said, 'Go in peace,' and I answered, 'Remain in the safe keeping of God.' It had started to rain when I left the house, and it rained all day.

Some months later, I met an English doctor, a heart specialist employed in Baghdad by the Iraqi Government. He had been in Basra when Falih was taken to the airport and, hearing of the accident, had gone there at once. After examining Falih he wanted to operate immediately, to relieve the pressure of blood congealing round the heart, but was told that Majid had given orders for his son to be taken to Baghdad. The doctor tried to explain that *he* was the Government heart specialist from Baghdad, the only one in the country, and assured them that the only chance of saving Falih's life was to let him operate at once. They refused. He told me that, in fact, nothing could have saved Falih. The post-mortem revealed that the pellet had bruised the heart, cut the big nerves and collapsed the lung. He was only amazed that

Falih could have lived for so long, saying that he must have been exceptionally strong.

Three days later I went back to Falih's village to join in the mourning, and arrived early in the afternoon. While still some distance off, I could hear the women wailing and the rhythmic beating of breasts. Many canoes were fastened along the bank and there was a large crowd outside the *mudhif*. Several tribal banners were set in the entrance, their long red folds and the silver ornaments on the poles brilliant against the reed walls in the spring sunshine. It was very silent inside and rather dark. Figures wrapped in black cloaks sat motionless round the walls. Someone whispered to me, 'There is Majid, over there.' I crossed the room, greeted him, shook hands and looked for a place. Some strangers moved slightly to make room for me. I recognized a few people in the *mudhif* but not many. There were *Sayids* in green head-cloths, divines from Karbala or Najaf dressed in black, with small tightly-wound black or white turbans; sheikhs of tribes from as far off as Kut and Nasiriya with their retainers; village headmen and elders, and townsmen and merchants from Majar, Amara and Basra; and there were Majid's relations, a whole clan of them. A boy dropped a packet of cigarettes in front of me. Abd ar Ridha got up from beside the hearth and, carrying his small, beaked coffee-pot, came over and gave me coffee. One or two people near by said quietly, 'Good afternoon, Sahib,' and then the small stir caused by my arrival subsided.

Occasionally someone spoke a few words in a low voice to his neighbour, but mostly they sat in silence playing with their rosaries or smoking. Half a dozen figures rose, went over to Majid, bade him farewell and left the room. Others came in, sometimes two or three together, sometimes twenty at a time. They greeted Majid as I had done, sat down and were given packets of cigarettes, coffee and glasses of tea. Before each party left, whoever was senior would announce '*Al Fatha*' and they would recite the opening verse of the Koran with their hands held out in supplication. I could hear the boats landing or being pushed off, on the other side of the mat wall. Overhead the sparrows chirped among the great reed arches, and in the doorway the shadows lengthened. More people left and fewer arrived; gaps appeared and widened among the figures round the walls.

Years of practice in Arabia had accustomed me to sitting on the ground, but when Majid rose at sunset and left the *mudhif* I was stiff and aching. The others prepared for the evening prayer and I went outside to find Dair. I asked how long it would be correct for me to remain. 'Everyone knows you were Falih's friend. I think they will expect you to stay another two days. Come now and sit with some of your friends.' He led me towards a long reed shelter that had been built in the last few days. The sun, a glowing orange ball, rested on the horizon ahead of us, beyond the same date garden where Falih and I had first gone shooting.

Inside the shelter several of Falih's retainers sat round a small fire, their headcloths dyed dark blue as a sign of mourning. They welcomed me kindly and poured me out more coffee. It was as well that Arabs only put a few drops in a cup, for I had drunk endless cups that day. All at once, from the twilit shore beyond the river, the brief evening chorus of the jackals started up. Rising, falling, and rising again, it shivered out across the listening land, to die away in a series of tortured screams.

I asked what had happened to Abbas. Dair answered contemptuously, 'He ran to Qalat Salih and threw himself on the mercy of the police. He is still there, God destroy him.'

'And Muhammad, his father?'

'He too went to Qalat Salih and asked the Government for help. They say he has engaged a lawyer.'

'A lawyer,' someone said, 'a lawyer won't help him much. Majid is furious that he went to the Government. Indeed, it was a disgraceful thing to do.'

'Yes,' someone else remarked, 'Muhammad should have brought Abbas here and handed him over to Majid. If he had done that, Majid would have spared him. Now, surely, he will kill him.'

'They have been very foolish,' Dair said. 'There will be big trouble.'

'Majid now says that Abbas shot Falih deliberately, because of a quarrel over the cultivation,' the same man said.

'I know he does,' Dair answered.

There were still about thirty people in the *mudhif* when I went back there. I knew none of them, but one asked me, 'Are you the

Englishman who was Falih's friend?' and when I answered, 'Yes,' he said, 'Welcome; welcome to Falih's friend.' Another asked if I had been with him when Abbas shot him and what happened. While I was telling them, dinner was brought in and we ate in silence as was customary. Afterwards we talked again until servants came with bedding, which they arranged round the sides of the room.

The *mudhif* was astir early. One by one the others rose and, after washing and saying their dawn prayers, ranged themselves along the walls. Servants rolled up the bedding and removed it. Coffee was brewed and drunk, a boy carried in a platter stacked with discs of bread, and dropped one on the mat in front of each person. With this we were served two or three small glasses of hot milk. We rose as Majid came in, accompanied by Khalaf, his younger son, and by Abd al Wahid and others of his family. He greeted us and sat in the same place as the previous day, while we ranged ourselves once more round the room. The first visitors arrived shortly afterwards and the *mudhif* gradually filled. Majid, grey and unshaven, looked very tired, his great stomach bulging in front of him, an old broken man filled with bitterness. 'Why did it have to be Falih? Why Falih?' he burst out. 'God, now I have no one left,' and I recalled that Kharaibid, his eldest son, had been murdered three years earlier.

Those next to him tried to comfort him, 'You have Khalaf and Abd al Wahid.'

But he cried, 'No, no, I have no one; now I have no son. My land, what will happen to my land when I die? What will happen to my land now that Falih is dead?'

Other visitors arrived. He returned their greetings and lapsed into brooding silence.

A commotion broke out behind me on the river bank; the sound of voices and the bumping of boats. A large party of men, all carrying rifles, filed in behind a tall, heavy figure in a gold-embroidered cloak of finest camel's hair. 'Who is that?' whispered a townsman from Basra. 'Sulaiman bin Motlog,' his neighbour answered. I had heard of Sulaiman, the paramount sheikh of the Azairij, rice cultivators whose lands adjoined Majid's, but had never met him when I visited his tribe. His face was pallid and fleshy, and he looked soft from years of easy living. Like many of the richer sheikhs he spent much time in Baghdad. He sat down next to Majid, and his followers settled themselves according to rank lower down the line. Under his cloak, each wore a dagger and crossed bandoliers full of cartridges. Coffee and tea were served to them, and the room relapsed into silence. Then Sulaiman called out 'Al Fatha' and he and his companions intoned,

> 'In the name of God, the Compassionate, the Merciful,
> Praise be to God, Lord of the worlds!
> The Compassionate, the Merciful!
> King of the day of reckoning!
> Thee only do we worship, and to Thee we cry for help.
> Guide Thou us on the straight path.
> The path of those to whom Thou hast been gracious;
> With whom Thou art not angry, and who go not astray.'

I was hoping that lunch would soon be served, so that I could stretch my legs, when a fusillade of shots and the sound of hysterical wailing heralded the arrival of yet another party. Through the doorway I glimpsed a tribal banner and a crowd of people with wet mud smeared on their heads and clothes. 'From Qabab,' someone told Majid. There were between forty and fifty from Bu Mughaifat as well as Qabab. One behind the other they went up to Majid, kissed his hand and withdrew. I recognized most of them. A little later came the sound of more shots and wailing, and a large contingent arrived from Al Aggar. They, too, were plastered with mud. By now it was long past midday, and three more bands of mourning tribesmen arrived before a servant informed Majid that lunch was ready. Forty or fifty at a time, as we were bidden, we filed out to the reed shelter I had been in the night before, where we fed from great dishes piled with rice and mutton. As each party finished, the dishes were replenished and another group was ushered in. Everyone was fed, both the visitors inside the *mudhif* and the waiting tribesmen outside.

Afterwards they danced the *Hausa*, the war dance of the tribes. From each village in turn, someone improvised a chant in praise of Falih, and the listening tribesmen took it up and roared it back, their rifles held above their heads as they stamped in a massed circle round the crimson banners. The men who held the banners, heads of families whose traditional right was to carry them into battle, shook the poles so that the silver ornaments clashed and jangled. Still stamping in time to their singing, they began to fire off their rifles, a few scattered shots at first, then massed firing such as I had only heard in war. The smell of powder, sharp and intoxicating in their nostrils, stirred them to wilder efforts. 'Enough,' Majid called out at last, and his servants pushed into the milling crowd shouting, 'Enough, the sheikh says enough.' We trooped back into the *mudhif*.

Hours later, at sunset, soon after Majid had left, I was talking to a group of people on the river bank. A boy hurried past crying out something, and I was aware of general excitement. Several men hurried away to their houses. 'What has happened?' I asked.

'Majid has sent a party to kill Muhammad,' someone told me.

'But Muhammad is with the Government in Qalat Salih,' I objected.

'No, they say he has returned to his house at Majar.'

I watched two canoes slip upstream through the fading light, carrying the avengers of blood, while the jackals yelled their refrain from the opposite bank. But Muhammad was still safe in Qalat Salih.

18. The Eastern Marshes

As Dair had advised, I remained for a further day, then took formal leave of Majid and left for Qabab with Amara and Sabaiti, who had joined me in the *mudhif* the previous evening. They too were deeply affected by Falih's death, and as they paddled our *tarada* towards the Marshes, the tears trickled down Amara's face. 'He was our father. My friend's friends, he called us, and sent for us whenever he came to our village, to ask if we were all right.' During the coming year I heard his death referred to with regret in places as far apart as the Persian frontier and the Euphrates near Nasiriya. 'Were you Falih's friend?' strangers would ask, and made me the more welcome. I had not realized how widely he was known by reputation and how greatly respected.

We planned to pass the next six weeks in the Eastern Marshes, and slept one night in Sadam's *mudhif* where his young son acted as host in his father's absence. Qabab too was in mourning. The few people who came in spoke little and soon went away. Next morning Yasin and Hasan joined us and we went on to the Al bu Bakhit where we spent two busy days doctoring in their small marsh villages. Passing under the girder bridge that carried the motor road from Basra to Amara and Baghdad, we reached the Tigris below Azair and paddled upstream past Ezra's tomb with its dome of green and blue tiles. The tomb was set among palms and flanked by a ramshackle dormitory for pilgrims. Azair itself was a squalid spot, used as a halting-place by lorries and buses. For some miles beyond the village, a succession of squat brick kilns, like sacrificial altars, dotted the otherwise empty banks (Plate 70). Such kilns may well have fired the bricks with which Babylon was built. These bricks would be used for bungalows in the suburbs of Basra.

Yasin broke in on my reflections. 'They say a man was seized in the river here recently by a shark and lost part of his leg.' I knew that sharks sometimes attacked people bathing at Basra, but Azair was a further eighty miles upstream and a hundred and fifty from the sea. When I expressed surprise, my boys assured me that Azair was known as a bad place for sharks. Another time when I was there, a villager told me that in his father's day a monstrous fish had blocked the river at low water and could only be got rid of by cutting it up where it lay.

As we paddled along, I asked if sharks were ever found in the Marshes, and Hasan said that a small one had been speared some years before. Amara interrupted. 'Did you hear that a man was killed by a hyena while you were away? He was sleeping in the open beyond Majar and it grabbed him by the face. He was dead when they found him and they could only recognize him by his clothes.' I had seen a hyena myself three years before. It was a striped hyena; the larger spotted species is found only in Africa. Forty years earlier there had been lions in these parts but they were wiped out when the tribesmen got modern rifles during the First World War. One of Falih's old slaves once told me how he had seen three near Majar, and another man described a lion hunt in which he had taken part, not far from Amara. A hunter had shot the lion with a muzzle-loader. Someone else I met had seen two cubs that a party of Madan brought to the sheikh, and a number of older men remembered lions roaring at night.

We turned down a broad waterway leading into the Marshes to the east and passed a large two-masted boat, loaded high with reed mats, being laboriously poled towards the Tigris. Later we passed a great raft made of dry reeds. Forty feet long and ten feet high, it was aground and temporarily abandoned. When the water-level rose, this stack of reeds would be floated downstream, perhaps as far as Basra, and there broken up and sold.

Baidhat al Nuafil, where we spent the night, was the largest village I saw in the Marshes. It comprised six hundred and forty houses, but not a single *mudhif*. The various groups of houses were built along ridges of dry land, separated by water. Sometimes, when the Tigris was very low, the water dried up and then the Nuafil left their village and camped along the river. With their neighbours, the Al bu Ghanam to the north and the Al bu

Bakhit to the south, they made up the Shadda, a large and unruly section of the Al bu Muhammad. The Nuafil kept some buffaloes, but their livelihood depended on the weaving of mats, which they exported in great numbers. Large sailing boats, like the one we had already seen, fetched the mats when the water was deep enough to make the passage (Plate 105). This year the water was exceptionally high.

We stayed with the headman and fed badly, which annoyed me as I had treated several sick members of his family. I thought the villagers as a whole were a churlish lot and parted from them without regret, a feeling shared by my companions, who grumbled that our host had given us no milk for breakfast and only two glasses of inadequately sweetened tea with our bread. Yasin said disgustedly, 'That did not loosen the spittle' – a pun, for in Arabic 'to loosen the spittle' and 'to breakfast' are the same phrase. However, it was a lovely morning and they soon cheered up. The air was crisp and clear, a gentle breeze blew from the north, the sun was pleasantly warm, and cirrus cloud marbled the pale-blue sky. We worked the *tarada* along a succession of narrow channels that twisted across an open plain covered with fallen sedge. In the Central Marshes, except on the occasional lagoons, the reedbeds always restricted visibility, sometimes to a few yards. Here we could see for miles. The ground had been dry throughout the winter and now, where still uncovered, it was as hard as baked clay and grey in colour. In other places the rising water covered it to a depth of several inches and the resulting mud was the colour and consistency of melted chocolate.

We disturbed many kinds of wader; some rose singly with shrill cries, others in dense flocks that wheeled and turned above the sheets of water and the bleached sedge. I recognized curlews and whimbrel, redshank, godwit, ruffs, avocet, stilts and various kinds of plover. There were duck, too, that took off long before we could get within range, and herons and ibises and egrets and spoonbills. Once, in the far distance, we saw a flock of cranes. Hasan made constant sorties after any bird that he considered edible, but never got close enough to shoot. He returned each time to be greeted with ribald comments on his inadequacy as a wildfowler. Meanwhile Yasin and Sabaiti walked along the banks on either side pushing the *tarada*, their poles wedged in the bows.

The watercourse was barely wide enough in places for the canoe, and sometimes made a right-angle bend. Then I thought we should have to go back, for our *tarada* was thirty-six feet long, but in the end the boys always managed to ease her round.

I was wearing a long Arab shirt and if I had to get into the water to help them, I tucked it round my waist. I have always suspected of exhibitionism travellers who adopt the local dress without good reason. Arab clothes, in particular, are not easily managed by anyone unaccustomed to them. I had worn them for five years in Southern Arabia because I would have been unacceptable to my companions otherwise. In Iraq the tribesmen were well used to the sight of European clothes – all Government officials were careful to wear nothing else in public – and I wore them when I first visited the Marshes. Later, when I felt accepted, I wore a headcloth and long Arab shirt for their obvious convenience – with a jacket on top, a fashion that was increasingly popular with the Madan themselves. Sitting in a canoe or in a house, the shirt protected my legs and feet from flies and mosquitoes. But I always changed into European clothes before visiting officials or going to a town.

We were crossing part of Auaisij, a stretch of ground only submerged during the floods. For twenty miles or more it separated the Tigris, and the swamp that bordered it in places, from the great Marshes to the east. Since these Marshes were generally too deep to be suitable for buffaloes, the Madan tended to build their villages along Auaisij, or in the estuaries of the Chahla and Masharia to the north. In autumn the nomad Rabia of the Feraigat crossed the Tigris with great herds of buffaloes, set up their encampments and wintered there. In spring they moved back across the Tigris and followed the Wadiya slowly northward, grazing their buffaloes on the harvested fields of barley and wheat on the way to Majar, which they were allowed to do free, in return for the manure. Then they moved westward to Jindala to pass the summer on the rich grazing that sprang up as the floods receded, but for this they had to pay the sheikhs fairly heavily.

Amara belonged to the Rabia and we expected to find his relations at Abu Laila, the largest of their winter encampments, which lay ahead of us. As we approached it we saw herds of buffaloes guarded by boys. Among them I noticed one almost white buffalo and several that were piebald. Impressed by the size of the herds I asked how many buffaloes an ordinary nomad family owned. 'Between twenty and thirty,' Amara told me, but Hasan insisted that most of them had far more, and named one of the Rabia who had a hundred and fifty.

'At what age does a buffalo first calve?'

'Usually in its fourth year,' Amara answered, and added, 'They carry their young for eleven months. A good buffalo will bear as many as fifteen calves.'

Knowing that the Bedu usually killed off male camels at birth in order to have more milk for themselves, I asked if the Madan did the same with their buffaloes. 'Yes, unless a man has very few. Then he usually keeps a bull calf to sell when it is grown up. If he has slaughtered the calf he often puts another one to suckle the cow as well as its own mother so that it will have more milk and do better. Otherwise he will smear the slime from the new-born calf on a cloak and wear this when he milks its mother. If a calf dies we place the stuffed skin in front of the mother before we milk her.'

'How much can you get for a buffalo?'

'The *Jallaba* were paying as much as fifty dinars for a good cow last month, and thirty-five for a bull.' The *Jallaba* were special traders who wandered among the Madan buying any buffaloes they could get hold of. I remembered that in the Sudan the word *Jallaba* had been used only of slave-traders. These merchants also bought the skins of animals that had died in the periodic epidemics of haemorrhagic septicaemia that decimated the herds. The Marshmen knew that these skins carried infection, but it did not stop them selling them, although they would protest furiously if a merchant brought such skins into their own village. Hasan said, 'A few years ago there was a bad outbreak of foot-and-mouth. Many of our buffaloes got it, and even the wild pig. We used to find pig that could not walk, their feet were so badly infected.'

At Abu Laila the watercourse widened out to thirty yards (Plate 68). Buffaloes were submerged in the water, others stood at its edge. Many canoes, most of them unusually large, were drawn up on the shore, and children paddled about on miniature rafts made from bulrushes. The hundred or so houses were scattered along either bank. Themselves small, with only five arches, they were dwarfed by the buffalo shelters attached to them, called *sitra* (Plate 64) and as much as forty yards in length. Unlike the house itself, of which it was a prolongation, a *sitra* was tent-shaped and not covered with matting. The *qasab* reeds, set close together to form the walls, inclined inwards and were fastened overhead to a ridge pole fashioned from more reeds. Manure and trampled *hashish* were piled along the walls on either side.

We stopped with one of Amara's cousins, a tall quiet lad, by name Badai. He embraced Amara warmly for they were great friends, and fetched rugs and cushions. We sat in the sun at the entrance to his *sitra* which led back like a tunnel to the house. His wife and sister were soon pounding rice, before boiling it for our lunch. Badai's father had died some years earlier and he was the head of a family that consisted of his mother, wife, sister and two younger brothers, who were both away at the moment with the buffaloes.

Badai was on bad terms with the family of a man called Radhawi who lived in a nearby encampment. Hasan, one of Radhawi's sons, was in love with Badai's wife, whom he had hoped to marry. But Badai, as her paternal first cousin, had prior claim, insisted on his rights and married her himself. Hasan vowed that he would take the girl even if he had to kill Badai. A few weeks before our arrival, the two lads chanced to meet and came to blows, but were separated. Everyone sitting with us agreed that Hasan had no right to the girl. An old man exclaimed, 'He is Radhawi's son; like father, like son, all of them lawless and bad. Has not Radhawi already murdered two men who opposed him?' Amara now persuaded three elders to go with him to Radhawi's house to try and effect a reconciliation. They came back in the evening having failed, and Amara said disgustedly, 'No one could have done anything with them, not even Sayid Sarwat himself. They just went on repeating that Badai must divorce his wife or take the consequences.' He warned Badai, 'Don't go near them, and keep your rifle handy, especially at night. They mean trouble.'

As the sun set and the air grew chilly, the last buffaloes, darker shapes on the darkening plain, moved towards the village. Diaphanous clouds, steeped in ever-changing colours, trailed across the sky above, and flight after flight of duck winged towards the west. We moved inside the house itself, and the long passage filled up with the herd, the ponderous bodies thrusting forward behind thick curved horns.

Amara belonged to these nomadic Feraigat. Vouched for by him and with my medicine to recommend me, we were welcomed in other of their encampments. Tied to no one place and heavily armed with rifles, these Rabia were arrogant and lawless. To provide a new growth for their buffaloes they used to fire the reeds on which the Nuafil of Baidhat depended for their mat-making, and were hated in consequence. They were always at feud too with the Suaid Madan, a people as lawless as themselves, who lived near the Persian frontier. Each tribe lifted the other's buffaloes whenever a chance occurred.

Leaving the Feraigat, we stopped for a night at Turaba, a large village that, like Baidhat, depended on the mat industry, but was inhabited by Al bu Ghanam. Among the nomads I had resigned myself to a diet of rice and milk. Here, I thought they might at least have killed a chicken for us, and when our host spent the evening abusing the Feraigat, I championed them to excess. Next morning a man from the Chahla asked us for a lift. We were glad to have him, to guide us through the reedbeds ahead. Yasin had asked for directions the previous evening but was told that we should get lost without a guide. Our route lay through high reeds and across small lagoons and was indeed seldom discernible. I remember that it was on this journey that I first heard a bittern boom. We took four hours to reach Dibin, the village for which we were bound, in the estuary of the Chahla.

My companions were skilled at remembering the way, and during the years they were with me acquired a knowledge of the Marshes that must have been unrivalled. But even in places where they had never been before, their instinct seemed to guide them. I noticed this especially when they were searching among reeds and islets, along the edge of a lagoon, for the entrance to some small estuary that was indistinguishable from a hundred others leading nowhere. The same kind of skill, acquired since child-hood, enabled them to track a swimming pig, tell one kind of fish from another by its wake, or recognize at a single glance a canoe they had only once seen. Curiously, however, they were hopeless at remembering names. Suffering myself from the same disability, I was always exasperated when not one of the four could recall the name of our last host.

As we paddled along one or other of my companions would sometimes call out to us to stop, and would then reach into the water and pull up a young shoot of *birdi*, their name for a bulrush. They would eat the crisp etiolated stem near the roots, but apparently only certain shoots of *birdi* were fit to eat. They would also occasionally chew the stems of selected pieces of *qasab* as if they were chewing sugar cane. In the spring, the Madan women gathered the heads of bulrushes and from the pollen made a hard yellow cake, much esteemed as a sweetmeat, though personally I found what little taste it had unpleasant.

We spent several nights at Dibin, setting off each morning to explore the Hawaiza Marshes. We found lakes as extensive as Zikri, hidden behind vast reedbeds, but never ventured far out on them for fear of sudden storms. As we pushed along ill-defined waterways, that seemed always to end against a solid wall of reeds, our guide kept urging me to have my rifle ready, saying repeatedly, 'Brigands could kill us here and no one would ever know.' These lakes were a natural sanctuary for wild-fowl; nowhere else did I see such numbers. They darkened acres of water and there was a roar when even a small part of this enormous gathering took wing. Apart from occasional smugglers or raiders heading for Persia, few men disturbed them.

But throughout the Marshes duck and geese were becoming fewer year by year. In 1951 I had seen duck flighting in at sunset to feed on harvested rice-fields near Saigal, in such numbers that they reminded me of swarms of locusts. When I left the Marshes in 1958 there were nothing like as many. A million cartridges were imported annually at that time into Iraq, and most of the people who used them counted on getting at least one bird with a shot. A heavy toll was also taken of wild-fowl by professional fowlers, who netted them a hundred or more at a time. They paid the sheikhs for the right to use certain ponds where they put down grain. There were many small reserved ponds round Amara alone.

The wild geese used to arrive in the Marshes in October.

Grey-lag and white-front, they came out of the north, returning from their breeding grounds in Siberia, and in their calling was the magic of wild places. Wedge-shaped formations followed each other, strung out across the pale sky, and as I watched I thought of the day when the last wild geese would be gone, and there were no more lions in Africa.

Each morning before starting out we would borrow a kettle, glasses and a dish from our host at Dibin and buy tea, sugar, salt and flour from the merchant. When we felt inclined to stop, we would choose a convenient spot on the edge of a lake, trample down reeds to make a platform to support us on the water, and cook a meal. Hasan roasted on a reed spit whatever birds we had shot, and in the embers Sabaiti baked discs of bread that were soggy and full of ashes. Afterwards we went on brewing tea until the sugar was finished, and I would watch the duck on the lake, or the halcyon kingfishers darting past. Once we noticed two otters playing together a hundred yards away, but Hasan reached for the gun and they saw us. They appeared to stand upright in the water eyeing us for a few seconds, before they dived and disappeared. I was glad they had seen us as otherwise Hasan would certainly have tried to shoot them. Their skins were worth a dinar apiece. His uncle at Bu Mughaifat once shot forty in two months.

Hasan told me that otters were very common round Zikri, where they bred on the floating islands, sometimes as early as January but more often in February or March. Three years later, in 1956, Gavin Maxwell, who wished to write a book about the Marshes, came with me to Iraq, and I took him round in my *tarada* for seven weeks. He had always wanted an otter as a pet, and at last I found him a baby European otter which unfortunately died after a week, towards the end of his visit. He was in Basra preparing to go home when I managed to obtain another, which I sent to him. This, very dark in colour and about six weeks old, proved to be a new species. Gavin took it to England, and the species was named after him.

19. Among the Sudan and the Suaid

In the evenings, as we returned to Dibin, Amara would chaff me, 'You had better look out, Sahib, the *Zaira* will be waiting for you.' The *mudhif* where we stayed was on a mound surrounded by water, and from it we could see the distant line of villages and palms along the Chahla. It belonged to Muhammad al Araibi's representative, an old man sick in bed with kidney trouble, who died the following year. He had four grown-up sons, but they were unceremoniously thrust aside on every occasion by the *Zaira*, their portly and ageing mother. Swaddled in a bundle of dark draperies, she bustled in and out of the *mudhif*, or settled down inside to preside. My conventional nature was offended by this breach of custom, the more so as I thought her a dreadful old woman and could never get away from her. She would even appear when I was treating my patients and offer advice, an embarrassment to us all on occasions.

At Dibin a boy was brought to me, paralysed from the waist down. He had had a fever the year before which had left him crippled. I came across a number of similar cases, presumably the result of poliomyelitis. The tribesmen were especially kind to the afflicted, and among them a major physical disability was perhaps less of a handicap than in some parts of the world. Also in Dibin was a boy who, though born blind, moved freely about in the village and even went out a short way by himself in a canoe to collect *hashish*. During the years I was in the Marshes I met several deaf-and-dumb boys and men, who were happy and friendly, and who fitted usefully into the life of the community.

One afternoon, some days after leaving Dibin, we arrived at a village on the mainland. The sheikh was away looking at his cultivations, but we were shown to his *mudhif* by a boy wearing a head-rope and cloak, with a dagger at his waist. He looked about fifteen and his beautiful face was made even more striking by two long braids of hair on either side. In the past all the Madan wore their hair like that, as the Bedu still did. After the boy had made us coffee and withdrawn, Amara asked, 'Did you realize that was a *mustarjil*?' I had vaguely heard of them, but had not met one before.

'A *mustarjil* is born a woman,' Amara explained. 'She cannot help that; but she has the heart of a man, so she lives like a man.'

'Do men accept her?'

'Certainly. We eat with her and she may sit in the *mudhif*. When she dies, we fire off our rifles to honour her. We never do that for a woman. In Majid's village there is one who fought bravely in the war against Haji Sulaiman.'

'Do they always wear their hair plaited?'

'Usually they shave it off like men.'

'Do *mustarjils* ever marry?'

'No, they sleep with women as we do.'

Once, however, we were in a village for a marriage, when the bride, to everyone's amazement, was in fact a *mustarjil*. In this case she had agreed to wear women's clothes and to sleep with her husband on condition that he never asked her to do women's work. The *mustarjils* were much respected, and their nearest equivalent seemed to be the Amazons of antiquity. I met a number of others during the following years. One man came to me with what I took for his twelve-year-old son, suffering from colic, but when I wanted to examine the child, the father said, 'He is a *mustarjil*.' On another occasion I attended a man with a fractured skull. He had fought with a *mustarjil* whom I knew, and had got the worst of it.

Previously, while staying with Hamud, Majid's brother, I was sitting in the *diwaniya* when a stout middle-aged woman shuffled in, enveloped in the usual black draperies, and asked for treatment. She had a striking, rather masculine face, and lifting her skirt exposed a perfectly normal full-sized male organ. 'Will you cut this off and turn me into a proper woman?' he pleaded. I had to confess that the operation was beyond me. When he had left, Amara asked compassionately, 'Could they not do it for him in Basra? Except for that, he really is a woman, poor thing.' Afterwards I often noticed the same man washing dishes on the river bank with the women. Accepted by them, he seemed quite at home. These people were kinder to him than we would have been in our society. Yet in some ways they were very callous.

Once as we were setting off on one of our daily expeditions, we were asked to look out for the body of a small girl drowned in the river. Coming back in the evening we saw the floating corpse, but when I suggested bringing it on board my companions refused to touch it, or even to have it in the *tarada*, for fear of ritual pollution. 'We should have to wash completely seven times,' Yasin said. 'And anyway it's not our child.' The most they would do was to push the corpse to the river bank and lift it out with their paddles.

Another time, an elderly *Sayid* arrived with his son, a child of nine, who had cut his hand deeply while gathering *hashish*. He reeled towards me, faint from loss of blood. When I asked the father indignantly why he didn't help the child, he objected that he might get blood on his clothes, which would make him un-clean. Luckily I remembered in time that he was a *Sayid*, for it would not have done for me to curse him. I must say some of his fellow Moslems were less inhibited.

The Chahla leaves the Tigris some miles below Amara, dis-persing into the Marshes twenty-five miles farther on. The villages in its delta, where we spent a few days after leaving Dibin, were inhabited by families from several tribes besides the Al bu Muhammad, to whose sheikhs they all owed allegiance. The villagers kept buffaloes and grew rice. Farther upstream, the Al bu Muhammad lived in a succession of villages along the various branches of the river and its numerous canals, cultivating wheat and barley which they sowed in November and reaped in April or May. Unlike the Majar, where the houses stood out starkly along the river bank in an otherwise empty landscape, the villages on the Chahla were interspersed with palm groves, small fruit gardens and thickets of willows. We wandered among them, travelling up one branch of the river and down another.

On each branch we had to negotiate a great earthen dam, which the sheikhs had built to supply water to their winter cultivation. The pent-up current poured like a mill-race through a narrow gap in the middle, forming eddies and whirlpools for thirty yards downstream. My companions fought their way up foot by foot and then inch by inch. The *tarada* never had more than two inches of freeboard and I was afraid it would be swept sideways and swamped. Coming down, we shot the other dam like a rapid with an exhilarating surge of speed. Often, in the small canals, we found the stream completely blocked and were faced with a sloping bank about four feet high. The *tarada* was far too heavy to carry. We splashed water over the bank to make it slippery and then, lifting the prow, dragged the boat laboriously up the slope till she balanced on the top, when we carefully eased her into the water on the far side.

Muhammad al Araibi was the richest and most powerful of the Al bu Muhammad sheikhs on the Chahla. A much venerated old man, he lived mostly in Baghdad or Amara, leaving his favourite son, a dissolute and arrogant youth, in charge of his estates. His other relations lived in varying degrees of poverty on small farms which he had allotted to them in the less fertile areas. We stayed with several and found them hospitable and unassuming.

Leaving the Chahla we crossed a marsh abounding with pig, of which I shot a number, and came to a branch of the Masharia, a river that leaves the Tigris north of the Chahla in the middle of Amara town. We were now among the Sudan, one of the nicest of the tribes and the most unfortunate. In the past they had been powerful and prosperous, but now they were scattered and their land was largely derelict. They maintained that the water-level had fallen ever since the barrage was built at Kut on the Tigris. Their late sheikh had installed pumps, but when he died his son sold them to meet the gambling debts he had incurred in Basra.

On the way I had counted sixty pig feeding outside one reedbed. The Sudan implored me to shoot them as they were devastating their small crops of wheat and barley that were nearly ripe. Pig seldom entered barley if there was wheat near by. At this season they fed in the fields at night and lay up in them by day. In places the corn was four feet high, which made hunting extremely dangerous, especially when a wind was moving the corn. I had been knocked down by a boar under similar circumstances the year before.

On that occasion I had already shot a dozen or so, kicking them out of bramble thickets along abandoned ditches, and shooting them as they broke across the open. A boy brought me news of a pig he had found in some nearby wheat and pointed out the exact spot. The hollow in the corn was obvious even from a distance, but the corn was breast high and I could not see into it until less than a yard away. Suddenly an ear flicked, and the pig was there, lying in the shadow with its back to me. I shot it in the neck and it never moved. 'Come on, let's return: we have a long way to go,' my host urged when I rejoined him.

As we were leaving, the boy ran up again with the news of another pig. 'Come and shoot it, Sahib, it is destroying all my crop.'

My host tried to dissuade me, but I said, 'Just this one and then I will be with you.' Again I stalked the hollow which the boy indicated and peered over the top of the corn straight into the eyes of a big boar – I still remember the white glint of its tushes. Before I could aim I was on my back, yards from where I had been standing, the rifle going off as I went down. Then the pig was on me again. I felt its weight on my thighs, saw its long snout and small angry eyes above me, and felt its breath on my face. It drove at my chest with its tushes, and instinctively I blocked the swipe with the butt of my rifle. Then the pig was gone. I sat up and looked at my rifle; there was a great gouge in the stock, and one of my fingers, slashed to the bone as by a razor, was pouring blood. I reloaded and got to my feet. The boar, a big one, was walking away on the edge of the cornfield. I shouted, it swung round, and I aimed at its chest. It dropped where it stood.

Then I had been alone and only responsible for myself. This time my four boys were with me and a crowd of Sudan, all plunging about in the standing corn and doing far more damage than a dozen pigs. Amara was armed with my shotgun (Plate 61), loaded with buckshot, Hasan carried a 9-mm. Browning pistol I had brought with me that year. Sabaiti and Yasin were armed only with their daggers. After killing several pigs and having two narrow escapes, I persuaded the villagers that we would hunt to better purpose among the flooded beds of bulrushes. Here we killed thirty-six pigs in two days, riding them down in our *tarada* and shooting them through the head with the Browning as they swam in front or turned to attack us. So long as they were swimming, they were powerless to hurt us. Once Yasin jumped into deep water beside a large boar and drowned it with his hands. The Sudan were sorry when we left them to visit the Suaid.

On our way across more marshes, we passed a bare black mound rising thirty feet above the reeds. Once the site of some long-forgotten city, it was now known to the Madan as Ishan Waqif, or Standing Island. Later the Suaid took us farther into the marsh and showed us another similar mound, Azizah, which I estimated was fifty feet in height. I remember seeing a mongoose scampering about on it. We stayed for a week with various sheikhs on the lower reaches of the Masharia. None was wealthy, but all were hospitable. One old man, the shape of a Chinese idol, was known as 'the Father of the Lamp', because every Friday, the Moslem Sabbath, he guided wayfarers to his *mudhif* by hanging a lamp on a pole. These sheikhs were friendly and informal with their villagers, and whenever a meal was served pressed anyone in the room to stay and share it. Even Amara and Hasan, who as Feraigat felt no love for the Suaid, admitted that their sheikhs were more open-handed than most of those of the Al bu Muhammad. However, when I had once criticized, in another tribe's *mudhif*, an Al bu Muhammad sheikh's lack of hospitality, I was severely taken to task afterwards. 'Say what you like of our sheikhs in front of us. We say the same. Most of them *are* mean, but don't criticize them in front of another tribe.' I was surprised at their loyalty, since none of them actually belonged to the Al bu Muhammad.

When feeding with the Suaid, we conformed to their custom of going down to wash at the water's edge afterwards. My four boys had adopted the Bedu habit, unknown in these parts, of rising all together when the five of us had finished. When questioned they said, 'This is *our* custom.' Often after a meal we challenged the sheikhs and their retainers to shoot against us with the air rifle, sometimes with my rifle or pistol. Amara had become an outstandingly good shot, and both Yasin and Hasan were better than most, but no amount of coaching could improve Sabaiti's deplorable performance.

'Aim at that *mudhif* over there and perhaps you will hit the target by mistake,' the others teased him. They were themselves easily provoked, but Sabaiti never minded their jibes. Yasin could be quarrelsome and Amara moody, but Sabaiti, the kindest of my companions and the most considerate, was intelligent and level-headed and invariably good-tempered. We all owed a great deal to him. I sometimes got angry with the others, but rarely with Sabaiti and, when I did, I always felt ashamed.

Leaving the Suaid sheikhs with regret, we turned east towards the Persian frontier and punted the *tarada* through shallow water among the bulrushes that grew between the *qasab* reedbeds and the desert's edge. Yasin was as always in the stern, with Amara in front of him, Hasan in the bows and Sabaiti behind him. Hasan maintained that he was captivated with a boy called Madhi (Plate 56) whose dancing had held the stage the night before. 'Madhi, oh Madhi,' he sighed with noisy exaggeration. The others laughed, and Yasin suggested we should put him ashore when we next saw a donkey.

We found ourselves in the van of a Suaid village on the move to a new site, the larger boats loaded deep with dismantled houses and other possessions. In the smaller canoes, herdsboys, many of them naked, shouted and yodelled as they drove the splashing buffaloes. These Suaid were not cultivators but lived in the Marshes with their herds. Unlike those of the nomad Feraigat, their headcloths were ochre in colour. Behind us more and more of their canoes emerged from the reeds. A man explained that the rising water, exceptionally high that year, had driven them earlier than usual from their winter site deep in the Marshes. 'Stop with us tonight, Sahib,' he said. 'We are going to set up our village on that dry ground over there.'

Within less than an hour of landing, the first house was up. The reed bundles to form the arches were planted opposite each other in two rows, each bundle inclining outward. A man then climbed on to a reed tripod and, as others pulled the tops within reach, bound them together (Plates 88 and 90). This was easily done since the bundles were already curved from previous use. When the five arches were in place, the Suaid fastened on the horizontal ribbing, threw the mats, sometimes only a single thickness, over the framework and tied them in position. All the bindings were made of *qasab*. While I was strolling about, watching houses being built and canoes unloaded, my new acquaintance invited me to his house, which I found already furnished, with tea ready and the rice for lunch on the fire. The youngest of his sons, a child of nine, wore nothing but a silver necklace set with a single large blue stone (Plate 79).

These nomadic Suaid gathered bulrushes and *kaulan* (*Scirpus brachyceras*), the sedge which covered most of the temporary marsh, for their buffaloes. As we watched them feeding on it, Yasin remarked that his own buffaloes at Bu Mughaifat would not have touched it. Many of the Suaid wanted medicine, so we stayed another day, and then visited other of their villages, one several miles inside the reedbeds. They were the least sophisticated of all the Madan, and the pleasure of their company was only marred by the taste of the water, which was brackish all along this edge of the desert. The Suaid on the mainland made salt by evaporating the water in shallow pits. At length we reached the Persian frontier which was as far as we could go in the Eastern Marshes and, after spending the night in a small Iraqi police post, started back for the Central Marshes.

20. Amara's Family

Auaisij was flooded and the Feraigat were gone when we got back there. As we forced the *tarada* through dark fields of sedge, only the occasional grey-lag, that had remained on to breed, recalled the massed wild-fowl of the winter months. In the reed-beds along the Euphrates a new growth was already high among the sapless old, while scented water-crowfoot covered the open water like a fall of snow (Plate 44).

At Azair we left the boat and hired a car to take us to Basra, which I generally visited every two months to collect my mail, have a bath and buy more medicines. A few days in a comfort-able house was a pleasant change and my friends at the Consulate were always good to me and my companions. Back once more in our *tarada*, Amara said, 'Now that Falih is dead you must stay with me instead. We have not got much, as you know, but what we have is yours. We will leave Yasin and Hasan with their families and send for them when we are ready to go on again.'

Four days later we entered the canal that led to Rufaiya, Amara's village. The current ran strong. Beyond the banks, men cleared the ground and floated great piles of vegetation farther into the marsh, working knee-deep to waist-deep in water. A tall boy, his shirt round his neck, splashed towards us and called greetings. 'That is Reshiq, my brother,' Amara said. 'Last year he helped others with their rice; this year he has his own land.' The boy washed the mud off his feet and legs, dropped into the *tarada* beside Amara, kissed him and then picked up a pole. Although nice-looking, with a lively rather cheeky expression, he lacked the air of breeding that distinguished his brother. A year younger, and nearly as tall, he appeared gangling but would prob-ably be the more powerful of the two when he filled out. We passed the first houses, and children began to follow us, scampering along the banks till I felt like the Pied Piper. By the time we stopped, a large crowd of them had gathered and were waiting to help us land. 'Hasan, run and tell father that the Sahib comes as our guest,' Amara said to one; and to Reshiq, 'See that the other chicks bring everything to the house, and don't forget the poles.'

Yasin and Hasan had remained for a few days in Bu Mughaifat. Accompanied by Sabaiti, and another lad who had come with us, we walked towards Amara's home on the outskirts of the village. Harvested fields of barley lay beyond, and in the distance a dark clump of palms. Amara's father, Thuqub, was an old man with a weathered face and untroubled eyes. Dressed in a clean white shirt and headcloth, he received us with quiet courtesy. He held himself erect but moved slowly and rather stiffly as he showed us into his house, which was small and low-roofed, each of its five arches only a few reeds thick. A worn carpet was spread on a tattered mat with two cushions. A lively, middle-aged woman with a kindly face greeted me. 'Welcome, Sahib, welcome to your home. Are you not Amara's father? God bless you.' Behind her stood a baby, two small boys and a girl of fifteen who half hid her face.

Amara sent Reshiq off to find a kettle and Sabaiti to his father's shop for sugar and tea. Then, assisted by his small brothers and a crowd of other children, he attempted to capture an old rooster. After escaping from the house and leading them round the village in noisy pursuit, it was finally cornered and slaughtered for lunch. Amara also produced a very stale fish, but in these parts no one minded if a fish smelt. To eat with it, Naga, his mother, baked bread for us in a circular clay oven, slapping the discs of wet dough on the inside wall. On the mainland, one of these ovens was to be seen in front of every house. In the Marshes, the women cooked their bread over a fire on round earthenware platters. Chilaib, another brother, arrived back from the Marshes. A solid silent boy, he was in charge of the buffaloes while Amara was away with me and, although only about twelve, worked from dawn till dusk cutting and fetching *hashish*. Reshiq helped him carry his load to the house from the canoe. In the evening the buffaloes were tethered to pegs before the house. They could not be left loose at night or they would wander into the cultivations. The herd comprised a wild-eyed bull, three cows, a heifer and a calf. Like Chilaib, Amara's heart was with the buffaloes. After milking, he said to me as he fondled a cow, 'Look at this one, she is a real beauty and in calf. I bought her with the money you gave me last year. Soon, God willing, we will have a proper herd.'

Reshiq, on the other hand, was only interested in his rice crop and grudged any time spent with the animals. He had a quick wit, little respect for his elders, and, egged on by his contemporaries, could be wild and irresponsible. But in the fields he did a man's job with passionate absorption and of an evening would sit against the wall, dog-tired but content. While he told us how his rice crop was doing, he worked his fingers as if he was still moulding the soil. Later in the year his legs would be covered with *shara*, an itch caught, during summer, in water round villages and cultivations, as well as in the shallower marsh wherever pig were common. The rice cultivators inevitably suffered from it and scratched their legs raw. The irritation usually lasted for about twenty-four hours and I knew how maddening it could be, for I often picked it up while hunting pig.

Arabic months are lunar and fall a little earlier each year. Like the cultivators in the Hadhramaut, these cultivators reckoned the seasons by the rising and setting of certain stars, the Pleiades and the Dog-star for instance. At the beginning of each new season, the land on either side of the canal below Rufaiya was marked off with reed pegs into plots of equal breadth, for which the villagers cast lots. Generally a man found himself with several plots in different places. He might then join up in partnership with others or cultivate his portion by himself or with the help of his family. In a normal year they cleared the ground in April and sowed their rice in the middle of May on the falling water. If the floods remained high after that date, the weeds came up on the cleared ground and choked it.

Before sowing the rice, they soaked the seeds in water for five days and then laid them under a weighted mat in the sun for a further two, until they began to germinate. They distinguished between the *nithar* crop, that was sown and then thinned out, and the *shital* crop, of seedlings that were transplanted after forty days. The Madan in the Marshes planted only *shital*, whereas the Azairij, whose lands were far from the Marshes, cultivated little rice except *nithar*. Here at Rufaiya, on the edge of the Marshes, the villagers grew both crops. Reshiq, who was single-handed, grew four-fifths *nithar* which required far less labour, but which gave only about half the yield of *shital* to an equal area. *Nithar* was usually harvested in the middle of October, *shital* a month later.

In 1956, which was to be a good year, Reshiq cultivated four *qabalas* of *nithar* and one of *shital*. A *qabala* is 0·62 of an acre. This yielded him about 3,500 kilos of rice. He gave Majid a quarter of his crop, kept enough to feed his family for the coming year, and sold the rest for about thirty dinars. Majid's share, collected in kind, was levied on the village as a whole. Sometimes he took a third of the *harvested* crop, but more usually a quarter of the *assessed* crop, in which case he fixed the amount as soon as he knew the flood level for the year. I was told that his judgement was generally very accurate.

High floods were welcomed by cultivators, like the Azairij, who grew their rice on land irrigated from the rivers, but were a misfortune to the Madan whose rice lands remained under water. Conversely, low water enabled the Madan to cultivate more extensively but was disastrous for the others. In 1951, a year of exceptionally low water, the Madan from Saigal, Al Aggar and the large villages in the Marshes off the mouth of the Adil cultivated far larger areas than usual. Unfortunately heavy autumn rains raised the water-level and swamped most of the crops before they could be harvested. In Amara Province the tribes only grew rice on land covered by fresh silt, but on the Euphrates below Suq ash Shuyukh some of them ploughed their rice lands. Here they sometimes grew rice under the palms on the same land where they had just harvested wheat or barley.

Hasan, a child of seven and one of Amara's four brothers, cut his hand the first evening and came to have it bandaged. Until then he had remained silently at the far end of the room and I had hardly noticed him, unlike his younger brother, Radhi, who sat chatting beside me. He struck me as looking seriously anaemic and his mother said he was always tired and lifeless. The blood that flowed from the cut was the colour of dirty water and hardly showed up on the tanned skin. I gave her a bottle of iron tablets for him and a month later hardly recognized him. He was a happy, affectionate child and I was soon very fond of him.

Thuqub's ambition was to make the pilgrimage to Meshed. He spent much time in prayer and meditation, content to leave the family's affairs to Amara, who often asked his mother's advice. The following year Amara consulted me about sending Hasan to school. 'We ought to have someone in the family who can read and write.' I agreed, though rather doubtfully, and next morning we sent him off to a school, which half a dozen boys from the village attended and which was two miles away on the main stream of the Wadiya. There was another school on the Adil below Majid's village, but none inside the Marshes. Hasan was very happy there. He trotted off in the morning with the other children and in the evening showed me his work with pride. When I was next in Basra I bought him a satchel and notebooks, coloured pencils, pens, an inkpot, a ruler and compasses. He was delighted and assured me that none of the others had anything of the kind. Nevertheless, I felt worried about the results. For the next five or six years he would spend the day sitting at a desk inside a house and at midday would be given a special meal as prescribed by UNESCO – an easy existence compared with Chilaib's in the reedbeds or Reshiq's in the rice-fields. But reedbeds and rice-fields would be his lot if he remained on in Rufaiya after leaving school. I only hoped that he would not later drift off to become a corner-boy in one of the towns, the fate of so many of the semi-educated throughout the Middle East today.

Few boys who had been at school were content to remain in their village. For years they had been influenced by teachers who hated the tribal life and encouraged them to think that the only respectable existence was in the towns. 'Take me with you to Basra, Sahib, and find me a good job there,' young men often pleaded. 'I hate it here where we live like animals – it is all right for my parents and brothers but I am educated.' If they stayed at home, such boys soon became bitter and discontented. Their belief that, if only they could escape, their meagre education would give them all they hoped for, was pitiful. They did not realize that there were hundreds of thousands of others in Iraq with the same qualifications. In fact, if they left home, they probably ended by selling newspapers or Coca-Cola in Basra or Baghdad, as well as stealing from cars and pimping for taxi-drivers to keep alive.

Nearly all parents were anxious to send their children to school, but I remember an old man, in a village on the Adil, saying to me, 'My son has a good job with the Government in Basra. We are poor, as you can see. I spent much money keeping him in Amara during the ten years he was at school. Later I thought he would look after us. We were happy with him when he was a child; he is our only son. Now he never comes near us or helps us. This education is a bad thing, Sahib, it steals our children.' An old woman in Qabab, however, whose husband had divorced her and worked in Amara as a night-watchman, had no such doubts. She was visited by her son who had been to school there. He wore a coat, and trousers with a large hole in the seat, and his hair was smeared with brilliantine and parted European-fashion. When he left, after his two days' visit, his mother went proudly round her neighbours, declaring, 'My son is civilized. He eats with a spoon, and pees standing.' Tribesmen always squat to urinate.

On one of our many visits to Qabab, Dakhil invited us to his wedding. When I had sent him to Basra the previous year I had thought he was dying. Since he recovered, I had run into him on several occasions, among the Fartus, at Al Aggar, and recently at Qabab, and was attached to this humorous, argumentative and slightly comic lad. I felt responsible for him, helped him with money, and now had paid most of the seventy-five dinars for his bride price. He was marrying his friend Wadi's sister, the girl with whom he had always been in love.

We reached Qabab at noon the day before the wedding and were glad to have arrived, for the passageways between the dark lifeless reedbeds had been stiflingly hot. Even sitting still the sweat trickled down my body, while my companions looked as if they had been bathing in their shirts. The water we scooped up to drink was tepid and tasted flat. Small spiders fell into the *tarada* in scores, mosquitoes swarmed round us, and the flies, although looking as innocuous as house flies, bit us savagely through our shirts. The village lay inert and seemingly deserted, steaming slightly under the summer sun. Sadam was on a visit to Majid, so we stayed with an elderly Feraigat who was a friend of mine and a cousin of Hasan. Dakhil was living next door with a Fartus family. He was busy extending the house by adding a couple more arches. When he had finished, he erected a red mosquito-net inside this to cover his bridal couch.

The following morning we heard singing and drumming from the far end of the village where Wadi had started to celebrate his sister's marriage. In the afternoon Dakhil's friends set off to fetch the bride in our *tarada*. Amara took the shotgun and Hasan the pistol, in order to fire off shots to celebrate the occasion. As was customary, Dakhil awaited their return in his house. Having no family, he asked me to remain with him, and we sat listening to the distant sounds. The singing stopped and then started once more, which he told me meant they had landed and that Wadi was now entertaining them. An hour later as the sun was getting low, the singing grew louder, and then we heard scattered shots. 'They are putting her in the boat,' Dakhil said. 'They will take her right round the village and stop to dance at various houses on the way here.'

At last we saw them coming slowly towards us. The *tarada*, in which the bride sat muffled in her new clothes, was surrounded by canoes. Men stood in them chanting as they paddled towards us. In front of the bride were stacked quilts, mattresses, pillows and other furnishings that Wadi had given her to take to her new home. As head of her family, he was entitled to spend as much, or as little, of the bride money as he chose. I was glad that he appeared to have been generous, for Dakhil was extremely poor.

As they landed, I fired shots with my rifle. Amara and Hasan jumped ashore and, while the bride was being led into the house, Hasan blazed off the entire magazine of thirteen rounds from the pistol, and Amara fired the shotgun as fast as he could load. Everyone came ashore, scrambling from boat to boat to reach the space in front of the house. Ajram improvised a couplet and repeated it twice. Then the crowd took it up, as they stamped round us, waving rifles, paddles and daggers over their heads. At intervals, we fired shots into the air to encourage them. They kept it up until the sun set, when they returned to their houses to feed. Afterwards we all collected again at Dakhil's house. Helu and others sang, various boys danced and Dakhil handed round cigarettes and tea.

About midnight, I suggested to Amara that Dakhil might be glad if the party broke up, so that he could go to his bride, but he answered, 'That is all right; he will go when he is ready.' Later, Dakhil borrowed the shotgun and one cartridge and disappeared. The party went on. Suddenly, and unexpectedly so far as I was concerned, a shot was fired at the far end of the room, but the others, who had evidently been waiting for it, grinned. It was a signal that Dakhil had consummated his marriage. He reappeared shortly afterwards looking very dishevelled. His shirt was torn and he had lost his head-rope. Yasin asked if his bride had proved too much for him, to which he replied, with comic indignation, 'But didn't you hear the shot?'

Next morning I visited Dakhil and he took me inside the net where, by tribal custom, his wife was confined for the next seven days. I sat beside her on the pile of quilts and cushions that she had brought with her. Resembling her brother in appearance, she was a pleasant-faced buxom girl of sixteen and not in the least shy. She drenched my clothes from a bottle of particularly strong scent and fed me on sticky sweets, while Dakhil brewed tea. As soon as this seven-day honeymoon was over, he built a small house in the village and they settled down. Even-tempered, hard-working and frugal, she made him a good wife. Within a year she bore a daughter, the following year a son. Whenever I visited him Dakhil used to produce them with the greatest pride and give me one of them to hold. I do not care for babies.

On our way back to Rufaiya we stopped at a large Madan village near the mouth of the Adil. A few days earlier, a father had left his small child with his old blind mother while he went across to the merchant's. When he came back, he found that the child had fallen into the water and been drowned. The mourning ceremony was in progress at his house, close to where we were staying. Canoes went past filled with men or women but never both, and the wailing rose and fell. Two boys stopped to talk with us. We had hunted pig together in the past. They sat chatting, until one said to the other, 'Come on, we had better go over there.' They got to their feet, said good-bye, and, without warning, started to wail loudly and continuously. I was reminded of an occasion with the Fartus, when Falih, Daud and Khayal took me shooting in the Marshes some distance from Jasim's village. We met a canoe from Qabiba and heard that a boy who was their friend had died that morning. All three abandoned themselves to hysterical weeping, until all of a sudden Falih said, 'That is enough.' Abruptly the wailing ceased and they picked up their paddles.

We knew the father of the dead child and went to pay our respects. The *Fatha*, as the mourning was called, was held for either sex and lasted for seven days, during which time the villagers took it in turn to provide the midday meal, including meat. People from the village would drink coffee at the *Fatha* but would not take tea or cigarettes, which were for visitors. Amara suggested that I should say the *Fatha*, but I refused, telling him to do so instead. It was often difficult to know which religious expressions should be used by a non-Moslem and which should not. Many are part of everyday speech, for example, 'The praise be to God', 'In the name of God', 'Remain in the safe keeping of God', and above all, 'If God wills'. No one can speak Arabic without such expressions. Others, however, are best left to Moslems. For example, after mentioning the Prophet's name, they add the words, 'on him be prayer and peace'. I always referred to him as 'Your Prophet'. During the ten days of Muharram, when the Shias mourn the death of Husain with passionate intensity, I often found myself in a *mudhif* for a 'reading' after dinner. Then, of course, I behaved like the others, rising when they rose and turning to right or left as they did.

The room, when we got there, was very full. We greeted the father, an elderly man with a crippled leg, the result of a bullet wound, and he invited me to sit beside him while we were given coffee, tea and cigarettes. Twelve years earlier, he had won fame in the battle between Majid and his brother-in-law Haji Sulaiman. I had never heard the real reason for this fighting but I knew that Haji Sulaiman's daughter had been murdered while she was Majid's wife. Years later Kharaibid, Majid's eldest son, was also murdered; this was said to be part of the same feud. In the battle itself, Majid's tribesmen had charged across open rice-fields and had taken and burnt Haji Sulaiman's village. A hundred and forty men were killed and wounded in that day's fighting, before a *Sayid* arrived and imposed a truce. The father of the dead child had been disabled carrying his tribal banner under the very walls of the fort, which they had failed to capture.

We sat beside him for half an hour, then I nudged Amara who called out '*Al Fatha*' and we left. It was customary to make a contribution to the expenses and when the father saw us to the door I gave him half a dinar.

21. 1954: The Flood

The winter of 1953–4 had been exceptionally severe. Although the deep snow on the Persian and Turkish mountains had not yet begun to melt, the Tigris was in flood as the result of heavy winter rains when I returned to Iraq in the middle of February. Amara and Sabaiti met me in Basra and, after a few days buying medicines, cartridges and clothes, we went back to their village. On the way we stayed the night with Abd al Wahid, Falih's son, a dull youth who never seemed to have anything to say. He was dominated by his interfering and parsimonious mother. Falih's old retainers would have stood by his son but she had got rid of them to save money. Dair was gone and Abd ar Ridha told me that he too intended to leave. Few people came to the *mudhif* nowadays and we sat most of the time in awkward silence.

We had left our *tarada* here and found it was leaking. We turned it over and sealed the cracks by warming them with a torch of reeds, but it needed repitching, so we decided to cross the Marshes of Huwair and get this done by Haji Hamaid himself. The current was very strong and the stream ran level with its banks, threatening in places to overflow them and drown the fields of wheat and barley which here, as elsewhere, lay below. We passed several gangs of men strengthening the banks before we reached Rufaiya, where as usual I stayed with Amara. He had rebuilt the house which was now spacious and well constructed. I noticed a new rug and several new cushions. Reshiq had done well with his rice crop and the buffaloes had calved, so that there were now two in milk. I was delighted to be back and everyone seemed as glad to see me. All the small boys in the village escorted me from the landing-place to Thuqub's house, where the elders urged Amara to 'turn those chicks out so that we can see our friend' – easier said than done. One seven-year-old called out cheekily, 'Leave us alone; he is our friend not yours.' I never saw a man strike or be unkind to a child, and only very occasionally did the children quarrel among themselves. Reshiq now appealed to the boys to help him catch some chickens. This was irresistible and they rushed off in pursuit like a pack of puppies. The chickens were owned by Matara, Amara's sister, and were decimated each time I came to stay. She sometimes sold a few to the buyers from the town who travelled round the villages.

I had bought Matara a green silk dress from Basra, chosen by Amara, so this time I felt less guilty about her chickens. She was a shy, silent girl, slim and graceful and with a lovely face. I once asked Amara what he and Thuqub would do if a sheikh asked for her and he said they would refuse. 'If a sheikh married her, I should be powerless to protect her.' A sheikh could marry anyone he liked, but his daughter could only marry a sheikh and the same was true of *Sayids*. Moslems were entitled to four wives, but in Rufaiya there were only three men with two wives, none with more. Similarly, in Qabab, only Sadam and two others had two wives.

I had at first supposed that a very large proportion of children must die in infancy. In one Fartus village I visited early on, five babies had died of whooping cough in a week. But in fact infant mortality was comparatively low. Of Thuqub's nine children, all but one had survived, and Sabaiti's seven brothers and sisters were all alive. Ten families at Qabab, whom I selected at random, had eighty children between them and of these thirteen died under the age of fifteen. I wondered how this compared with Victorian England.

We stayed at Rufaiya for another day before going on to Bu Mughaifat. It poured during the night, and in the morning the sky was overcast and threatening. As we arrived within sight of Hasan's house, the rain came down again, and it continued all day. We were drenched before we could get our things inside the house, which was well-built with several thicknesses of matting on the roof. Hasan himself was out shooting but Afara, his mother (Plate 63), welcomed us and built up a fire to dry our clothes. A large woman, with grey-green eyes set wide apart in a squarish face, she was influential in the village, devoted to her son, and came from the well-known family of Bait Makenzie.

When I first heard the name, I almost expected to meet some off-shoot of a Scottish clan, wearing a tartan shirt, but in fact the Bait Makenzie were Feraigat of unimpeachable descent. Afara's grandfather had called his son Makenzie as a compliment to a Scotsman whom he had met and admired in the First World War.

Hasan came in soaked to the skin, his small canoe half-filled by the rain. He brought back four shoveller that he had killed with one shot. He said the duck were very wild and he had only got near these by holding a small clump of reeds in front of him and wading up to his neck.

Yasin turned up shortly afterwards from the reedbeds. Both he and Hasan were anxious to come with me again. After getting the *tarada* mended at Huwair, we planned to cross the Tigris at Qurna and to travel north through a part of the Eastern Marshes that none of us had yet seen. 'Don't go near Zikri in this weather,' Sahain counselled. 'Go down to the Euphrates through the Al bu Bakhit villages, and see if you can get hold of Tahir bin Ubaid as your guide. He lives by smuggling and knows every water-course in the Eastern Marshes.' Yasin said, 'Yes, I met him last year at Azair. If he is with us, we can go anywhere.'

We lunched at Daub next day with the man whose son had been savaged by his dog three years earlier. Neither the boy nor his father would hear of us going on in the afternoon, and they kept us for the night. Some days earlier, thieves had stolen buffaloes from the village during the night. Dogs gave the alarm, the thieves were chased, and fired several shots, hitting a boy in the chest and killing him, before escaping. I had known the dead boy and went over to the *Fatha*. Sahain had talked about this incident at Bu Mughaifat and suspected that the thieves were Feraigat from Auaisij. Now we heard that they were Suaid. They had been identified by their voices. A Marshman could always tell a stranger's tribe by his accent.

Tahir was at home when we arrived the following evening. He was a powerfully built man of thirty, distinguished by a growth the size of a walnut over his right eye. He agreed to come with us as soon as I suggested it.

Tahir's eldest son had died recently and now he only had two small children. His nephew, a lively boy of twelve who lived next door, helped him to entertain us. His father was Tahir's younger brother, who resembled him somewhat in appearance and also lived by smuggling. I was always surprised how quickly news got about that I was in a village, and I had to remain another day with Tahir, as more than the usual number of patients turned up, some having come a long way. One was an unfortunate boy with his penis under his scrotum.

On the way to Huwair, Tahir told us that his last venture had not been a success. He had been caught by the Persian police who confiscated his sugar and tea and questioned him about the disappearance some months earlier of two policemen. After two days they bastinadoed him and allowed him to go, but warned him that he would be shot out of hand if caught again. Tahir grinned and said, 'I could have shown them where their two missing policemen were. I had pushed them under a floating island in the Marsh. They surprised us while we were getting away with a load of grain and chased us in the dark. Two of us stopped behind and ambushed them. We got a hundred dinars each for their rifles. I am keeping away from Persia for the time being.'

Huwair was a short distance up a creek to the north of the Euphrates. The houses and numerous *mudhifs* stood under palms on an island of high ground surrounded by marsh. We stayed with Haji Hamaid himself in his small *mudhif* next to his boat yard. He was an energetic middle-aged man, and at once set children to stripping the *tarada* while he took me round the village. Everyone seemed to be directly or indirectly concerned with building boats. Planks, logs of wood and bamboo poles were stacked in the yards behind the shops. Inside the merchants sold tools and packets of nails as well as their usual wares. Under some palms, men worked putting the finishing touches to a large two-masted boat, before rolling it down to the water on logs. Most craftsmen worked in their own yards behind reed fences, stripping and recoating small boats and canoes, mending the broken frames or building new ones. We watched an old man start on a canoe. He outlined the bottom with transverse slats of wood, an inch or so apart, and then nailed a single long plank down the centre. While we drank tea he fashioned the ribs, selecting suitable pieces of wood from a pile beside him. He used an adze, and his only other tools, a small saw and a bow drill, lay on the mat beside him with a heap of nails. The smell of warm tar drifted to us from the yard next door; shafts of sunlight came through the palms above, and two pied crows sitting in the branches watched our every move (Plates 71–75).

At last Haji Hamaid said, 'We had better get back. They will have finished stripping your *tarada*. After lunch I will put a new coat on it. Stay the night and it will be properly hard in the morning.' He made us new paddles and we painted the blades red, so that they would be less easily stolen, for anyone would be glad to acquire one of the Haji's paddles. From now on red paddles became our distinctive badge. They looked well, I thought, dipping together in the water, as we glided downstream next morning past banks lined with palms. Tahir had taken Hasan's place in the bows and Hasan had replaced Amara, who sat opposite me as a passenger. We passed two or three motor-launches before we arrived at Qurna. The pontoon bridge on the Euphrates, where it enters the Tigris, was open. The Tigris was running high and we lunched in a *mudhif* on the far side. The date was 4 March, and we remained on the east side of the river for the next five weeks.

At first we visited tribes that I had not previously met, such as the Dukhainat, or the Haliki, whose name meant 'the Cormorants'. Later we were back with old friends among the Al bu Muhammad, the nomadic Feraigat and the Suaid. Often it rained, especially at night, heavy thunderstorms that swept across the Marshes. Few of the houses we slept in had more than a double, and many had only a single, thickness of matting on the roof. The household sometimes added the matting from the floor, but this seldom kept the rain out and it left us lying on the ground. It was cold, too, and we slept in pairs, sharing our blankets. And all the time the floods rose.

We were out shooting one afternoon when black clouds massed quickly, presaging a tremendous storm. Yasin said anxiously, 'God, I hope there is no hail in that,' and the others echoed his prayer. The storm broke and before we were home we had to bale to keep afloat. My companions were frightened of hail, with good reason. The following year a hailstorm cut a swath right across the northern half of the Marshes, smashing even the largest reeds and killing countless pelicans, geese and other birds. Their corpses were scattered everywhere. It also killed a number of buffalo calves, and battered a man and his son to death on Dima.

'With this high water, we shall kill many pigs this year,' Amara said, and sure enough we did. Before recrossing the Tigris, I had shot two hundred and five. It was always exciting work, and sometimes dangerous, but I did not hunt them solely for sport. They were the Marshman's natural enemy, and I had had to sew up too many men savaged by pigs to feel any compunction killing them. Yet I should have hated to have seen them exterminated here, as the lions had been. Their massive dark shapes, feeding on the edge of the reedbeds at evening, were for me an integral part of the Marsh scene. Without the constant risk of encountering them, life here would have lost much of its excitement.

The pig could be astonishingly bold. Once, in the Amaira country, the villagers assured me that the pig came back to the village with the buffaloes and spent the night in empty houses. I did not believe them until we saw two walking through the shallow water towards the village at sunset. We chased and killed them and, when we got back in the dark, a family who were sitting outside by a fire, said quite casually, 'There are some more in there,' pointing to the next door house a few yards away. I thought they must be joking. However, we landed on the *dibin* and were nearly knocked over by five pig as they charged out and plunged into the water.

Turning north in the *tarada*, Tahir guided us to Auaisij, the long ridge of slightly higher ground that runs parallel with the Tigris. Owing to the unusually high floods, most of it was already awash and great numbers of pig were lying up there by day. My companions were easily able to slide the *tarada* through the sludge in any direction while we were hunting. One afternoon I killed ten that were walking across our front in single file. I was shooting exceptionally well that day and dropped the rearmost each time with a single shot. We found four more. When I killed one, the other three gathered round it as it kicked convulsively on the ground, and for some odd reason remained like that until I had killed them too.

The next two we saw were very big boars and they stood watching us from two hundred yards in front. Tahir and the others turned the canoe sideways and stood behind it. Sitting in

the canoe, I fired and hit the larger boar. He spun round, gal-
loped off about twenty yards, then swerved and came straight at
us with the other close behind him. I fired again and heard the
bullet smack, but he never faltered. Then again, and still he
came on. By now he was very close indeed. I fired, and this time
he dropped. Four shots, one left . . . I worked the bolt and
swung to face the other boar which would be on top of me with
two more bounds. I fired my last shot and he went down, skid-
ding right up to the boat. I reloaded, but neither moved. Leaning
out, I touched the nearest pig, the other was a foot or so out of
reach. I had been too busy to be afraid. But the double charge and
the seeming ineffectiveness of my shooting must have been very
alarming to my five companions who were unarmed, the shotgun and pistol being in the boat beside me. I turned to find them
half-crouched, their daggers in their hands.

'What would you have done if it had got into the boat?' I
asked.

'We were going to jump on it and kill it with our daggers,'
Amara answered.

Next day we chased another big boar through water eighteen
inches deep. He was only forty yards ahead and we were gaining
on him when he whipped round and charged, coming very fast
through the water in a smother of spray. I failed to stop him
from the still moving *tarada* and he was alongside before I could
fire again. Tahir had borrowed a fishing spear that morning and
he now drove it straight into the boar's face. From the corner of
my eye, I saw him lifted on the end of the shaft, right out of the
boat. I fired again and this time the boar collapsed, knocking the
tarada sideways through the water. Dripping from head to foot
with liquid mud, Tahir got up spluttering.

'Why did you jump out of the boat?' Yasin asked him inno-
cently. 'You would have been quite safe in it. Didn't you see the
Sahib was getting ready to shoot?' Tahir was not amused.

'Another foot and it would have smashed our *tarada* in half,'
Amara remarked. 'Like the boat we saw the other day that a pig
had broken up.'

This boar, one of the largest I ever shot, had long matted hair,
dark brown in colour. The coats of some were almost black,
of others reddish, while a sounder we once saw were all so pale

in colour that, for a moment, we wondered if they were sheep. Many, however, had only a few coarse bristles on their bare hides. The piglets, born between March and May and usually five to a litter, had soft striped coats and were attractive little beasts. When shooting pig I found that it was generally useless to stalk them downwind. They had good eyesight, but seemed hard of hearing when they were asleep. Once, hunting them on horseback in tamarisk scrub, some mounted Bani Lam shouted to me to come over to where a large boar was snoring in a bush within a yard or so of a dozen trampling horses (Plate 62). The Madan maintained that pig ate carrion. On Auaisij, I certainly saw the partly devoured bodies of boar I had shot some days before, but they might as easily have been eaten by jackals of which there were many. I was afraid all the jackals would be drowned that year, for there was little ground still uncovered and the floods would continue to rise for at least another two months.

Often we slept in small villages where the surrounding water was only kept out of each house by a slight mud wall, hastily thrown up. I always expected it to collapse while we slept and let in a couple of feet of water. Most nights there were violent storms, with much thunder and lightning, and we were quickly soaked, the rain splashing down on us from the leaking roof. On a fine morning we soon dried out; otherwise, chilled and miserable, we continued on our way across an expanse of mud and water under a lowering sky.

The villages at the mouth of the Chahla were flooded out when we got there. In one, the surrounding mud wall had been swept away during the night, and families were groping about in the water for their possessions. All along the Chahla the river had burst its banks and poured out over the uncut fields of wheat and barley. When at last we recrossed the Tigris, we did not need to look for a bridge in order to pass under the main road, for the floods were already level with the top of the embankment. We splashed water on the earthen road and slid the *tarada* across it.

Here Tahir insisted that he must leave us, to help his family. 'This year the water will be too deep for the buffaloes to feed in the marsh. We shall have a job cutting them enough *hashish*.' By now he had become one of ourselves, guiding us deep into the vast reedbeds along the Persian frontier by ways known to few others. And always, even under the most trying conditions, he had been good-tempered and obliging, sharing the work equally with my companions who were young enough to be his sons. He promised to come with us again, but when I asked for him the following year, a man said in surprise, 'Have you not heard that Tahir is dead? His young nephew killed him last month.' Apparently Tahir and his brother lost their tempers over some trifle and came to blows. The same twelve-year-old child we had seen the previous year rushed to his father's assistance, seized a fishing spear and drove it into Tahir's back. A barbed prong penetrated his kidneys and he died in agony some hours later. 'His brother was frantic with grief,' the man told me. 'He cursed his son. The child too had always loved Tahir as a father. Indeed it was a tragedy.'

In the Marshes we were completely out of touch with the rest of the world and had no idea of the disaster that was befalling Iraq. Vast areas were already flooded and Baghdad itself was in serious danger. But the floods had not yet closed the road to Basra when we paid a quick visit there in April. We hired a car, leaving the *tarada* at Azair. Before coming to Iraq I had bought a second-hand ·275 rifle from Rigby's, not wishing to take the ·275 they had made specially for me before the war. In 1954, however, I brought my best one as well, leaving the other at Basra. I now presented that to Amara, and bought Sabaiti, Yasin and Hassan a shotgun each. Two months later, when we again visited Basra, we poled our *tarada* down the main road as far as Qurna where we hired a launch to take us down the river.

Even on our return to Qabab in April we found the water only a foot below the entrance to Sadam's *mudhif*; it had been six feet below on the first occasion I saw it, in an exceptionally dry year. Soon afterwards he had to surround the building with a wall. The phenomenally high water was certainly a great inconvenience to the Madan but life went on as usual. Families just piled more and more reeds on the floors of their houses to keep themselves dry. From Qabab, we set off to visit the Muntifiq tribes along the lower Euphrates, and then to travel northwards up the Gharraf river. We stopped for two days with Jasim al Faris on the way. At this time of year the country to the west of the

Fartus villages was always flooded and we had, in fact, nearly been drowned the previous year crossing from Awaidiya to Hamar. Jasim, therefore, insisted on sending his son Falih and two other Fartus with us in a *balam*. We left his village of Awaidiya on 29 April. A strong north-west wind blew and a big sea was running on the open water. Amara, Sabaiti and myself had transferred, with my luggage, to the *balam*, leaving Yasin and Hasan to manage the *tarada* which, lightly loaded, rode the waves magnificently, smashing down into the troughs and up again.

The floods were already far above the level of any normal year, and would go on rising for another month at least. But it was only when we found most of the village of Hamar submerged that I realized how serious the situation was. We could go wherever we wanted, poling our *tarada* and the larger *balam* across fields of uncut corn and between the trunks of countless palms. Whole villages had been abandoned and, as we passed by, stray dogs howled in despair from the rooftops. Occasionally we saw a cow, belly-deep in water on the top of an embankment, where it had eaten every palm frond within reach. But a few *mudhifs* and houses on higher ground, or where the embankments held, were still inhabited. Whenever we exchanged greetings with their occupants they shouted to us to stop with them and, if we did, prepared coffee and tea and slaughtered chickens for our meal, sitting and chatting with us as if nothing were wrong. Some I had met on previous visits; all had heard of the Englishman who lived with the Madan. But even if I had been unknown to them they would have made us equally welcome, for we were guests.

Turning back to Nasiriya, we entered the main course of the Euphrates and were swept downstream on its racing current. In one place the remains of a dam formed a shelf over which the torrent poured in an ugly swirl. We still carried my heavy boxes in the *balam* and, without them, the *tarada* sat lightly on the water. Even so I thought for a moment we were going to upset, but Yasin knew exactly what he was doing and steered us deftly through, while the others paddled for all they were worth. The town of Suq ash Shuyukh, which we passed, was half under water.

After staying for two days with the Al Juaibar, we returned

to Hamar and later watched the market of Fuhud (Plate 86) being evacuated. As the shopkeepers climbed into boats, the mud walls of their shops collapsed behind them. We then followed the Gharraf upstream to within a few miles of Shatra. In places the water had breached the banks, in others they still held and men worked without rest to save their crops. We stayed with Mahsin in his great guest tent among the Al bu Salih. Even under such conditions he kept open house with a lavishness that became the son of Badr. We stayed with others of the Muntifiq sheikhs, but more often spent the night with simple shepherds or cultivators, sometimes in black tents, at others in reed huts or small mud houses, all marooned in the surrounding sea.

At Awaidiya again, we parted from Falih and his two companions and set off to visit the Bazun. Five years earlier Dugald Stewart and I had left their encampment and ridden south across a dusty desert to reach the tents of the Al Essa. Now I went back to them across the same desert in a *tarada*.

22. 1955: The Drought

On the other hand, 1955 was a year of drought. Little snow had fallen on the mountains in the north, and by April the Tigris had scarcely risen above its winter level. The phenomenal floods of 1954 had devastated the wheat and barley crops on the Gharraf, the Euphrates and elsewhere, and in the Marshes had prevented the villagers from cultivating the rich rice-growing areas between Saigal and the mouth of the Adil. Whereas tribes like the Azairij, whose rice lands lay outside the Marshes, were able, as the waters subsided, to sow and reap a bumper crop off large areas, not normally flooded, but which that year were thickly carpeted with silt. Now, the exceptionally low water would enable the Marshmen to clear and plant far more ground than usual, while the Azairij in their turn would be hit.

The Azairij were a tribe of rice cultivators numbering some forty thousand who lived on the lower reaches of the Butaira, a branch of the Tigris that leaves the main river ten miles above Amara and, after dividing into three important streams, disperses into the Marshes north of Saigal. We passed through their country in mid-April. Prosperous villages succeeded one another along the banks almost without interruption. A special feature of them was the T-shaped *raba*, one arm being used as a dwelling by the family, the other reserved for guests. Round the headmen's houses great bins, made from matting and sealed with a roofing of dried buffalo dung, held the sheikh's share of the previous year's rice. From the number and size of these bins, we could tell how rich the harvest must have been.

Nevertheless the villages were half empty. I knew that numbers of Azairij migrated in the spring to help reap the wheat and barley on the Gharraf. At first sight I assumed that more than usual had gone there, anticipating a bad year with their rice crop.

When we stayed among them, however, we noticed that many of the larger and better-built houses were standing empty. Their owners were unlikely to be harvesting on the Gharraf, an occupation of the poor, and I soon found out that, in fact, fewer Azairij than usual had gone harvesting this year. We asked what had happened and were told that large numbers, both of the poor and the well-to-do, had migrated to Baghdad and Basra. This was the start of a movement in Amara Province that was to resemble an old-fashioned gold-rush and was to leave many villages wholly or partly deserted. All the cultivators were affected by it, not only the Azairij but also the Al bu Muhammad, the Suaid and what were left of the Sudan. Only the Madan, and shepherd tribes like the Al Essa, remained largely unaffected.

When I first went to Iraq in 1950 the Basra oilfields had not yet opened, but by 1955 they were in full production and money was pouring into the country. In Baghdad whole quarters of the town were being pulled down and rebuilt, new roads were being made everywhere and bridges constructed. Casual labour was in great demand and exaggerated accounts of the money to be earned circulated among the tribes. The cultivators from Amara Province left with their families in tens of thousands. When they went off harvesting on the Gharraf or elsewhere, they moved with their animals and all their possessions. Now they sold their boats, their buffaloes, their grain, in fact everything, except what they could carry with them on a bus or lorry – for they had no intention of returning.

They were not driven from the land by want. In particular the Azairij, who left in greater numbers than any other tribe, had harvested an exceptionally good crop of rice in November. They were faced, it is true, with the certain failure of their crops in the coming year, but they had plenty to tide them over, and those who stayed behind suffered no real hardships. 1951 had also been a year of very low water, but then I had noticed little sign of destitution among the Azairij or Al bu Muhummad. The truth was that the low water of 1955 precipitated this mass migration to the towns, but did not cause it.

During recent years, small numbers of the Azairij and the Al bu Muhammad had already migrated to Baghdad and Basra, where they lived together in their own quarters and kept in touch with their kinsmen in the villages. Some managed to set up as shop-keepers or go into small businesses, and did well. Stories of their success lost nothing in the telling. Besides it was common know-ledge that any able-bodied man could now find work in Baghdad and earn five shillings a day. That alone sounded like wealth to these villagers.

A further and more important cause of the migration was the discontent resulting from education. Among the cultivators many of the most enterprising young men had been to school and in consequence had learnt to be critical of the accepted values of village life. They also resented the sheikhs' authority and grum-bled openly at their extortions. They dreamed of escaping to Baghdad, to a world of greater opportunities and greater rewards, with more variety and excitement. The parents respected the book learning which they themselves lacked and were influenced by their sons, but were usually too set in their ways to move. When, in 1955, the young saw that only a small part of the land would be cultivated, they renewed the pressure on their elders. 'Why stay here and wear ourselves out trying to raise a crop for the sheikhs? Why should we work for them anyway? We are freemen, not slaves, yet they treat us like dogs. What right have they to the land? A proper Government would take it from them and give it to us. There will be no cultivation this year; there is no water anyway. If we stay here we starve. If we go to Baghdad we can all get work; in a few months we shall be rich. Look at Wawi; he went off two years ago with nothing but his shirt. Now he owns a car and a house. Ali and Abbas and Zair Chasib have all gone. Ghanim too is selling his buffaloes and leaving. Come on, Father, soon we shall be the only people left and then the sheikhs will make us do all the work. Let's go before they send for us to build the big dam at Abu Fahl.'

The sheikhs themselves were seriously concerned. This exodus of tribesmen threatened to leave no one to work their fields. Their authority over those who remained had been weakened and might soon disappear. Before setting off for Baghdad, the villagers of a particularly unpleasant Azairij sheikh paraded in front of his *mudhif* and chanted '*hammal wa la and Inkal*' (Any work in the town rather than work for Inkal).

In many cases the sheikhs had only themselves to blame, for

they were intolerably arrogant. In 1953 one of Majid's slaves struck the brother of the Shaghanba *qalit* at Al Aggar. The slave was set upon and half killed by the infuriated villagers, for a *qalit* and his family were very much respected. Majid sent his representative, who flogged several of the village elders. In consequence most of the Shaghanba left Al Aggar and went to Saigal. When Majid heard of this he exclaimed publicly, 'The dogs have gone. I will find other dogs to put in their place.' But by July 1955 he was not finding this so easy. When I asked him then if half his cultivators had left, he thought for a moment and answered fatalistically, 'No, I don't think as many as that yet.' I asked what he would do if more left and he said he would give up his rice cultivation and concentrate on growing wheat and barley with machinery. His land was what had always mattered to him, never his tribe. I recalled his anguished cry at the mourning for his son, 'My land! Now, when I die, what will happen to my land?' I thought it sad at the time that he put his land before his tribe.

Among the Al bu Muhummad and the Azairij the old relationship between the sheikh and his tribesmen had disappeared and both were the poorer in consequence. Among the shepherd tribes the bond still held. Maziad of the Al Essa had encouraged his tribe for years to plant barley on the mainland, but conditions were unsuitable. Sometimes there was too much water, sometimes too little. It was a tribal venture but it was Maziad who sank ever more deeply into debt to the Government. However, in his hour of need, the tribe collected the money among themselves and paid his debt. Again, Mahsin bin Badr of the Al bu Salih asked me one morning to take him at once in my *tarada* to the District Headquarters, two hours away up the Gharraf. When we landed, he strode into the office where the *Mudir* was trying a case and, after greeting him, said sharply to the prisoner, 'Go and get into the *tarada* outside.' To the *Mudir* he said, 'This does not concern you. That man belongs to my tribe; I will deal with him.' He then sat and chatted urbanely for a while before asking to be excused.

By the spring of 1956 the stampede to the towns was over. Although families continued to leave for Baghdad and Basra, the reports were no longer enthusiastic, and a few had returned to their villages disillusioned. A quarter of a dinar a day sounded a magnificent wage beforehand; when they got there they found that it barely sufficed to keep a man and his family, however frugally they lived. Moreover, in bad weather, work might stop for a week or more and then there was no wage at all. And everything cost money. Even water, some said.

What was the point of going? A man who stayed at home and worked in his rice-fields could harvest enough grain to feed his family for a year and, after the sheikh had taken his share, still have thirty-five dinars' worth in hand – which, after all, was the equivalent of two shillings a day for the whole year for only six months' work. In the slack season he could go harvesting with his family and earn corn, which would enable him to sell more of his own rice. He could keep buffaloes for milk and chickens for meat. Fuel, building material and fodder for his animals, were all to be had for nothing. There were fish in the rivers and lakes, and water-fowl in the marshes.

Besides, there was little contrast in these villages between the lives of the rich and the poor. The sheikh lived in the same manner as his tribesmen, only better. But in Baghdad and Basra the contrast was overwhelming. Next door to expensive hotels and villas, the new slums, consisting of mat shelters, were squalid with empty tins, broken bottles and scattered paper and, since there was no open country near, were far dirtier than any village.

It is easy enough to leave tribal life and go to a city, but it is almost impossible for the down-and-out to return to his tribe. In 1936, while in Morocco, I visited a large slum on the outskirts of Casablanca, known to the French as Bidonville, where indigent Berbers existed in hovels made from flattened petrol tins. They had originally come to Casablanca from their mountain villages during the boom years after the First World War, when there was a great demand for labour. Then, in the thirties, came the slump. At the time of my visit, these Berbers scavenged round the gutters for scraps to keep themselves alive, and were dying in scores of starvation.

In Iraq, many of the immigrants left their villages to escape the tyranny of the sheikhs. But in Baghdad or Basra they encountered the police. Having set up their mat shelters among a clutter of others, on waste land inside the city, they began to feel at home and to know their way about – until the police arrived with orders to clear the site.

'Where are we to go?'

'Anywhere, but don't stay here. Go back to your villages if you don't like it here. Come on, pull down that house. Hurry! We are busy.'

So, with difficulty, they would move their possessions to another site and again the police would shift them. If they settled on the outskirts, they had to spend money they could ill afford on bus fares to and from their work. The authorities, alarmed by this mass immigration, were anxious to stop it and encouraged the police, who in any case regarded these rustics as fair game, to harass them. 'Show me your discharge papers. You have not got any? Then come with me to the police station.'

In Iraq every man was supposed to serve two years in the army, but very few of the immigrants had done so. I was staying once with Falih when a stout middle-aged captain arrived at the *mudhif*, accompanied by a sergeant and two privates with a mass of files. Falih had been warned of the visit and been asked to have the conscripts ready. It was July and very hot. The captain and his staff gratefully accepted drinks of sherbet and lime tea. The captain's uniform was tight, not designed for sitting on the ground. He rose and went over to the chair and table that had been prepared at the end of the room. The conscripts were brought in; sixteen boys, all but two under the age of puberty. They were lined up in front of the table. Their parents and other visitors sat round the walls. The captain consulted the files, mopped his face, put on his glasses and read out, 'Alwan bin Shinta?' No response. He repeated the name. A man sitting by the wall answered, 'He went with his family to Basra last year.' The captain fumbled with his lists, made a note and read out 'Chilaib bin Hasan?'

'He died last year,' came the prompt answer.

'Maziad bin Ali?' A twelve-year-old was pushed forward.

'Are you Maziad bin Ali?'

'No,' the child replied promptly, and then, after an obvious dig in the back, 'Yes.'

'Are you Maziad bin Ali?' the captain repeated doubtfully, referring to his lists.

'Yes, I am Maziad bin ... bin Ali,' the boy said with more assurance.

'But you're down on my list as eighteen. Lift up your shirt, boy.'

Mopping his face harder than ever, the captain then turned to Falih. 'There must be some mistake. This *can't* be Maziad bin Ali.'

Falih answered blandly, 'These people have a tough life. The boys develop late.'

So the captain made another note on the list and said, 'Tell him to come back next year.'

After a good lunch, he and his staff at length departed with the two victims who had all along been selected for them. Apparently the other thirty-two in the files had either died, moved elsewhere or been obviously still too small.

With the sheikh to back his villagers, the interview had been a good-natured affair. But it was altogether a different matter when a man was asked for his papers in a police station in Baghdad, by police who intended to frighten him and were prepared to use violence to extort money.

23. Berbera and Mudhifs

In the last week of April, we left the Azairij villages behind and, approaching Saigal, could see Abdullah's *mudhif* across the lake. We had flushed several marbled duck that morning, which came here in the spring to breed. I was surprised at the number of pochard, for I would have expected them to have left by now. Yasin insisted that we hug the reedbeds for fear of sudden storms. A few days earlier a hurricane of wind stripped the matting from many houses in the village where we were staying. The year before, at this season, we had been storm-bound for more than two hours in these same reedbeds, enveloped by an eerie red murk.

Far out on the lake, Berbera were fishing from boats. We could hear the beating of tins, and the smack of poles on water as they drove the fish into their nets. The Madan had a profound contempt for the Berbera and, except that they would eat with them, despised them hardly less than the Sabaeans who were at the very bottom of the social scale. Yet no tribesman ever suggested to me that the Berbera were of a different origin. The prejudice was solely against their occupation. At first sight this appeared to be illogical, since the Madan themselves caught fish. But the Berbers netted fish to make money, whereas the Madan speared fish for food. It was true that in recent years Madan had begun to sell fish, but this was a departure. In the past none of them would have sold fish any more than they would have sold milk. Now circumstances forced some of them to do both; for example, women of the nomad Feraigat sold milk and butter in Qalat Salih and Majar when they were camped near those towns. The original prejudice against the Berbera for selling fish had now become associated with their methods of catching them. A parallel would have been 'Damn it, sir, a gentleman may have to sell his pheasants, but he still doesn't shoot them sitting!'

There were no Berbera among the Fartus, Shaghanba or Feraigat, but there were many among the Al bu Muhammad and even more among the Azairij. Among the Bani Assad, at Kubaish, there were others who fished along the western edge of the Marshes, camping for months on a small island near Jasim al Faris's village. Buyers, known as *saffat*, bought their fish, salted it and transported it to Basra. The Berbera generally fished with seine nets, but I also saw them using drift nets on rivers and long fixed nets attached to *qasab* poles in flooded country outside the Marshes.

Occasionally boys from Majar al Kabir used cast nets on the banks of the river near that town but I never saw these nets anywhere else, except in Basra. The Suaid cultivators in the Eastern Marshes would sometimes set a piece of netting across a fast-flowing channel, and once I watched two of them fishing thigh-deep in a stream with a scoop net, shaped like a stretcher and of about the same size. Villagers living on the edge of rivers often erected small mats in the water below their houses, to provide a shelter from the current, and set up a number of reeds immediately downstream. When a fish lay up, it moved the reeds and thus gave itself away to the waiting spearman.

In spring, before the water rose, the Madan collected in parties of forty or fifty canoes. They swept up and down a lagoon, in line and some four or five yards apart, while the spearmen tried to impale the fish as they broke back under the canoes (Plate 92). In summer they speared fish at night by the light of reed torches. But poisoning fish with datura produced the best results.

As we paddled towards Abdullah's *mudhif* I told my companions that I had once seen a fish five feet long, caught in the Tigris near Kirkuk, and asked how big the *qatan* and *binni* ran in the Marshes.

'We catch them as long as my arm,' Yasin answered. 'A *shabut* is probably what you saw. They live in flowing water and some of them are more than twice as long as that. There is another fish even bigger, which we call *gessan*. It's like a giant *qatan* and is found under the floating islands. We swim under the island and catch it with our hands. We have a rope tied to one leg and the man in the canoe holds the other end. Once, somebody mistook the swimmer for the fish and speared him in the bottom and tried to lift him out of the water. We had to cut the prongs out with our daggers and we had an awful job, because he would not lie still.'

Shabut were barbel, and *gessan*, since they resembled *qatan*, were probably another kind of barbel.

'If God wills, this will be like the year of Al Binni,' Yasin remarked. 'There is even less water now than there was then. In two days I speared enough fish to fetch four dinars. By God, I would have made a fortune if Majid had not interfered.'

Hasan agreed. 'Yes, I went to Umm al Binni with my uncle two days before Majid closed the lake to everyone but the Berbera. I saw you there with some Fartus,' he said to me. 'You were all camped with the Berbera. I did not know you then, but you gave my companion medicine for his stomach.'

I remembered the occasion well. It was 1951, my first year in the Marshes. In the last week of November I and three Fartus had arrived at Al Aggar, to find the village practically deserted. The water was exceptionally low that year, but, as the result of rain in the north, had risen in the past few days and threatened to swamp the rice-fields that were being harvested. Most of the villagers were away trying to save their crop. Every other man and boy had gone to spear fish at Umm al Binni where we heard that phenomenal catches were being made. We went there too. The passage of many boats and canoes had driven a wide track through the heart of the reedbeds, and some of the *qasab* stems that lay trampled in the mud were as thick as my wrist. The water was shallow and sometimes we had difficulty in keeping even our canoe moving. Yet we met two large unwieldy *balams* loaded deep with fish, the crew of six laboriously dragging the boat along. Later I heard that the merchants were offering as much as a dinar a day each to the crew for this gruelling work.

Three hours after leaving Al Aggar we came to a small cleared space, where a merchant was camped under a rough shelter of mats. His name was Mullah Jabar and with two others he was buying fish for the Baghdad market. He had been there for six days, and advised us to spend the night since we could not hope to reach Umm al Binni before dark. He was paying three dinars for a hundred fish, irrespective of size, and was buying them in thousands. Recently, he said, the numbers had fallen off considerably. They sent the fish in *balams* to the mainland where lorries waited to take them to Baghdad, packed in ice. We slept beside his shelter on a heap of reeds that kept us out of the water. The mosquitoes were very bad, but the weather was cold and I buried myself in my blankets. Other parties on their way to Umm al Binni camped round us, sitting by their fires and singing late into the night. Three more *balams* passed in the dark and the merchant inspected their loads by the light of reed torches.

In the morning it took a further three hours' work to reach Umm al Bini. The lake proved to be about two miles long and a mile and a half across. It was encircled by almost impassable reedbeds and was hardly ever visited. The Berbera were camped on platforms of beaten-down reeds at the mouth of the track. Spare nets were stretched to dry in the sun and one or two boys remained on guard at each camping site. Their boats, about fifteen in all, were fishing on the lake and we paddled across to watch (Plate 93). The crews were in and out of the water the whole time and in most cases had taken off their shirts and worked naked. Using seine nets, with a diameter of roughly forty yards, they were making big hauls of barbel, nearly all *binni* (*Barbus sharpeyi*) averaging four pounds. One grizzled old man, who told us that his boat had been the first to reach the lake, said, 'All my life I have been fishing but never have I seen anything like this. In our first haul we took nine hundred. Truly, I never thought we would get them all in the boat. Now the fish are fewer.'

A couple of hundred canoes belonging to Fartus, Shaghanba, Feraigat and Al bu Muhammad skirmished round the edges of the lake. Each canoe had two occupants; one paddled, while the other stood in the bows and jabbed unceasingly in the weeds. Ordinarily Madan count themselves lucky if they take a dozen fish in a day, unless they are poisoning them. Here, however, they were getting one with every three or four stabs. These fish were mostly *qatan* (*Barbus xanthopterus*), another kind of barbel.

We joined a group of Fartus. They were wild with excitement as they plunged their spears into the water and lifted the shining fish into their canoes. 'You can't miss,' they shouted. 'They are lying one on top of the other.' They concentrated on one spot for a while, their canoes clustered together; then they would decide that somewhere else was better and race off, the spearmen urging the paddlers to hurry. When some Berbera came near, the Fartus left the lake's edge, swept down upon them, yelling, and drove their canoes over the top of the seine net to spear the fish inside. The Berbera shouted abuse but the tribesmen laughed and taunted them. Some of them must have complained to Majid for two days later he closed the lake to the Madan and only allowed the Berbera to fish there.

From Saigal, we went on in the *tarada* and stopped a few days with Jasim at Awaidiya. Normally at this season all the country between the western edge of the Marshes and the Gharraf was under at least four feet of flood, but in 1955, owing to the drought, we had to go south, almost to the Euphrates, to find enough water to float even a *tarada* outside the Marshes.

We stayed at Hamar, an Al bu Shama village among the palms on the lower Gharraf. Other sections of the same tribe lived in the Marshes as nomadic Madan, and we passed a group of them migrating to the cornlands, to graze their buffaloes on the stubble. On the Gharraf we also stayed with the Amaira. Part of the tribe lived at Mabrad and other Madan villages and earned money by selling boatloads of dry reeds at Suq ash Shuyukh. The neighbouring Fartus did the same, but more often went there with loads of mats.

In May, we had bright and sunny weather as a rule, but sometimes the sky was overcast for days on end, and there were three or four heavy rainstorms with thunder. In general the wind blew strongly from the north and west, filling the air with dust. With this wind, it was cool and pleasant, but without it the days were already hot and very sticky. We spent the month among the Al Juaibar, Al Hasan and other Muntifiq tribes, travelling along the Euphrates. We made constant excursions down side channels lined with willows, often reaching the verge of the Marshes to stay in *mudhifs* to which we had been invited. All this time we were in a land of palms, which grew in serried ranks on any ground that was not flooded annually, even on islets among the beds of bulrushes. The palms also covered the line of islands to the south, showing up dark against the shining waters of Haur as

Sanaf. The only signs of the disaster that had befallen these tribes the previous year were the flood marks clearly visible on the trunks of the palms and the walls of their *mudhifs*.

On the Tigris, the few date gardens were tangled jungles through which we had to force a way while hunting wild boar, but here the trees were carefully tended and each desquamated trunk rose from ground cleared for tillage. We visited the islands along the edge of Haur al Hamar, separated from the Marshes to the north by open water that, later in the season, would be covered with the flat leaves of the fringed water-lilies or *kaiba* (*Nymphoides peltata* and *indica*) and myriads of brilliant yellow and white flowers. In September I had seen buffaloes grazing belly-deep among these plants, thrusting their heads under water to pluck the trailing sprays. From a distance, they looked like cattle feeding in a meadow of buttercups. In autumn there would be other water-lilies (*Nymphaea caerulea*) in the Marshes, some white, others mauve.

The Muntifiq tribesmen did not live in villages but each separately on his own land. They were traditionally hospitable and there were almost as many *mudhifs* as dwelling-houses among the palms. Many had constructed small loopholed mud forts beside their houses, for they were also warlike and much addicted to blood feuds. Every man and boy wore a dagger and most possessed rifles with plenty of ammunition. Whenever there was a wedding, and there seemed to be one every night, the firing went on till almost dawn.

Sometimes our things were put in a *sarifa* before we were shown into the *mudhif*. A *sarifa* was a small rectangular building with trellis-work walls. The pitched roof, covered with matting, was supported on two reed pillars. Among the Muntifiq the ridge pole was usually the trunk of a small palm, but in the Marshes, where this type of building was favoured by the merchants as a store (Plate 104), it consisted of reed bundles. The entrance was in the side of the building. I was always glad when I could retire to a *sarifa* for a while, from the communal life of the *mudhif*. Even after years of living with Arabs, I found the complete lack of privacy very wearying. After a long morning, dealing with crowds of clamorous patients, I often felt exhausted, especially as the weather was getting hot. If my companions felt tired when they arrived at a *mudhif*, they would get up from their places as soon as they had drunk the formal cups of coffee, go to the other end of the room, wrap themselves in their cloaks and fall asleep. Their host would waken them when the meal was ready. This was a perfectly normal procedure, but I would have felt awkward doing the same. To be entirely by myself was more than I could hope for, but probably only my companions and two or three others would follow me to the *sarifa*, where I could get in a corner with a book, or doze.

Unlike the Tigris, where *mudhifs* were traditionally built with either nine or eleven arches, those on the Euphrates had more. The largest one I saw, though it had only fifteen arches, was eighty-four feet long, fifteen feet wide and fifteen high. Many had seventeen arches and I saw one with nineteen, which measured sixty-nine feet in length, and fifteen in width, but which was only twelve feet high, having been shortened. The *mudhifs* on the Tigris were usually eighteen feet wide and eighteen feet high, whereas on the Euphrates fifteen feet was the normal width and height. There, if a *mudhif* showed signs of collapsing, the owner and his friends reduced its height by the following method. They first dug a trench outside up to the base of an arch, to uncover the two feet of the reed bundle in the ground, and, fastening ropes round the base, pulled it into the trench. They then cleared out the hole, cut off the bottom two feet of the bundle, allowed it to sink back into place, and filled in the trench. The process was repeated with each arch, first on one side and then on the other.

On the Euphrates a *mudhif* could be cut down twice, but the practice was unknown on the Tigris where suitable reeds were easier to come by and where a *mudhif* was always entirely rebuilt. Normally a *mudhif* needed rebuilding every ten years, but the length of time depended on the state of the ground and, under good conditions, it might last fifteen years. To construct a large one took a hundred men twenty days. Only the master builder was paid. The workmen expected a large meal at midday, and that the owner would slaughter an animal each day to provide them with meat. The core of each bundle to form the arches consisted of reeds which had been used before and which made the bundle more pliable. The surface was then covered with a casing of thin reeds to give a smooth finish. In the Muntifiq country, the available reeds were too short for the full height of an arch and were therefore married. In consequence the arches tended to be elongated (Plate 99) instead of horse-shoe shaped, and could not be subjected to the same strain as among the Al bu Muhammad, who used single lengths of reed. It was customary, when a *mudhif* was finished, to mark each pillar with a hand dipped in henna. The imprint was often renewed for a festival. At the New Year, or *Nai Ruz*, they adorned the pillars with small bunches of green reeds.

Among the Al bu Muhammad, the Azairij and the other tribes on the Tigris, *mudhifs* varied little in general appearance. The roof, as with all *mudhifs*, was made of overlapping mats – and on one the bottom layer consisted of a single huge mat that covered the entire roof. The lower walls consisted of single mats that hung down like flaps to the ground behind the arches and could be propped up in hot weather and lowered in cold. The south-western end, facing Mecca, had three open entrances between the great pillars, with windows sometimes cut in the matting above them. The north-eastern end was a blank wall.

Among the tribes on the Euphrates, the design of the *mudhifs* was more elaborate and more varied. The whole length of the lower walls consisted of a reed lattice, attached to the outside of the arches and joined by a strip of matting to the roof. In front of this lattice on the inside was a guard rail, less than a foot high, for the occupants to lean against. In the centre of the south-west end, there was invariably a pointed arch entrance, surrounded by lattice windows (Plates 97 and 98). The design of the north-east end was the same, but usually without an entrance. The arrangement and pattern of the lattice windows varied with the fancy of each builder. Above the entrance there was generally a lattice of the same size and shape as the doorway, flanked by two smaller lancet windows. In one *mudhif*, a single circular window alone pierced the blank upper half of the wall. In this case the wall's lower half was horizontally divided in three, with a blank section of matting between the upper and lower lattices, the whole being vertically divided by two central pillars (Plate 101).

Sitting in the Euphrates *mudhifs*, I always had the impression of being inside a Romanesque or Gothic cathedral, an illusion enhanced by the ribbed roof and the traceried windows at either end, through which bright shafts of light came to penetrate the gloom of the interior. Both on the Euphrates and on the Tigris the *mudhifs* represented an extraordinary architectural achievement with the simplest possible materials; the effect of enrichment, given by the reed patterns, came entirely from functional methods of construction. Historically, too, they were important. Long familiarity with houses such as these may well have given man the idea of imitating their arched form in mud bricks, as the Greeks later perpetuated wooden techniques in stone. Buildings similar to these *mudhifs* have been part of the scene in Southern Iraq for five thousand years and more. Probably within the next twenty years, certainly within the next fifty, they will have disappeared for ever.

24. Amara's Blood Feud

Every year I spent June, and often July, among the tribes along the Tigris north of Amara, and twice I followed the river almost as far as Kut. Except in 1954, when we passed through this country in our *tarada*, crossing the flooded desert from Saigal, only Amara and Sabaiti accompanied me. We always travelled on horseback, our hosts lending us horses to the next village or encampment. Neither of them had ridden before and, the first time they mounted, their horses walked off in opposite directions, but with practice they became reasonably proficient. As I was hopeless in a canoe, it pleased me to be able to show off on a horse, though we went mostly at a walk for we carried my medicine in our saddle-bags. By midday it could be almost unendurably hot, but in June it was still chilly at night and I was glad of two blankets. The north-west wind blew, often with gale force all through the month, and there were dust storms when it was impossible to see a couple of yards. In July the wind died away and then, even at night, there was no relief from the humid heat, which could reach 126° F. in the shade.

Of my four regular companions, Amara and Sabaiti were my favourites, and, away from their fellow tribesmen and the familiar setting of the Marshes, the three of us were drawn still closer together on these expeditions. By 1956, I found myself becoming more and more involved in their affairs. Yasin and Hasan had married the year before. Now Amara and Sabaiti were engaged. They said they would only marry after I had left, as they wished to be with me till then. Having agreed with a publisher to write a book about Southern Arabia, I could not be back the following year.

Amara was engaged to Sabaiti's sister, and five months earlier, on his behalf, Sahain and I had gone to Lazim, Sabaiti's father.

Lazim's brother also had to be consulted for, by custom, his son had prior claim to the girl, and he had only agreed to Amara's engagement after endless discussion. We fixed the bride price at 75 dinars. Both Amara and Sabaiti were delighted and, that evening at Bu Mughaifat, we had celebrated the occasion with dance and song and the firing of rifles.

That year, as always, our journeying had no goal. We knew we should be welcome in any of the small villages ahead for as long as we rode north. We stopped where we wished, turned back when we felt inclined. The Al bu Daraj, an agreeable tribe who grew rice along streams that dispersed into an isolated marsh, entertained us for a while. From them we borrowed canoes to visit the nomadic Kaulaba and Aqail who grazed their buffaloes among the dwarf *qasab* or in patches of inundated thorn scrub. We rode on again past the rice-fields of the Al bu Ali, a section of the Al bu Muhammad who followed Haji Sulaiman north after the battle with Majid. Then we reached the Bani Lam.

The muddy river flowed through a dusty landscape and an orange sun rose and set on a flat horizon across an empty plain. Only at dawn, near the tomb of Ali al Gharbi, could I occasionally see the faint outline of the Pusht-i-Kut. Some of the time we slept among shepherds in small black tents, where sheep and goats trampled us and flies swarmed over us from dawn till dusk. But I always enjoyed being with these nomads and there was magic in the evenings when herdsboys played their pipes sitting round flickering fires. At other times we unsaddled in scattered villages along the river bank where the many small sheikhs proved excellent hosts and congenial companions. Outside at noon, the wind struck with a scorching heat, but the small mud houses were deliciously cool inside, for the windows were covered with thorn-bush mats, kept drenched with water.

This stark land gave me the same feeling of freedom that I had known so strongly in the desert. There was the same endless empty space, and even the few houses contained only the bare necessities of life. There was much medical work, which was always interesting and often gave me a definite sense of achievement. I liked the Bani Lam too, many of whom, after my previous visits, had become my friends.

Several times we saw wolves and one man told us that he had

ridden down and killed a hyena. It takes a good horse to catch a hyena as I had learnt twenty years earlier in the Sudan. Another man told me how he and his friends had dug out a honey-badger. It attacked and severely bit two of them, seeming impervious to their blows until someone hit it on the snout. We occasionally saw wild cat, one of which was a ginger colour, quite different from the others. There were no gazelle, but plenty to the east along the Persian frontier, where they were unfortunately being decimated by parties that chased them in cars. By law this practice was forbidden; in fact, Government officials were often the culprits. Riding down that way from Kurdistan, I had seen herds of fifty and more gazelles, but soon they would all be wiped out in Iraq, as the onager and the lion had been before them.

We ourselves only hunted pig, which abounded in the tamarisk scrub along the water-courses, as well as in the matted carpets of salt bush, three feet high, that covered whole acres beside the Tigris. This would have been ideal country for pig-sticking, but I had no spear and made do with my rifle, firing it like a pistol with one hand as I rode alongside. I enjoyed the exhilarating gallops, but otherwise I was sick of slaughtering pig and, when we hunted them on foot, let Amara shoot. He seldom missed. He had already won a reputation as a crack shot which was soon to stand him in good stead.

Returning to Majar at the end of June, we were greeted by the news that Amara's cousin Badai had killed one of Radhawi's sons, a brother of the same Hasan who had coveted Badai's wife and had tried to break up the marriage. I recalled the day we had spent with Badai on Auaisij three years earlier, and how Amara had then gone to Radhawi to try and effect a settlement. Now blood had been spilt.

Amara had already told me that, earlier in the year, Badai's wife had left him and gone back to her father. A man could divorce his wife by just saying 'I divorce you,' but, if so, he did not normally get back the bride price. A wife, on the other hand, could not divorce her husband. She could, however, run away and seek refuge with her father or brother. If she remained obdurate, they would try to induce the husband to divorce her by offering to return part or all of the bride price. In this case,

Badai refused to divorce his wife so that she could marry Hasan, and blamed him entirely for the trouble between them.

We now learnt that, while Badai was camped on a canal near the Wadiya, Hasan, his younger brother Khalaf and one of his cousins had gone there intending to kill him. Their own camp, the usual collection of mat shelters, was some distance off, near Qalat Salih. Badai happened to be away searching for a stolen buffalo, so they lay up, waiting for his return. He came back on the third day. They approached his shelter late that night, but were seen and challenged by one of his neighbours who called out, 'Why do you come every night looking for Badai? He hasn't killed anyone in your family,' and fired a shot over them. As they made off, Badai's dog rushed out and chased them, followed shortly by Badai himself. Guided by the dog's barking, he caught up with them as they stopped to light a cigarette, and heard Hasan say, 'Let's shoot his dog anyway.' Badai then fired and missed, and the three of them scattered and ran. He fired again and one of them dropped. Approaching the fallen man, he recognized Khalaf, who was wounded in the thigh, the bone being shattered. 'You want blood? Then you can have it!' he said, and shot him again through the head.

Meanwhile Hasan and his cousin joined up, discovered that Khalaf was missing, went back to look for him, and eventually found his body. Bent on immediate vengeance, they hurried to Badai's encampment. Standing on the canal bank opposite, Hasan shouted a challenge and Badai took it up. The moon had set and it was now very dark. Neither was prepared to put himself at the other's mercy by wading across the canal so they fired at each other's rifle-flashes. Before dawn, neighbouring Feraigat prevailed on Hasan to withdraw, saying the sheikh would arrest him if he was still there in the morning and the Government would certainly imprison him until his father, who was already wanted on two charges of murder, gave himself up. Hasan and his cousin carried away Khalaf's body. Badai himself had been slightly wounded, but he pulled down his house at first light, loaded everything into his boat and disappeared with his family and animals into the Marshes. No one knew where he had gone.

When we heard the news, Amara looked grave. I tended to dismiss it as only another killing among these lawless nomads, until

Sabaiti said, 'Don't you realize that Amara is Badai's nearest relation and that Radhawi and his family may now try to kill him?'

I planned to spend three months in Nuristan, that wild little-known area of mountains on the borders of Chitral, and was due to leave for Afghanistan in ten days. Before going, I had to do what I could to ensure Amara's safety. We went straight to Rufaiya, to Amara's family. I asked Thuqub if he and Reshiq were also in danger. He said, 'No. But if Radhawi can't kill Badai, he will certainly try to kill Amara.' He suggested that I should ask Majid to arrange an *atwa*, or truce, for Amara. 'If only you can get an *atwa* for six months, Radhawi may have cooled down. Later it might be possible to get him to accept blood money.' I agreed to go to Majid in the morning and see what I could do.

I knew that no sheikh, however powerful, and no *Sayid*, however revered, could finally settle a blood feud. Only the *qalit*, or headman, could seal the pact by binding the headcloth round the reed and handing one end to either party. His position was heredi-tary, even if he was senile or half-witted. Only if he was a child could his nearest male relation act in his stead. I asked Thuqub whether Sahain, who was the *qalit* of the section of Feraigat con-cerned, would need to come with us in order to conduct the negotiations for the truce, provided we could get in touch with Radhawi. He assured me, however, that an *atwa* could be made by a sheikh or anyone else without the presence of the *qalit*.

I lent Amara my pistol, and advised him to get a good watch-dog and to change his place in the house each night. He also had the ·275 I had given him two years earlier and plenty of ammuni-tion. Recently he had bought a rifle for Reshiq which, though old, was as good as most. As we were going to bed Thuqub said, 'I will keep watch. I am an old man now and I need very little sleep. I can rest during the day.' Reshiq said laughingly, 'Shoot us a wolf, Sahib, and give us one of its eyes. We will sew it on a skull-cap and whoever wears it will not go to sleep.'

We took no chance that night. I lay down between young Hasan and Amara, with Reshiq beyond him. Amara and I had our loaded rifles by our sides. Their old father sat in the doorway with Reshiq's rifle across his knees. At the end of the room

Matara sang quietly to herself as she tidied things away. The smallest child was fretful and Naga, the mother, picked him up and nursed him by the fire. From where I was I could see the tethered buffaloes, a respectable-sized herd, feeding in the moonlight on the shoots that Chilaib had gathered for them in the marsh. Hasan pressed my hand as a sign that he was glad I was back. Earlier he had fetched the satchel I had given him to show me his books. Up to now, everything had been going well for Amara's family. Reshiq had sown more land than ever before and the previous year had harvested a good crop in spite of the shortage of water. Now, through no fault of theirs, a man with a loaded rifle might be skulking in the shadows outside, waiting his chance. Unless I could arrange an *atwa* they would hardly dare to sleep. Even tonight, Amara lifted his head every time a dog barked in the village.

25. My Last Year in the Marshes

Early next morning I went to see Majid at the new house he had built near Majar. He sent me in a car with his personal representative and a letter to the sheikh on whose land Radhawi was camped, near Qalat Salih. I asked the sheikh to secure me a year's truce for Thuqub and his family.

'Radhawi is wild with grief and rage. I do not think he will agree to an *atwa* at all. He certainly won't if you include Badai,' he said.

'Badai must look after himself; he does not concern me. I want an *atwa* for Thuqub's family.'

'I will do my best but I do not think we shall succeed. Stay here in the *mudhif* and I will go there with Majid's representative.'

I sent Sabaiti with them to represent me. They were away for hours and I began to fear that they had failed. The coffee-maker was not encouraging. 'Radhawi will never agree to an *atwa*. He has sworn that he will have blood for blood. By God, there is no good in any of that family.'

But at last they came back with the news that, after endless arguments, they had succeeded in persuading Radhawi to grant a truce for six months to Amara, his father and his brothers. I had never hoped for more.

Three months later, in September 1956, I stopped off for a fortnight in the Marshes on my way back from Nuristan and stayed for several days at Rufaiya. Amara had married Sabaiti's sister but was still living with his parents, as was usual. His wife, a slim gentle girl with large dark eyes, had already endeared herself to his family, and she and Matara were inseparable. As we watched her going to the stream to fetch water, old Thuqub said to me one day, 'The praise be to God, my son has got a good wife. But for your kindness he would have been too poor to marry for

many years. I would like to thank you for what you have done
for us.'

I was not free to return to Iraq again until the beginning of
1958. As we flew in, I could see the Marshes below and looked
forward eagerly to the next six months. Amara and Sabaiti met
me at the airport in Basra and hurried forward to embrace me as
I came through the customs. I asked after their families and my
other friends, and to each inquiry they gave me the formal answer,
'He sends his salutations.' Sabaiti, who by now was also married,
seemed unchanged, but I at once sensed a difference in Amara. He
was more mature and strangely reserved.

It was not till we reached the Consulate that Sabaiti took me
aside and told me that both Amara's father and wife were dead.
I asked immediately if Radhawi had killed Thuqub, but Sabaiti
said he had died in the summer of a sickness of the stomach,
following a long illness and much pain. From what Amara later
told me, I had little doubt that it was cancer. 'If you had been
with us, Sahib, you could have given him medicine to stop the
pain. I could do nothing and he was my father.' A fortnight after
Thuqub's death, Amara's wife had gone to her father's house for
the birth of her child, according to custom. She had died a few
minutes after it was born. The child, a boy, was alive, but ailing.
Amara told me that his mother, who had had a baby herself two
years earlier, was suckling him, 'but she has little milk left and all
our buffaloes are dry at present.'

Having consulted various people in Basra, we bought Farex
and other baby foods to take with us, but, when we reached
Rufaiya, we had some trouble persuading Naga to use them.
'They may be all right for sheikhs' sons, but the proper food for
our children is rice paste, and, if there is no milk, water with a
little silt in it from the river.' We enlisted Matara's support. She
was devoted to the baby and undertook to feed him as we
directed. The child certainly put on weight as the result of this
new diet. He had looked half starved when I first saw him, and I
am sure he was. Once he gave us a bad fright. We had been away
for two months in our *tarada* and arrived back to find him suffering from violent diarrhoea and vomiting. Amara was sure his
son was dying, but I gave him a penicillin injection and the next
morning he was all right.

Hasan had joined us at Bu Mughaifat, bringing his cousin Kathir to replace Yasin who was settled down with his family. We revisited nearly all the villages and I was much moved to find how glad people were to see me back. Many said, 'We thought our doctor had left us and gone to live in his own country. God preserve you, Sahib, now you are here again we shall be all right.' And I felt more than rewarded for all the exasperation, frustration and weariness that they had so often caused me. Government officials might still think I was a spy, though it was difficult to imagine what military secrets I could be unearthing in the Marshes. But the villagers, who had come to rely on me, knew that I was simply there to enjoy myself, and help them if I could.

The blood feud still threatened. Several times I was warned that Radhawi had given up trying to kill Badai and meant to get Amara instead. Our party was too well-armed and we had too formidable a reputation as marksmen for Radhawi and his family to try and kill him while we were together, but I feared what they might do after I had left. Badai was safe among the Fartus in the west, where Radhawi would be instantly noticed as a stranger. But at Rufaiya, within an hour or two of Radhawi's camp, Amara was very vulnerable and I was convinced that sooner or later Radhawi would strike. I suggested that Amara should move to Saigal, but, as I expected, he refused. 'I won't be driven into hiding. If Badai prefers to lie up among the Fartus, that is his affair. I am staying here, where my friends are and where Reshiq has his land. I have my rifle and you have lent me your pistol. I don't want trouble; Thuqub's family only want to live in peace. But if Radhawi comes looking for me, I shall kill him.'

Sayid Sarwat himself had gone in vain to Radhawi, to ask him to accept blood money. In fact he had been so provoked by Radhawi that he had struck him with his cane. I was determined to find Radhawi myself and force him to give Amara and his brothers another truce, this time for a year. That would see them through until I was back again.

The trouble was to locate Radhawi. Twice we went to look for him and each time our information was wrong. Then, at the end of May, we heard that he was near Azair, on the land of an Al bu Muhammad sheikh called Shinta. We arrived there in the afternoon and found Shinta, an elderly man, in his *mudhif*. After the usual formalities I said, 'I have come to get an *atwa* for Amara from Radhawi. I want him brought here now to this *mudhif*.'

'Where is he?' asked Shinta, feigning ignorance.

'Over there in those houses on the edge of the dry ground.'

Shinta called one of his men. 'Go to Radhawi and tell him I want him. Bring him back with you.'

We waited on the grass outside in the shadow of the *mudhif*, for the weather was very hot. Half an hour later the messenger returned alone.

'Radhawi refuses to come.'

I looked at Shinta who shrugged and said, 'What more can I do, if he won't come? Tomorrow, I will order him off my land.' He quite obviously had no intention of helping us.

'What good is that to me?' I said angrily. 'Sabaiti, Hasan, Kathir, come on, we will go and fetch him ourselves,' and I picked up my rifle.

Shinta got hurriedly to his feet, 'Don't go, Sahib, Radhawi is a bad man.'

'If you do not bring him here, I will.'

'No, I and my son will go. You and your companions stay here.'

Followed by a crowd of his retainers, Shinta went towards the distant houses. An hour passed, then two, and it was getting late. At last we saw them coming back. When they were close, Amara said quietly, 'Radhawi and his son are with them.'

We stood up and exchanged greetings. Radhawi and his party sat down opposite us. He was a small scrawny man with a wisp of beard and ruthless eyes. Hasan, his son, aged about twenty, was thickset and surly. Eight other Feraigat were with them. All were unarmed except for their daggers, but I was taking no chances and laid my pistol on the mat beside me.

'Sahib, this is Radhawi,' Shinta began. 'He has come because he hears you wish to speak to him.'

'I want an *atwa* for two years for Amara and his brothers. I am not concerned with Badai,' I said.

'Never. I will give no further *atwa*,' Radhawi answered flatly.

'For *two* years,' I repeated, never taking my eyes off him.

'Never!'

We watched each other in silence and no one spoke.

'We are asking for an *atwa* only for Thuqub's family,' Sabaiti said at length.

'Never, for no one, now or ever.'

Again we sat in silence. Beside me, Amara played with his beads. A file of buffaloes went past, coming home from the marsh. The sun was setting and the sky was a blaze of colour. Mosquitoes buzzed round us.

'Never!' Radhawi repeated.

I learnt forward. 'Listen, Radhawi, and listen carefully. Either you give me an *atwa* now, or I go in the morning to see the Government. You are already wanted on two charges of murder. If you are arrested you will spend the rest of your life in prison. Hasan, your son, helped you in the last killing and he will be arrested too.'

I paused, then went on, 'I will offer a reward of one hundred dinars for your arrest. Every policeman in the Province, and a lot of other people too, will be looking for you both. Make up your mind for, by God, Radhawi, I mean what I say. I swear it on my life. And, what is more, if you *had* killed Amara while I was away, I would have made sure that you were killed too, whatever it cost me.'

I sat back. After a few moments, a grey-bearded Feraigat who was with Radhawi, said to him, 'Come, let us go apart and talk it over.'

All of them withdrew a hundred yards and sat down. I could hear their murmuring, then Radhawi's curiously shrill voice raised in anger. Dusk had fallen and a servant brought a lamp. Shinta told him to fetch coffee. An hour later the Feraigat rejoined us. The grey-bearded man spoke.

'Radhawi is a good man. He and his son have agreed to give the house of Thuqub an *atwa* for one year. It is not the custom to give an *atwa* for longer. As for Badai, Radhawi will grant him no *atwa*, now or ever.'

Shinta urged me, 'Take it, Sahib. In truth, it is not tribal custom to give an *atwa* for longer than a year. When the time is up, you can renew it. Take it, Sahib.'

'Who will guarantee it? I want four men from different tribes.'

'I will arrange that,' Shinta said.

I consulted the others and said, 'All right, then we accept.'

When the formalities were completed, the Feraigat departed and Shinta sent for dinner. I was leaving for London shortly, still having six months' work to do on my book, before I would be free to return. Now at least I could go with an easy mind. Though I did not then know it, I was not to see or hear of Amara again.

Amara and Sabaiti saw me off from Basra. My plane left at midnight and we waited in the Airport Hotel. On the wall opposite, a tattered poster depicted a spry young man being served with a meal by an exotic air hostess. Underneath was written: 'See the world from an arm-chair.' The plane landed and, while it was re-fuelled, a crowd of weary passengers were shown into the room and settled down resignedly. A waiter handed them Coca-Cola. They had left that morning or the night before from Bangkok or Sydney. Now I was joining them and in eight hours would be in London. Time enough to travel from Qabab to Qurna and have lunch with the Al bu Bakhit on the way.

The loudspeaker erupted. I could make out odd words, 'Passengers ... BOAC, flight number ... Rome ... London ... passports ... passport control.' There was a general stir. I got up and collected my things. 'I must go now,' I told my companions.

Amara and Sabaiti kissed me farewell and Amara said, 'Come back soon.'

'Next year, if God wills,' I replied, and joined the queue.

Three weeks later I was having tea with friends in Ireland. Someone entered the room. 'Did you hear the four o'clock news? There has been a revolution in Baghdad and the Royal family have been murdered. The mob burnt the British Embassy ...'

I realized that I should never be allowed back, and that another chapter in my life had closed.

Glossary

AFA	a mythical serpent believed by the Marshmen to live in the Marshes.
ANFISH	another mythical serpent reputed to inhabit the Marshes.
ARAQ	a distilled liquor.
ATWA	a temporary truce agreed to by both parties in a blood feud.
BALAM	a flat-bottomed carvel-built boat generally about thirty-five feet long, usually punted but sometimes sailed.
BERBERA	professional fishermen who use nets. Despised by the tribesmen.
DIBIN	a KIBASHA with one or more coverings of earth.
DINAR	the equivalent of £1 in Iraqi currency.
DIWANIYA	a brick-built guest house used for entertaining Europeans and Iraqi officials.
FALLAH	a cultivator.
FASL	compensation or blood money.
FATHA	the opening verse of the Koran, also the mourning following a burial.
FIJIRIA	one of the other women handed over in settlement of a blood feud in addition to the TALAWI.
FILS	a thousandth part of a DINAR.
HASHISH	green newly cut fodder for buffaloes or other animals.
HAUSA	a tribal war dance.
HUFAIDH	a legendary island in the Marshes.
JALLABA	a merchant who travels round the villages buying buffaloes.

KABAB	small pieces of meat grilled on a skewer.
KAULAN	a sedge (*Scirpus brachyceras*). The predominant vegetation in areas of temporary inundation.
KHASARA	acute pains due to stone.
KIBASHA	a soggy platform made from reeds and rushes and used as the foundation of a house in the Marshes.
MADAN	the Marshmen.
MAHAIBIS	'Hunt-the-ring'. A favourite game played in the evenings.
MASHUF	the generic name for all types of canoe except a TARADA
MATAUR	a small single-man canoe used for wild-fowling.
MUDHIF	a barrel-vaulted guest house built of reeds and matting.
MUDIR	a Government official administering a NAHYIA, the smallest administrative unit in a province.
QALIT	a hereditary headman. Some tribes, for instance the Shaghanba, have one QALIT for the whole tribe; others, for instance the Feraigat, have one for each section.
QASAB	*Phragmites communis*, a giant reed growing to a height of twenty-five feet.
QUFFA	a circular coracle used on the Tigris.
RABA	a dwelling house with an entrance at either end, part of which is used as a regular guest house.
RAMADHAN	the Moslem month of the fast.
SARIFA	a building of reeds and mats which has the roof supported by a ridge pole.
SAYID	a descendant of the Prophet.
SITRA	a reed-built extension to a house in which the nomadic Madan shelter their buffaloes in winter.
TALAWI	a virgin of marriageable age handed over in part settlement of a blood feud.
TARADA	a sheikh's canoe, often thirty-five feet long. Distinguished by rows of decorative flat-topped nails along the inner planking.
TUHUI	a floating island of vegetation.

ZAIMA   a coracle made of QASAB and coated outside with bitumen.

ZAIR   a man who has made the pilgrimage to the tomb of the eighth Imam at Meshed in Persia. A woman who has made this pilgrimage is known as a ZAIRA.

Index

Abbas, cousin of Falih bin Majid, 139, 142–3; accidentally shoots Falih, 143–4; goes to the police for protection, 151

Abbasid Caliphate, the, 95, 100

Abd al Wahid, Son of Falih bin Majid, 27, 29, 143–4, 152, 182

Abd ar Ridha, 34, 138, 140, 141, 150, 182

Abdullah, uncle of Maziad, 120–21, 200

Abu Bakr, Caliph, 51, 52

Abu Laila, 158, 159

Abu Shajar, 82, 83 ff.

Abud, of the Al bu Abud, 74

Abyssinia, 59

Adil, River, 132, 193

Afa, the (a monster), 118

Afara, mother of Hasan, 183–4

Afghanistan, 213

Ahwaz, ninth-century capture of, 100

Ajram, 49, 54, 65–6, 67, 130, 131; duck-shooting, 76; refuses to accompany Thesiger across the Marshes, 78

Al Aggar, 84, 123–9, 153, 202; rice crops in, 175; the Shaghanba leave after quarrel with Majid, 196

Al bu Abud, the, 74

Al bu Ali, the, 210

Al bu Bakhit, the, 155, 156–7

Al bu Daraj, the, 210

Al bu Ghanam, the, 156, 161

Al bu Muhammad, the, 25, 68, 100, 120, 121, 124, 157, 166, 186; comparison with Bedu of Arabia, 28; origins of, 74; meanness of some sheiks, 169; migrations to Baghdad and Basra, 194–5; Berbera among, ·201; *mudhifs*, among, 207

Al bu Salih, the, 22, 192, 196

Al bu Shama, the, 204

Al Essa, the, 21, 22, 138, 192, 194, 196; fighting with the Fartus, 118–9

Al Hasan, the, 204

Al Juaibar, the, 191, 204

Al Madina, 95

Alexander the Great, 97

Ali, Caliph, 52–4, 95

Ali ar Ridha, 8th Imam, 55

Ali ibn Muhammad, 100

Alwan, 81–2

Amaira, the reed-selling by, 204

Amara, of the Feraigat: joins Thesiger as canoeboy, 136, 137–8, 139; sadness at Falih's death, 155; tries to effect reconciliation between Badai and Hasan, 160; pig-shooting, 168; his ability as a shot, 169; moodiness, 170; invites Thesiger to stay with his

Amara – *contd*
family, 172 ff.; at Dakhil's wedding, 178; meets Thesiger on his return to Basra (1954), 182; again invites him home, 182–3; presented with gun, 190; engaged to Sabaiti's sister, 209–10; marries her, 215; his bloodfeud, 213–14; six months' truce arranged, 215; again meets Thesiger at Basra (1958), 216; loses father and mother, 216; sees Thesiger off from Basra for last time after further truce, 220

Amara Province, 134; rice-growing in, 175; migrations from to Baghdad and Basra, 194

Amara (town), 25, 43, 110, 115, 167, 209

Amorites, the, 94

Anatolia, 94

Anfish, the (a monster), 118

Animal life, 210–11. *See also* Buffaloes, *and* Pig-shooting

Anopheles pulcherrimus, 109

Anopheles stephensi, 109

Aqail, the, 210

Arabia, warring tribes in, 52

Arabs: hospitality of, 71; overrun Iraq (seventh century), 95; later immigration by, from neighbouring deserts, 97; difficulties of wearing their clothes, 158. *See also under* Madan, *and names of individual tribes*.

Arbid, the (a snake), 117

Archaeological objects of interest, 84

Assad. *See* Bani Assad

Assyrians, rise and fall of, 94

Auaisij, 158, 172, 187, 189

Auda, Son of Sadam, 49

Awaidiya, 113, 121, 191, 192, 204

Azair, 155–6, 172, 190

Azairij, the, 115, 121, 138, 175, 193–4; migrations to Baghdad and Basra, 194–5; Berbera among, 201; *mudhifs* among, 207

Azizah, 169

Babylon, rise and fall of, 94

Badai, cousin of Amara, 160; kills Khalaf, 212; escapes Radhawi, 217

Badr, 114–15

Baghdad, 32, 148, 155; becomes capital of Iraq, 95; capture of (1258), 95–6; sacking of (1401), 96; in danger from floods (1954), 190; rebuilding and reconstruction in, 194; migration to, 194–5; slums in, 197; revolution in, 220

Baidhal al Nuafil, 156

Bait Makenzie family, 183–4

Balam, 47

Bani Assad, the, 100, 104, 201

Bani Lam, the, 22, 100, 189, 210

Bani Malik, the, 100

Bani Umair, the, 100

Barbus sharpeyi. See Binni

Barbus xanthopterus. See Qatan

Basra, 150, 155, 190; story of Madan youths in, 71–2; sacking of (ninth century), 100; oil-fields, 194; migrations to, 194; slums in, 197

Bats, in the *mudhifs*, 123

Bazun, the, 19, 22, 192

Beads, habit of playing with, 82

Bedu, the, of Arabia, 28; comparison of eating habits with the Madan, 50; interbreeding among, 97–8; their life and character, 98–100

Berbera, the, 92; as fishermen, 200, 203

Bilharzia, 85

Binni, 91, 201, 203

Birdi. See Bulrushes

Bird life in the Marshes, 157, 162-3, 200. *See also* Duck-shooting

Blood money, 73-4

Bu Mughaifat, 57, 64 ff., 70, 128, 131, 132, 153, 183

Buffaloes: the milking of, 67; use of, to make tracks through reeds, 70; grazing of, 70; freedom of movement for, 89; eating of pitch on canoes by, 126; among the Madan, 158-9; their shelters (sitra), 160

Bulrushes, 171; the eating of shoots of, 162

Butaira, River, 193

Byron, Robert, 55

Cassites, the, 94

Chahla, River, 166; estuary, 158, 161; villages on, 166; floods, 189

Chaldeans, the, 94, 99

Chilaib, brother of Amara, 173-4

Chitral, 213

Circumcision, operation of, 105-7, 136

Coot, shooting of, 80

Cormorant, as food, 114

Cyperus rotundus, 70

Cyrus the Great, 94

Dair, a canoeman, 143-8, 151, 155; leaves his village, 182

Damascus, 95; Omaiyad Caliphate of, 52

Darius, 97

Daub, 130, 184

Daub, cousin of Falih bin Jasim, 114, 115-16, 117, 129; accompanies Thesiger, 120; sets out to avenge father's murder, 122

Dhakar binta, 46, 125

Dibin, 161-3; blind and paralysed boys in, 164

Dibin, 75

Dima, 80, 187

Ditchburn, 61

Duck-shooting, 76, 80, 114

Dukhainat, the, 186

Edmonds, 61

Education, effect of on boys from the tribes, 176-7, 195

Elam, 94

Empty Quarter, the 30

Euphrates, River, 32, 126, 190, 204; early settlements in delta, 94; rice-growing beside, 175; *mudhifs* on, 206-8

Ezra, tomb of, 155

Falaij, of the Al Essa, 119, 120

Falih. *See* Falih bin Majid

Falih bin Jasim, 113-15, 118-19; as guide to Thesiger, 191; returns home, 192

Falih bin Majid, Sheikh of the Al bu Muhammad, 25-6; his judicial powers, 28; his hospitality, 27, 29, 32-3; 142; pig-shooting, 34 ff.; visits paid to, by Thesiger, 135-6; his popularity, 136; has *tarada* built for Thesiger, 137; dislike of town life, 138-9; his death, 143-8; mourning for him, 150-54; his reputation, 155; tactics when ordered to produce conscripts, 198-9

Fallah, the, 68

Fartus, the, 68, 114, 121, 201; fighting with the Al Essa, 118–19; their country, 111 ff.; fish-spearing by, 203–4; mat selling, 204

Fasl. See Blood money

Fatha, the, 180, 184

Feraigat, the, 68, 186, 201, 218

Fijiria, the, 73

Fodder. *See* Hashish

Fowlers, netting of birds by, 162–3

Fuhud, evacuation of market due to floods, 192

Fulanain: *Haji Rikkan: Marsh Arab*, 58

Gallinule, as food, 115

Geese, wild, in the Marshes, 162–3

Gessan, 201, 202

Gharraf, River, 8; in flood, 191, 192

Greeks, Ancient, 95

Grimley, 60

Gutti, the, 94

Hafadh, brother of Sahain, 73, 131

Hailstorms, damage done by, 186–7

Haji Hamaid, the boat-builder, 127, 182, 186

Haji Sulaiman: feud with Majid, 165, 180–81, 210

Haliki, the, 186

Hamar, 204; floods in, 191

Hamud, father of Hatab, 147

Hasan, son of Caliph Ali, 52, 53

Hasan, of the Feraigat, canoeboy, 131, 132, 134, 135, 137, 138, 139, 170, 173; lack of skill as wildfowler, 157; as a cook, 163;

pig-shooting, 168, 169; at Dakhil's wedding, 178; reunion with Thesiger, 184; presented with shotgun, 190; marriage, 209

Hasan bin Radhawi, 160, 211

Hasan bin Thuqub, brother of Amara, 175–6, 213–14; sent to school, 176

Hashim, father of Daud, 121; release from prison, 121; murder, 122

Hashish, 45, 48, 57, 78, 79

Hatab, cousin of Falih, 147

Haur al Hamar, 205

Hawaiza Marshes, 162

Hazaras, the, of Central Afghanistan, 55

Hedgecock, S. E. *See* Fulanain

Helu, 79, 130

Hit, pitch from, 126

Hittites, the, 94, 99

Holly-leaved Naiad. *See Najas marina*

Hufaidh, 23, 84–5

Hulagu, capture of Baghdad by, 95

Husain, father of Ajram, 64–5, 131

Husain, Son of Caliph Ali, 53; martyrdom of, 53, 95

Huwair, 127, 182, 184, 185

Hyenas, striped, 156

Iraq: weapons in, 37; changes in, 58–9; early history, 94 ff.; destruction of irrigation system, 96; becomes pastoral country, 97; system of local government in, 103; nature of officials, 103–4; danger from floods (1954), 190; mass migrations to towns, 194–5; harassing of

migrants by police, 197–8; revolution, 220
Ishan Waqif, 169
Islam: Sunni and Shia divisions in, 50–51 (*see also* Shiism); as bond between nomad tribes, 95

Jahaish, 45–7, 49, 50
Jallaba, the, 159
Janghiz Khan, 96
Jasim. *See* Jasim al Faris
Jasim al Faris, 64, 113–14, 115, 190, 201, 204 ff.
Jasim bin Muhammad al Araibi, 136
Jindala, 158
Jussiaea diffusa, 70

Kaab, the, 100
Kaiba. See Water-lilies
Karaim, 119
Karbala, Holy City of, 54, 95; titles of pilgrims to, 55
Kathir, replaces Yasim as canoe-boy, 217
Kauban. See Jussiaea diffusa
Kaulaba, the, 106, 210
Kaulan. See Sedge
Kausha, wife of Muhammad of the Zubaid Aza, 74
Khalaf, brother of Hasan bin Radhawi, 212
Khalaf, son of Majid, 47, 152
Khamisiya, 105
Kharaibid, son of Abid. 105–7
Kharaibid, son of Majid: murder of, 152, 180
Khasara, 129
Khayal, 115–16
Kibasha, a, 75
Kubaish, 100, 102–4, 110, 201
Kufa, 95
Kurdistan, Iraqi, 20, 104, 127, 211

Kurds, the 20, 21
Kut, 209; barrage at, 167

Lam. *See* Bani Lam
Lazim. Sabaiti's father, 209–10
Lions, 156, 211
Lisan al thaur. See Potamogeton lucens

Mabrad, 111, 204; fire at, 112–113
Madan, the, 30, 194; customs and habits of, 44–5, 49–50, 54, 100; comparison of eating habits with the Bedu, 49–50; bad reputation of, 58; thefts by, 65; houses of, 75; lack of privacy among, 88; habits of prayer, 88; sickness and accidents among, 108–10; belief in the *anfish* and the *afa*, 118; their buffaloes, 159; kindness to the afflicted, 164; callousness in other ways, 166; reckoning of months and seasons by, 174; child mortality among, 183; contempt for the Berbera, 200; spearing of fish by, 201
Mahsin, village headman, 111
Mahsin bin Badr, Sheikh of the Al bu Salih, 114, 192, 196
Majar. *See* Majar al Kabir
Majar, River, 132, 166
Majar al Kabir, 25, 43, 46, 54, 110, 132, 147, 158, 200, 201, 211
Majid al Khalifa, a Paramount Sheikh of the Al bu Muhammad, 68, 124, 132, 136; his land, 28; his powers, 28; visited by Thesiger, 133; his *mudhif*, 133; his competence, 133–4; second visit to, 134–5; mourns death of Falih, 149–54; quarrel with the Shaghanba at Al Aggar, 196;

Majid al Khalifa – *contd*
closes Umm al Binni to the
Madan, 202, 204; feud with
Haji Sulaiman, 180, 210; The-
siger arranges truce for Amara
through, 215
Malik. *See* Bani Malik
Manati, attacked by a sow, 40–43,
136
Marshes, the: earlier history of,
99–100; Eastern, journey to,
155 ff., Central, restricted visi-
bility in, 157; storms and floods
in, 186–7, 189 ff.; drought in,
193 ff.
Marshmen. *See* Madan
Masharia, River and estuary, 158,
167, 169
Mushuf, the, 37
Matara, sister of Amara, 183, 214,
215, 216
Mawalis, 95
Maxwell, Gavin, 163
Maziad bin Hamdan, Sheikh o
the Al Essa, 21–3, 120, 196
Medes, the, 94
Medicine, the dispensing of, 43,
61, 76–7, 86, 105–10, 111, 117,
129–30, 135–6, 155, 185
Meshed er Ridha, 55
Mittanians, the, 94
Mongols, the sacking of Baghdad
by, 96
Morocco, slums in, 197
Moslems: habits of prayer, 32;
prohibitions among, 80–81;
their wives, 183
Mosquitoes, 109, 138
Muaiya, Caliph, 52
Mudhifs, 26–9, 48, 71, 133;
nuisance of bats and sparrows
in, 133; along the Euphrates
and Tigris, 205–8

Muhammad, the Prophet, 51,
52–4
Muhammad, founder of the Al
bu Muhammad, 74
Muhammad, youngest brother of
Majid, 139, 151, 154
Muhammad al Araibi, a Para-
mount Sheikh of the Al bu
Muhammad, 68, 136, 167
Muhammad al Mahdi, 53
Mulberry wood, use of in boat-
building, 127
Mullah Jabar, 202
Muntifiq Province, 103
Muntifiq tribes, 100, 190, 192,
204–5
Mustarjils, 165

Naga, mother of Amara, 173, 214,
216
Najaf, Holy City of, 53
Najas marina, 91
Nasiriya, 103, 110, 155
Nineveh, fall of, 94
Nuafil, the, 156, 157, 161
Nuristan, 213, 215
Nymphaea caerulea. See Water-
lilies
Nymphoides peltata and *indica.*
See Water-lilies

Omar, Caliph, 52
Othman, Caliph, 52
Otters, 163

Pakistan, 139, 141
Parthians, 95, 97
Pelicans, 91
Persia, 20, 185
Persians, 95, 96
Phragmites communis. See Qasab
Pied Flycatchers, 25
Pigs, the boldness of, 187

Pig-shooting, 32, 39–42, 139, 167–8, 186–9, 211
Polygonum senegalense, 70
Potamogeton lucens, 70
Pusht-i-Kut, the, 210

Qabab, 30, 44, 46–8, 68, 128–9, 132, 153, 177; burnt baby in, 76–7; mourns Falih, 155; floods in, 190
Qabiba, 118, 120, 123
Qalat Salih, 151, 154, 200
Qasab, 39, 45, 47; used as fuel, 49; used in room divisions, 56; punting poles made from, 92; used in mat making, 92–3; the chewing of, 162
Qat. See Polygonum senegalense
Qatan, 201, 203
Qubur, 71, 81
Quffa, the, 128
Qurna, 100, 138, 184, 185, 190

Raba, a, 71, 193
Rabia, the, 158, 161; hated by the Nuafil, 161; and by the Suaid Madan, 161
Radhawi, of the Rabia, 160, 213; agrees to six months' truce for Amara, 215; persuaded to give Thuqub's family further truce, 217–19
Radhi, brother of Amara, 175–6
Ramla, 92–3
Reshiq, brother of Amara, 172–3, 182–3, 213; his rice-growing, 172–5, 182
Rice-growing, 64, 174–5; stopped by floods, 193
Riza Pahlevi, Shah of Persia, 37
Romans, Ancient, 95
Rowunduz, 20

Rufaiya, 172, 182, 213, 215; rice-growing in, 175

Saad, of the Amla, 74
Sabaeans, 127
Sabaiti, a canoeboy, 136, 137, 138, 139, 157, 170, 173, 209; sadness at Falih's death, 155; as a cook, 163; pig-shooting, 168; lack of ability as a shot, 169; character, 169–70; rejoins Thesiger, 182; presented with shotgun, 190; meets Thesiger again at Basra (1958), 216; sees him off from Basra for last time, 220
Sadam, 30, 44, 47, 54–7, 141, 155, interrogation of Thesiger, 60–64; on the Madan, 65, his unpopularity, 69; removed from his post, 70; as companion across the Marshes, 78, 81–2, 83, 85, 89–90; welcomes Thesiger back to Qabab, 129, 130; his wives, 183
Saffat, the, 201
Sahain, headman of Bu Mughaifat, 57, 73, 184, 209, 213; on Basra, 72; his house, 75; in journey across the Marshes, 79–80, 89, 91; habit of prayer, 88
Saigal, 115, 118–21, 138, 193, 196, 200, 204; rice crops in, 175
Sargon, Assyrian king, 99
Sarifa, a, 205
Sayid Sarwat, 44; asks Radhawi to accept blood money, 217
Sayids, 44, 71, 74, 75, 124–5, 129, 166
Scirpus brachyceras. See Sedge
Sedge, 70, 171
Seleucids, 95
Shabut, 202

Shadda, the, 157
Shaghanba, the, 68, 83, 84, 121, 123, 196, 201
Sharks, 156
Shatra, 192
Shatt al Arab, 13
Shatt al Gharraf. *See* Gharraf
Sheikhs: ownership of land, 28; powers, 28, 69, 134; rights, 68; hostility of official class to, 134; resentment of educated young men at, 195; relationship with tribes, 196
Shias: and ritual purity, 105; and Muharram, 180
Shiism, 50–51, 53–4, 95
Shinta, a sheikh of the Al bu Muhammad, 217–20
Sijal. See Sedge
Sitra. See under Buffaloes
Slaves, status of among the tribesmen, 69
Snakes, 117
Steele, Frank, Vice-Consul at Basra, 138
Stewart, Dugald, Vice-Consul at Amara, 19, 21, 25, 113, 118, 135, 192
Suaid, the, 106, 169–71, 186; thefts of buffaloes by, 184; migrations to Baghdad and Basra, 194; methods of catching fish, 201
Subba. *See* Sabaeans
Sudan tribe, the, 167, migrations to Baghdad and Basra, 194
Sulaiman bin Motlog, Paramount Sheikh of the Azairij, 152
Sumer, fall of, 94
Sumerians, 96, 97
Sunnis, 50–51, 52–4
Suq ash Shuyukh, 103, 128, 137, 175, 204; serious floods in, 191

Suq at Tawil, 122
Suwaika. See Najas Marina

Tahir bin Abdullah, 121, 123
Tahir bin Ubaid, 184; acts as a guide, 185, 186, 187; spears a boar, 188; leaves Thesiger, 189; killed, 190
Talawi, the, 73
Tarada, 34, 90, 127, 135, 137–8
Thuqub, father of Amara, 136, 173, 176, 183, 213, 215, 216
Tigris, River, 24, 100, 155, 158; floods in, 182, 186, 187, 189; drought, 193; *mudhifs* on, 206–8
Timur-leng, the sacking of Baghdad by, 96
Turaba, 161
Turkomans, 96
Turks: the taking of Iraq by, 96

Umair. *See* Bani Umair
Umm al Binni, fishing at, 202–3
Urmia, 20

Van, 20

Wadiya, River, 132, 158, 176, 212
Water-lilies, 205
Water pollution, 85–6
Woolley, Sir Leonard, 23

Xerxes, 97

Yasin, of the Shaghanba, a canoe-boy, 131, 132, 135, 137, 138, 139, 161; rejoins Thesiger, 155–7; pig-shooting, 168–9; a good shot, 169; quarrelsome nature, 170; reunion with Thesiger

(1954), 184; presented with shotgun, 190; warns of storms, 186, 200; on catching fish, 201–2; marries, 209; settles down with family, 217

Yezid, Caliph, 53

Yunis, of Al Aggar, 124–5

Zaima, a, 128

Zair Mahaisin, 35, 36, 136

Zaira, 164

Zairs, 50, 55–7, 88

Zanj, the, 100

Zikri, Lake, 64, 89–92, 184

Zubaid Aza, the, 74

More about Penguins and Pelicans

Arabian Sands

Wilfred Thesiger

In *Arabian Sands* Wilfred Thesiger records the many journeys he has made by camel through and around the parched sands of Arabia's Empty Quarter. This is among the greatest books on Arabian travel.

'Following worthily in the tradition of Burton, Doughty, Lawrence, Philby and Thomas, it is, very likely, the book about Arabia to end all books about Arabia' – Lord Kinross in the *Daily Telegraph*

'Wilfred Thesiger is perhaps the last, and certainly one of the greatest, of the British travellers among the Arabs. . . . The narrative is vividly written, with a thousand little anecdotes and touches which bring back to any who have seen these countries every scene with the colour of real life' – Sir John Glubb in the *Sunday Times*

'For all who love travel and for whom the desert preserves its mystique this splendid book, magnificently illustrated with the author's photographs, is a feast' – George Millar in the *Daily Express*

'*Arabian Sands* is that rare thing, a really great travel book' – Hammond Innes

a Penguin Modern Classic

Seven Pillars of Wisdom

Lawrence of Arabia

'It describes the revolt in Arabia against the Turks, as it appeared to an Englishman who took part. Round this tentpole of a military chronicle T.E. has hung an unexampled fabric of portraits, descriptions, philosophies, emotions, adventures, dreams. He has brought to his task a fastidious scholarship, an impeccable memory, a style nicely woven of Oxfordisms and Doughty, an eye unparalleled ... a profound distrust of himself, a still profounder faith' – E. M. Forster

'It ranks with the greatest books ever written in the English language. As a narrative of war and adventure it is unsurpassable' – Sir Winston Churchill

'As certain of immortality as anything written in English for half a century' – John Buchan

No collection of modern classics would be complete without *Seven Pillars of Wisdom*. It remains – like its creator – brilliant, controversial, and finally inscrutable.

a Pelican book

Islam

Alfred Guillaume

The cultural background of the Arab peoples, who are
playing an ever larger and larger part in the modern
world, has been formed as much by a great missionary
religion, Muhammadanism, as has that of Europe and
America by Christianity. The great awakening of the
Muslim world which is now in progress, the emergence of
new Muslim states such as Pakistan, Libya, Jordan, Saudi
Arabia, and the ever closer contact between the West and
Middle East makes an understanding of the spirit of
Islam essential to the informed Westerner. Professor
Guillaume provides the essentials for such an
understanding in this book. He deals in turn with
Muhammad, the founder of Islam; the Qurān, its holy
book; the evolution of Muhammadanism as a system of
faith, law, religion, and philosophy; the varying schools
of thought and the intense devotional life that have grown
up within it; and discusses the changes which are now
taking place in the Islamic viewpoint as the Muslim
peoples prepare to take their full part in the modern
world.

a Penguin Classic

The Koran

Translated by N. J. Dawood

The Koran, as Mr Dawood claims, 'is not only one of the
greatest books of prophetic literature but also a literary
masterpiece of surpassing excellence'. Unquestioningly
accepted by Muslims to be the infallible word of Allah as
revealed to Mohammed by the Angel Gabriel over thirteen
hundred years ago, the Koran still provides the basic rules of
conduct fundamental to the Arab way of life. Mr Dawood
has produced a translation which retains the beauty of
the original, altering the traditional arrangement to
increase the understanding and pleasure for the uninitiated.